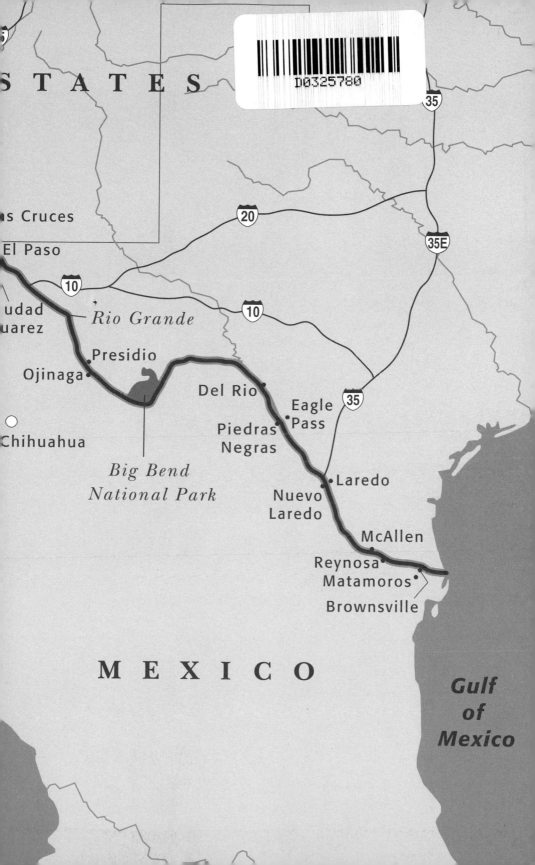

# THE BORDER

# THE BORDER

## EXPLORING THE
## U.S.-MEXICAN DIVIDE

### DAVID J. DANELO

STACKPOLE
BOOKS

Published by
STACKPOLE BOOKS
5067 Ritter Road
Mechanicsburg, PA 17055
www.stackpolebooks.com

Printed in the United States of America

10  9  8  7  6  5  4  3  2  1

FIRST EDITION

**Library of Congress Cataloging-in-Publication Data**

Danelo, David J.
    The border : exploring the U.S.-Mexican divide / by David J. Danelo. — 1st ed.
        p. cm.
    Includes bibliographical references and index.
    ISBN-13: 978-0-8117-0393-2
    ISBN-10: 0-8117-0393-2
    1. Mexican-American Border Region—Description and travel. 2. Danelo,
David J.—Travel—Mexican-American Border Region. 3. Mexican-American
Border Region—History. 4. Mexican-American Border Region—Social conditions.
5. Mexican-American Border Region—Economic conditions. 6. Border patrols—
Mexican-American Border Region. 7. Illegal aliens—Mexican-American Border
Region. 8. Drug traffic—Mexican-American Border Region. 9. Smuggling—
Mexican-American Border Region. 10. Borderlands—United States. 11.
Borderlands—Mexico. I. Title.
    F787.D36 2008
    917.2'10484—dc22
                                                  2008009887

*To our grandparents, but especially*
*Joseph & Yolanda Danelo*
*Melvin & Selena Thompson*
*and*
*In memory of my cousin*
*Mario Danelo*

# PROLOGUE

The border between the United States and Mexico is the most frequently traversed national boundary in the world. Over 250 million people legally transit the U.S.-Mexico border each year. An unknown number—perhaps as many as 10 million—do so beyond the law. "For decades, we have not been in complete control of our borders," said President George Bush in May 2007, when advocating an immigration reform bill that stalled in Congress. The president added that many have lost faith in the government's ability to even defend the border at all.

In 2007, I spent three months navigating the 1,951.63 miles of the U.S.-Mexico border. I went from the easternmost point, a spit of beach south of Boca Chica, Texas, to Border Field State Park, California, where a rusty fence spills into the Pacific Ocean at the border's western limit. I wandered from Brownsville to San Diego and Matamoros to Tijuana. This can be hazardous country for curious writers; in recent years, journalists have been intimidated, threatened, and even shot along the line that Mexicans call *la frontera*. Thanks to good fortune and some good advice, I emerged unscathed.

Is it possible to secure one of the most complex borders on the planet? On my first road trip in May, the same month that President Bush was arguing for immigration reform legislation that Congress would eventually reject, I tried to answer this question for myself. Beyond security, I had also wanted to make sense of the border; to find some logical, empirical reason beyond the statistics why McAllen and Laredo were bustling and prospering, why Douglas and Nogales were empty and corrupt, and why the cross-border urbanization of El Paso/Ciudad Juárez had evolved so differently than San Diego/Tijuana.

I talked with small business owners as well as community organizers who framed immigration law, border security, and the North American Free Trade Agreement through the lens of their own experiences. I met a Mexican tourism official who said he had spent almost two decades in jail for murder. I spent a day with three Catholic humanitarians who drop backpacks filled with water and medical supplies along trails in an effort to relieve suffering in the Arizona desert. I watched drugs being smuggled over the border in Nogales.

I wanted to know what the border was, but I found myself stymied each time I attempted to draw conclusions. I returned home with more questions than answers. I consulted a fellow writer for advice, who, in a single-sentence e-mail worthy of an oracle, illustrated both my problem and its solution: "Do not understand the border too quickly."

Fortified with that Zen, I plunged back in. The second trip in August and September took me back and forth along the border twice. I met a middle school principal whose students say the pledge of allegiance to the United States in both English and Spanish. I had coffee with the president of the Minutemen Civil Defense Corps. I was pulled over for speeding by Sheriff Ronny Dodson, whose jurisdiction includes 182 miles of border that is routinely violated by drug cartels and a town whose democratically elected mayor is a beer-drinking goat.

I took an unusual route for a gringo in reporting this story. My background as an Annapolis graduate, Marine Corps officer, and Iraq veteran caused me to reflexively examine the border as a tactical problem. My journalism forays to Vietnam, the Horn of Africa, and Iraq made me see it as an academic and legal one. Having spent much of my youth in San Antonio, I'm comfortable with Cinco de Mayo celebrations, enjoy mariachis, and am thoroughly fluent in Spanglish. *Sí, señorita. Dos fajitas, por favor. Gracias.* Unlike some gringos, the growing Latino population in the U.S. does not cause me grave concern.

My slow, poorly accented Spanish should have been a liability, but it turned out to be an asset for the man-on-the-street reporting I did along *la frontera*. Respect, gesture, and appearance are more universal as communication tools than words. With my big smile, broad shoulders, and a shaved head, the Mexicans I spoke with did not seem to believe I was a writer. They thought I was a businessman's bodyguard, an athlete on vacation, or a hit man. In much of Mexico, those professions are more popular, and safer, than investigative journalism.

There is no other place like it on the planet: this 1,952 mile strip of river and earth where the developed world meets the developing; where rich meets poor; where law can mean so much on one side and so little on another. In some regions, the border is a cultural estuary; 12 million binational residents produce a diverse blend, and the biological fusion becomes impossible to cleanly separate. Others could not seem more divided—by class, by economics, by their legal system. Some Mexican cities survive on the garish border party scene; the (barely enforced) drinking age in Mexico is eighteen. Others have established a thriving middle class through windfalls from NAFTA. Some have become hubs for smuggling marijuana, heroin, and cocaine. Others remain hovels of poverty.

When they flee, they run north. From 2000–2005, the United States accepted more migrants, legally and illegally, than any other country in the world. During those five years, according to the United Nations Population Division, an average of 1.3 million, the majority from Mexico, drifted annually into the United States. By 2007, one in eight people—37.9 million—living in the U.S. was an immigrant. About half had arrived illegally. The runner-up for immigration, Spain, logged a comparatively distant 569,000 migrants per year. No other country came close.

For every person who emigrates, another is not so lucky. In the same five-year period, the U.S. Border Patrol apprehended an average of 1.1 million per year attempting to sneak into the United States from Mexico—more arrests than any other law enforcement organization in the world. Known as *La Migra* to Mexicans, the Border Patrol creates continuity on both sides of this perplexing piece of terrain. Like an apparition or mythical deity who pays visits with sun, wind, or rain, *La Migra* has come to personify to the Darwinian cat-and-mouse game a migrant who endures in his or her attempts to find fortune. The undocumented flee *La Migra* when scrambling for economic freedom, but scream for them when dying of dehydration. In a paradoxical way, the men and women in green offer common ground on both sides of the border in a way that nothing else can. Their existence makes the border a reality.

Throughout the 1990s, demand and supply costs for the illegal commodities of drugs and migrant labor increased. This drove smugglers to establish more robust networks spanning both countries and charge higher rates to move their commodity. Partnerships uniting narcotics and migrant smuggling proliferated, pushing through long-established channels to sate the American appetite for marijuana, heroin, and cocaine (not to mention housekeepers, meatpackers, and strawberry pickers). The Border Patrol fought back with surges of stadium lighting, infrared cameras, and ground sensors. Stretches of fencing made from military scrap metal were installed south of San Diego, Nogales, and Douglas. From 1995 to 2006, funding for the Border Patrol increased tenfold, and the number of agents went from 5,000 to over 12,000.

As Border Patrol initiatives resulted in local success, smugglers adapted to the systemic changes. Operation Gatekeeper (1994; San Diego), Operation Hold the Line (1993–95; El Paso), and Operation Rio Grande (1998; Brownsville-McAllen) pushed the flow of migrants into Arizona's Sonora Desert. Instead of sprinting north through Tijuana along highways or bridges, migrants came through national parks, Indian reservations, and private ranches.

The violation of private land in southern Arizona, coupled with the attacks of 9/11, renewed the public rallying cry to "get the borders under control." Terrorists, we were warned, not just drugs, gangsters, or migrants, could stream through our porous south. Despite statements from security experts that the threat of Islamist terror would likely come from Canada—Toronto and Montreal are both less than 400 miles from the heart of Manhattan—the Border Patrol and the electorate remained absorbed with the influx of Mexican migrants.

After 9/11, the Border Patrol, along with several existing federal agencies, was subsumed into the Department of Homeland Security as part of the largest and most expensive federal government reorganization since the creation of the Department of Defense. Responsible for border security and the 317 air, land, and sea ports of entry into the United States, the Office of Customs and Border Protection bill themselves as "America's first line of defense." They have 40,000 employees and an annual budget of $7.8 billion. In 2003, the Border Patrol became "the mobile, uniformed law enforcement arm of Customs and Border Protection," making Border Patrol agents, effectively, the Department of Homeland Security's infantrymen. Although their primary task is counterterrorism, agents spend most of their time seizing drugs and illegal aliens.

If Border Patrol agents are the infantry in the war on the border, the Immigration and Customs Enforcement, or ICE, are the spooks and spies. Rival siblings to Customs and Border Protection, ICE special agents investigate smugglers, raid businesses, and deport the undocumented. Their annual budget is also $7.8 billion. Not counting the contributions of other federal agencies, the government spends $15.6 billion per year to prevent people who want to plot terror, sell drugs, or work for almost nothing from entering the country.

Despite the investment, the Border Patrol has only achieved "operational control" of 449 miles along the border, according to a September 2006 internal report. One reason why authorities say they can regulate only 23 percent of the border is because U.S. government spending pales next to the opposing market forces of labor and narcotics. Mexican expatriates send home $24.6 billion per year, a source of revenue that accounts for 3 percent of Mexico's estimated $840 billion gross domestic product. In 1995, the drug trade brought Mexico an estimated $30 billion; that figure has doubled since the passage of NAFTA. Globally, the drug trade is a $300 billion annual business. In 2007, President Bush asked Congress for a paltry $500 million to fight drugs in Mexico. But next to oil and tourism, drugs are Mexico's leading industry.

After the signing of NAFTA in 1994, it was thought that Mexico's poor would, in fact, run to the north. But they were supposed to stop at Mexico's *maquiladoras*, working for what bureaucrats promised would be fair wages. *Maquiladoras*, also simply known as *maquilas*, are Mexican factories that make raw materials into industrial imports in border cities like Juárez, Tijuana, or Matamoros. This economic development, it was thought, would encourage Mexicans to seek opportunity in their own country instead of a foreign one.

The *maquilas* have prospered, growing 15.5 percent since the NAFTA treaty. Some border communities in both nations, particularly in south Texas and northeastern Mexico, saw their fortunes increase. Since 1994, Mexican exports to the U.S. have increased fivefold, from $40 billion to $200 billion. The trade agreement has caused the national income for Mexico's richest 10 percent—including Mexican billionaires like Carlos Slim Helú, the third wealthiest man in the world, and Maríasun Aramburuzabala, the richest woman in Latin America—to exponentially rise.

Simultaneously, many critics argue, NAFTA has forced rural Mexican farmers into unfair competition with gigantic American agriculture corporations. Since one quarter of Mexico's 106 million survives on $1 a day, NAFTA did little to staunch the flow of humanity into the world's richest nation. In some places on the border, particularly Arizona, both the trade agreement and stronger border security only caused migration to increase. With both America and Mexico squeezed by globalization, population demographics continue to favor the south. Many Americans fear becoming a bilingual nation.

The United States, however, is not the global giant thwarting the future for Mexican workers. Although NAFTA created 1.3 million Mexican jobs and fueled an export boom, the overall cost of production in the early twenty-first century was still four times higher for a corporation in Mexico—despite its poverty—than hiring a work force in China. In the first two years of the millennium, 300,000 *maquila* employees were fired; their jobs outsourced across the Pacific. Mexican leaders call on the Americans to scrutinize Chinese labor practices, but critics shrug, saying that Mexico is at fault for the economic loss because they failed to remain competitive. Porfirio Díaz, who ruled from 1884–1911, summed up the dilemma best: "Poor Mexico! So far from God and so close to the United States."

I found the exception to this fatalistic despair in northeastern Mexico, a corridor that appeared to represent NAFTA's definitive middle class success story. The links between Houston, Texas, and Monterrey, Nuevo León, have grown to symbolize the degree that the economic fortunes of the U.S. and Mexico are intertwined. From Matamoros to Monterrey and Tampico to Saltillo, the GDP is 2.3 times higher than the rest of Mexico combined. Growth has resulted from the region's connectivity to Texas, the presence of oil in eastern Mexico, the dependence upon Brownsville, McAllen, and

Laredo for trade, and the cultural ties that Texans possess as former Mexican citizens.

The border in south Texas—a wide, friendly river—is more stable than the combustible line in the sand separating Arizona's wealth from Sonora's poverty. After seeing the difference, I understood why the Minutemen had trumpeted their call to arms in Tombstone. The Anglos I met in San Antonio, Del Rio, and Eagle Pass abhorred the thought of a border fence, but those in Tucson, Phoenix, and San Diego demanded immediate action against the "invasion" they confronted daily.

For non-residents of border states, the public view of the U.S.-Mexico border is sculpted almost entirely by its westernmost limit. Delegations from every country in the world visit San Diego, California to see how America guards her gates from Mexico. I met with a U.S. Border Patrol medial officer who had talked with officials from Thailand, Australia, Romania, and Poland over the latest thirty-day period. During the carefully scripted tours, visitors take pictures of San Ysidro, the largest non-commercial port of entry on the border, where cars stacked across twenty-four lanes wait hours to cross from Tijuana into San Diego. Dignitaries watch maintenance contractors repair the cuts along the two stacks of mesh wire fencing installed as part of Operation Gatekeeper in 1994. They enjoy a night out in San Diego's entertainment quarter called the Gaslamp District. Then, they go home.

In this way, both the U.S. Congress and the Border Patrol's San Diego Sector have colluded in a similar sales operation. San Diego is the only city on the U.S.-Mexico border that offers direct flights to and from Washington, D.C. airports. Congressional delegations can fly out of Washington in the morning, learn the "real story" of the border in an afternoon, and be back in the capital by dinnertime. At the San Diego Sector headquarters, the Border Patrol has a dozen media representatives, a full-time Congressional affairs staff, and media liaison officers designated for each of the sector's eight stations. This is over four times the public relations staff of any other sector.

The Mexican government casually patrols *la frontera*, but since crossing from Mexico into the U.S. is not illegal for a Mexican citizen, the *federales* do nothing to stop migrants. Grupo Beta, a government-sponsored welfare organization for migrants, runs twelve aid stations in cities on Mexico's northern border. Their charter: offer assistance to those preparing to cross or returning from a failed attempt. Some suspect that Grupo Beta's offices are merely fronts for smugglers and *coyotes*. Absent a law against crossing, enforcement is not a concern.

And why should Mexico's federal police care about stopping migrants from going north? The Mexican government has other things to worry about—primarily the threat of drug cartels. And even the poorest Mexican knows the story of how the United States "stole" the rich land of *El Norte* a century and a half ago after the Mexican-American War. For some, this enhances the sense that evading the Border Patrol is also a conquest on behalf of their Hispanic, Latino, or Chicano brethren. Others strive only for the humbler goals of money for home and hearth.

Beyond economics, historical and cultural factors also explain Mexico's lack of interest in stopping people from leaving their country. Hidden in plain sight is a bizarre but authentic satisfaction in turning our "*gabacho*" hypocrisy upon us. We consume drugs while spending billions campaigning to stop them. We want clean hotels, cheap food, and our children bathed and clothed by caretakers, but protest when we see too many signs printed in Spanish. Labor and smuggling are not just about providing for family; the *narcotraficantes* are celebrated on street corners, compact discs, and YouTube. The *machismo* of personal and national honor plays a role, as does the innate human drive for superiority against a competing tribe.

Ironically, even victory in the border battle brings negative consequences. Stronger border security appears to have brought more chaos to the other side. After the 9/11 attacks, fewer Americans ventured south of the border for weekends or holidays. Lines along the border grew, slowing trade and decreasing tourism. The aggressive approach has also placed Border Patrol agents in an awkward no-man's land. As security has tightened, patrolmen are assaulted with rocks, sticks, and occasionally bullets.

Farmers, growers, and gardeners throughout the U.S. face worsening labor shortages. Some American companies are shifting their operations to Mexico, cultivating crops where the farmers live rather than risking the backlash of immigration officials. "It's because of enforcement," said a vice president of a Texas garden produce company in a recent issue of *U.S. News and World Report.*

In the meantime, this economic vacuum has been exploited by drug cartels. Two years ago, the Sinaloa Federation moved into Nuevo Laredo, killed the chief of police, and imported their own "police force." They jockeyed violently for power with the Gulf Cartel, at times using rocket-propelled grenades and Kalashnikov rifles. "This city is becoming a ghost town," lamented a sixty-year-old merchant who faces bleak economic prospects because of the drug lords, and worried that I would use his name. "If this menace remains, there will be nothing left."

I started out wanting answers, but in the end, I realized that the same questions have been asked as long as Americans and Mexicans have been trying to discover, befriend, conquer, or subvert one another. My journey taught me to distrust anyone with glib responses to immigration, security, drugs, health care, free trade, citizenship, and water rights. Some are local issues; some are regional; some are international. But all are layered with complexity.

The border is entirely a man-made construction: an enormous fissure of nature demarcated by water, steel, concrete, and *La Migra.* Rising mountains, stagnant rivers, and scorching deserts are traversed day and night by four-wheel-drive trucks, all-terrain vehicles, and even horses as hunters seek their elusive prey. Cameras peer, sensors radiate, helicopters dart, and fences block. Without a Border Patrol, there would only be a mark on a map—no walls, no barriers, no fences. And no illegal aliens.

But even without *La Migra* and the fortifications, the line would still matter. As long as America exists, admirers and antagonists will classify the border as a beautiful place with a bicameral, binational state of mind. It will remain a point of unity and separation beyond the number of fences erected on either side. Its 1,952 miles mark North America's greatest divide. And her greatest opportunity.

## U.S. Border Patrol Sector Map

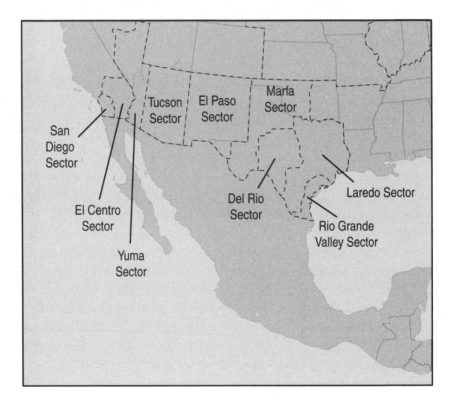

# 1

The border begins five miles south of Boca Chica.

Reaching the mouth of the Rio Grande in south Texas means driving thirty miles east until the road ends at the Gulf of Mexico. A stop sign is inexplicably there, as if beach-bound motorists might ignore the obvious and continue driving until plummeting into the ocean. The nearest collection of hamlets, Boca Chica Village, is an eclectic shantytown marked only by a white sign with blue paint, a pile of electric cables, some bamboo poles, and a few rusty cars. The village is less than a mile from the coastline, five miles north of the Rio Grande.*

To get to the actual border, where the Rio Grande empties into the ocean, I turned south at the stop sign and drove along the beach. The tide had scattered seaweed, shells, rocks, and beer cans over the wet, compacted sand. Three tents were pitched on the shore, including one that appeared to be a hobo's permanent dwelling.

There was no signpost or historical placard left here by either Mexican or American authorities. No screaming instructions in Spanish or English to warn the ten bronzed men who were wading toward the United States in chest-deep water that they were about to conduct an illegal crossing. No marker of any kind to say that this place of *terra firma* was where the southeastern limit of the U.S.-Mexico border began.

---

* In Mexico, the Rio Grande is called the Río Bravo del Norte (Great River of the North), or just the Río Bravo. For simplicity, I will use the American name exclusively in this narrative.

The Mexican men sloshing in the Rio Grande were not coming into America to stay. They were fishing. Because the border runs down the middle of the river, they crossed back and forth between countries many times, violating the law with impunity and determination until their nets were full. Segregated by age and gender, their women and children huddled on the Mexican side of the river's mouth around a blue sedan and flatbed pickup, busy with conversations and chores. A few hours later, they got in their vehicles, drove south, and presumably returned to their homes.

There were no Border Patrol agents that day on the beach south of Boca Chica. The group I saw fishing on the American side—thirty-five miles from Brownsville, the largest city within walking distance—was apparently not cause for a security alarm. The vegetation beyond the beach was thick enough, said the Border Patrol, to force people to walk along the road where they have manned a checkpoint if they attempted a permanent crossing. Helicopters with U.S. government markings buzzed every few minutes, watching for signs of infiltration.

Other than helicopters, the only sign that this was anything beyond a normal beach came from a lighthouse on the Mexican side. It was a tall white pillar with a blue platform on top. A small building was next to it. Set against the backdrop of river and sand, the lighthouse reminded me of the minarets I had seen in Iraq jutting skyward next to mosques amid the canals from the Euphrates. The beach on the Mexican side of the river is called *Playa Bagdad.* No one I spoke with, American or Mexican, knew the name's origin. It gave me déjà vu.

Boca Chica and Playa Bagdad are at the southeastern tip of the Rio Grande Valley. It was hot when I was there, not the dry heat of Arizona's Sonora Desert or California's Mojave, but the sticky humid haze of a subtropical climate. It was the kind of heat that can generate passion, poetry, and hordes of mosquitoes. This sauna is not actually a valley at all, but the northern side of a river delta. Half of the delta is American soil—52.1 percent, according to one hydrology table—and the rest is Mexican. Sediment and nutrients wash into the flats when the river floods, creating a menagerie of life in the resulting estuary of alluvial silt, soil, and loam.

I saw foliage growing in multiple canopies throughout the steamy region, which is home to more bird species than any other part of the

United States. According to local legend, the Valley—*el Valle* for many residents—was so named because original settlers thought the term more inviting than its scientific synonym. They hoped that a "valley" would draw investors and tourists.

Brownsville, the largest city in the Valley, is about thirty miles from the beach of Boca Chica and an hour east of McAllen. Maj. Jacob Brown, a U.S. Army officer, was killed during the 1845 Mexican-American War at an outpost that was then called Fort Texas. Gen. Zachary Taylor renamed it Fort Brown, and the city grew up alongside the base. During the Civil War, Fort Brown became a Confederate outpost. In May 1865, over a month after the war had officially ended at Appomattox, Virginia, Union forces attacked Confederate troops at Palmito Ranch, a garrison near the fort. The Confederates rallied, killing or wounding over 100 Union soldiers while losing none of their own. It was the last major battle of the Civil War. Two international bridges are now less than half a mile from the site.

In the early twentieth century, Fort Brown made national head-lines as the site of the Brownsville Affair, a 1906 racial uprising against an all-black Army regiment. A white bartender was killed, and many locals, lacking evidence, decided to blame his death on the black soldiers. Witnesses told the Army that the men planted spent cartridges at the crime scene and convinced investigators, pos-sibly through bribes, to frame the black men. Against the recom-mendation of the white officers in the chain of command, and overriding a personal plea from Booker T. Washington, President Theodore Roosevelt ordered 167 soldiers dishonorably discharged. In 1972, almost three decades after the fort shut down, the Army reversed its decision. Although the soldiers' honor was restored, the Nixon Administration refused to grant back pay to the families. Only one man, Dorsie Willis, was alive to receive the $25,000 pension.

Farming has been the economic mainstay of river deltas since the Sumerians and Egyptians developed their respective floodplains, and the Rio Grande Valley is no exception. Parallel levees protect the farms, creating a barrier against the irregularly perennial floodwa-ters. The levee snakes alongside the river, providing a dirt thorough-fare for farmers, smugglers, and Border Patrol agents. The three disparate groups, I was told, are constantly transiting the area, trying to either find or avoid each other. The felines of the cat-and-mouse game, agents profile their prey as brown, ageless, faceless, and anonymous. The hunters are men and women like Agent Walter King.

Field Operation Supervisor Walter King, Caucasian, fifty-two, had brown eyes, sandy hair, and a dimpled chin. Outside, he wears tinted police sunglasses. He has been with the Border Patrol for almost twenty years and is approaching retirement eligibility, though he plans to stay in as long as he can. King did a stint in the Navy, a few years as a flight attendant, and then burned out as a social worker before he discovered the Border Patrol. He entered the Academy at thirty-two, which was just under the maximum age. King, who is married with two children, told me that the Border Patrol is his dream job. When I said he looked good for an officer his age, he corrected me. "We're agents, not officers." He felt strongly about the distinction.

Walter King is a good-humored man who seems wholly identified with his work at the Brownsville Station in the Rio Grande Valley Sector. When he would agree with you on something—your fondness for the coffee he had offered you, or the next order of business for the day—he would reply "Ten-four" a few times, nodding and smiling until you were satisfied with the concurrence. The jokes and witticisms plastered on his office walls included a Western-style poster of Geronimo and his mates. The Indians were on the warpath, and the picture proclaimed: "Homeland Security: Fighting Terrorism Since 1492." It was not a poster I had expected to discover inside a federal building—the style suggested militant Native American teenager—but I would find it more than once inside *La Migra's* cubicles. To me, it suggested a renegade streak of anarchy in the Border Patrol; they were not only guardians in the fight against aliens, but also rugged individualists raging against the machine.

Like all Border Patrol agents, Walter King speaks fluent Spanish. The motivations are both tactical and humanitarian, and the mandate for agents to learn Spanish—few nations require their national guardians to maintain bilingual skills—says something about the way Americans want their law enforcement to be portrayed. Like our military personnel, we want our cops to be the good guys, able to communicate easily with our neighbors and harmoniously diffuse any situation. Americans want to win and be loved at the same time. Both aren't always possible.

Agent King wears a gold oak leaf on his collar, which signifies his rank. The insignia for Border Patrol agents, I learned, is similar to that of the U.S. military. Silver bars, or "railroad tracks," are for supervisory patrol agents, oak leaves designate senior managers, an eagle is a station chief, and stars are for sector chiefs. As in the military, silver is more valuable; the tinseled insignia always outranks the gilded one.

It seems appropriate that the Border Patrol's emblems of authority, ideology, and training methods originated in the Army; the organization has walked the line between official law enforcement and secretive paramilitary brotherhood since its inception. King's training started at the Border Patrol Academy, which, in his day, was headquartered in Georgia (it has since been moved to Artesia, New Mexico). At a 2004 ceremony, Commissioner Robert Bonner of Customs and Border Protection said that when new trainees arrived, they would soon become "modern-day centurions, charged with guarding our country from all those who seek to harm us or violate or laws." In an effort to quickly deploy more Border Patrol agents in 2007, two classes of fifty trainees started every week the entire year. Some were completed in as little as eight weeks. As in King's time, all new graduates are sent to the U.S.-Mexico border for their first duty station, where they remain for at least five years.

The Border Patrol traces its roots back to El Paso as a late-nineteenth-century spinoff from the Texas Rangers. According to their own historical records, Jefferson Davis Milton, a stout white man who had a thick mustache, was the first Immigration Border Patrolman. Whatever his qualifications were as a gunslinger, they were enhanced by robust political connections. He was the son of John Milton, governor of Florida from 1861–65 when the state was part of the Confederacy. Milton's mission was to enforce the new tough labor laws Congress had passed in 1885 to protect American workers against migrant competition—from the Chinese. Mexicans and Canadians could come and go without any restrictions for another thirty years, but all "Chinamen" who sought work were banned from entry.

During World War I, the authority of soldiers stationed along the border was augmented by tougher immigration laws, which were the first to restrict Mexican transit. Fearing a backlash of postwar global refugees, Congress passed the (anti-)Immigration Act of 1917, overriding President Woodrow Wilson's pro-immigration veto in the process. The legislation mandated a literacy test for all immigrants, placed an $8 "head tax" on new arrivals, and banned all persons from the Middle East, Persia, India, and Southeast Asia from entering the United States. The 1917 Act also denied entry to "all idiots, imbeciles, feeble-minded persons, epileptics, and insane persons." The irony of such categorizations was clearly lost on the lawmakers.

The end of World War I marked the creation of the documentary world that now defines the international nation-state system. By agreement with the Wilson-inspired League of Nations, states were supposed to become sovereign, define their borders, grant citizenship persons within their boundaries, and issue passports that would serve as authorizations to travel to other lands. After the victors of World War I carved the world into nation-states, a person became "legal" only by possessing the proper documents, photographs, or papers.

Suddenly, visas, passports, and medical evaluations were required worldwide for any migrant to complete their journey to a new land. Without the right documents, a man or woman could be expelled from a nation. Phrases like "deportation," "proof of citizenship," and "undocumented worker" first entered the American cultural, legal, and political lexicon. Forgery blossomed as a cottage industry. Thus did President Woodrow Wilson, through his globalist ambition in forming the League of Nations, unwittingly start an international domino effect that created "illegals" in America and throughout the world.

In 1920, after decades of lobbying, social conservatives won approval to "dry out" the country, prohibiting the manufacture, sale, or transportation of intoxicating liquors with a constitutional amendment. This upset many World War I veterans, whose ranks included federal immigration officials. Unable to vote in the Congressional elections because they were fighting overseas, they returned home from liberating France—where wine flowed like water—only to find their own libations banned. But alcohol remained legal in both Mexico and Canada, and, almost overnight, savvy businessmen united with border residents in rebellion against their government. After Prohibition passed, smuggling grew along the entire border.

The combination of alcohol smuggling and growing fears about immigration spurred legislators to action. On May 28, 1924—two days after Congress had lowered the immigration quota for Europeans, still barring all Asians from entry—legislators ordered the disparate bands of immigration inspectors, mail clerks, and quarantine officers along the southwest border to be consolidated into the United States Border Patrol. The 450 newly commissioned inspectors, who fell under the Immigration Bureau in the Department of Labor, were issued a badge, uniform, revolver, and paid $1,680 a year. Each man had to provide his own horse and saddle. After consideration through committee, Congress allocated funding for hay and oats.

Department of Labor and Immigration Bureau officials divided the 450 inspectors into three districts, which were subdivided into sectors. Fifty inspectors were assigned to each of the nine sectors. The San Antonio District supervised the Brownsville, Laredo, and Del Rio Sectors. The El Paso District, which was seen as the "border capital" by virtue of population and location, owned the Marfa, El Paso, and Tucson sectors. The Los Angeles District finished the distance with the Yuma, El Centro, and Chula Vista sectors. Even in the 1920s, the Chula Vista Sector was responsible, as it is today, for guarding the smallest portion of the border but the largest grouping of population (the reverse was true, then as now, for the Marfa Sector in west Texas). Although the districts no longer exist, the nine sectors—with minor changes in nomenclature and boundaries—have not been significantly revised since their original design.*

The day we met, Agent Walter King took me on a somewhat scripted tour of the Brownsville border area called a ride-along. We were in a white Suburban with a running board, green stripe, and official markings. Like many law enforcement vehicles, the door handles in the back seats had been disabled so arrested persons could not escape. An ivory-and-black push-button microphone was tethered to an analog radio below the dashboard that King could use, if necessary, to call headquarters.

---

* The district levels were eventually eliminated and the Border Patrol partitioned the entire continental U.S. into twenty sectors, all reporting to a headquarters in Washington. Puerto Rico is also designated as a sector.

Although he was not raised on the border—atypical for a Border Patrol agent—King spoke of his adopted hometown of Brownsville with affection in a way that employees of other federal services might not. By virtue of the remoteness and austerity of their duty stations, officials who serve on the border appeared to be more integrated with rhythms of their local communities than any other federal law enforcement agency in America. Most agents have lived and worked in their respective sectors for years. For some, this offered a sense of making them even more invested in the safety and stability of their neighborhoods. For others, this created an incentive to accept bribes and payoffs from smugglers for looking the other way.

I met some agents along the border who struck me as the corruptible type, but Agent King was not one of them. King came across as a man who had remained with the Border Patrol because it was a secure government job, because it offered meaningful work, and because he wasn't cooped up for the day in his office. Beyond the formal bluster about how proud he was to be on the front lines fighting terrorism, Agent King seemed happiest about the chance to get paid to run around, breathe fresh air, and possibly take down a bad guy. First and foremost, King enjoyed the hunt. Everything else was just part of the job.

King and I started along the levee road that paralleled the river. Periodically, he stopped the Suburban so he could point out trails leading up from the Rio Grande. The footpaths cut through a noxious weed called carrizo that had become the kudzu along the riverbanks. The carrizo had taken over both American and Mexican sides like ivy on a brick building, providing smugglers and migrants with concealment from the agents.

Dotted along the trails that led up from the river, we found discarded trash bags, as well as t-shirts, shorts, and underwear. Most of what we saw was damp, but not wet. "That stuff's been here at least a week," King said nonchalantly. He didn't seem worried about it.

But farther down the road, King saw another pair of wet trash bags. At that, he furrowed his brow. "This concerns me," he said. "This is fresh." The water was still beaded on the black plastic. Clothes and shoes had been discarded.

King squatted like a baseball catcher and peered into the ground. He was engaging in a process that he called sign-cutting. To cut sign was to track, in Border Patrol lexicon. King was inspecting for footprints, matted leaves, broken branches, or any other "sign" that could confirm the direction where the trail was cut.

Seconds later, the agent stood up. "It was a drug load," he announced. "Backpackers came through a few hours ago. They were packing over sixty pounds." He pointed to the shoes. "Dope runners always bring another pair with their change of clothes, and discard the wet ones after swimming across. Migrants can't afford extra shoes."

Then King pointed to the tracks. They were formed as impressions into grass; an untrained eye would not notice the footprints. "You can tell this guy was carrying something heavy," he said. "The grass is pushed further into the ground. And he was obviously in a hurry."

We returned to the Suburban. King called in the report, exchanging ten-fours with the dispatcher to end the conversation. He was not talking as much. I sensed that he was thinking about the route the backpackers took into town or maybe the safe house where they were seeking refuge. He would probably prefer if I was not around, I thought. Moments later, another pair of agents would be detailed to chase down the backpackers. But King would still be stuck with the reporter.

Although Agent King conducted the ride-along with personal candor, it was obvious that this tour would illuminate only a fragment of the overall picture of the Rio Grande Valley. Officials preferred that media be escorted along routes likely to guarantee their safety—rocks were often thrown at Border Patrol agents by smugglers from the Mexican side for either diversion or defiance. I had signed a waiver releasing the Border Patrol from any liability, but agents—even nice guys like Walter King—were still unlikely to "be themselves" in the presence of a camera and notepad. The privilege to report was not restricted, but the opportunity to find the unvarnished truth was also not readily available.

And I wasn't the only man seeking information that day about the Border Patrol's daily routine. A few moments after King reported the possible drug load, we noticed a shiny, red Chevy pickup with tinted windows parked on the Mexican side of the river. The two men inside, a driver and passenger, were watching for activity. Their engine was off, but the headlights were on. In patroller's argot, the men were "sitting on an X": maintaining a stationary position for observation or deterrence. It was a tactic that agents often employed themselves. After we arrived, they turned on the engine, cut the lights, and drove away.

The men could have been alien smugglers inspecting for new routes. They might have been conducting surveillance on Border Patrol cameras and vehicles. Perhaps they were waiting to pick up a "mule," a backpacker who had just deposited his cargo of marijuana. They might have been looking for a spot to drop someone off. They might have been Mexican policemen.

We would never know. They were in Mexico, and—unless we could proffer a *mordida*, or bribe—there was no trustworthy authority on the other side to call; no one to share what little information we had found about this suspicious behavior. Even though we were standing thirty yards away from a man in a terribly poor country who was wealthy enough to own a very nice truck, we could just as easily have been looking at a video screen or watching YouTube.

The sun set as we had finished the ride-along, and King offered to let me inside the Brownsville Station Command Center. Digital monitors and the cameras that feed them are often the primary source of information that agents have in their endless quest to enforce federal law. Two soldiers from the Texas Army National Guard and a civilian Border Patrol employee were sitting at the terminals. Combined, they were looking at the feeds from thirty or more cameras. They controlled the field of vision, zoom, depth, and angle of observation from a joystick or mouse at their workstations. They were the eyes for the Border Patrol.

One of the soldiers, who asked that I not mention his name, noticed something on the screen and pointed. "There's a group of eight running south," he said. Because the camera had an infrared heat-seeking lens, humans showed up against the dark background as fluorescent white orbs. In an odd twist, the Rio Grande snakes so wildly in the Valley that an illegal crossing of the river could take place in almost any cardinal direction. At more than one peninsula near Brownsville, the switchbacks are sharp enough that migrants often swim south or west into the U.S. before sprinting for refuge.

The soldier picked up an intercom microphone and pushed a black button. He identified himself as "Charlie," which was the command center's call sign. He zoomed and turned the camera with his joystick. He told the agents in the field what he saw and advised them where to go in order to apprehend the group that just came across. They were identified as suspected illegal aliens. Marijuana smugglers, King said, do not normally cross here in packs.

I asked Agent King if he thought the illegal aliens would be caught. He nodded, saying that once they have them on camera, they can tell the agents in the field where to find them and "talk them on to the target." King was proud of the station's command center, and he credited it, in part, with changing the Border Patrol's performance in the area. Illegal traffic, he said, has been cut in half over the last ten years.

The immediate past was not nearly as stable, King said. A decade ago, illegal aliens were flooding into Brownsville at a rate that no barrier seemed able to block. On the ride-along, King had pointed to a neighborhood of newly constructed houses adjacent to the border in Brownsville. "It used to be a no-man's land," he said, telling stories about shadowy encounters with knife-wielding aliens hidden in rail yards and boxcars.

In 1998, the Border Patrol started Operation Rio Grande, their effort to take control of the river. Patterned in part after the successful Operation Gatekeeper—a 1994 federally funded surge of sensors, floodlights, fencing, and additional Border Patrol agents that plugged the porous San Diego Sector—Operation Rio Grande added each of those elements, in varying degrees, to the Valley. One year later, apprehensions had fallen 32 percent and crime by 20 percent (the Border Patrol measures a drop in apprehensions as a metric of success). Children could play in neighborhoods along the Rio Grande again. Downtown merchants no longer complained about shoplifting. The next year brought more of the same.

"Given the personnel, technology, and infrastructure, we've proven that we can do the job," King said. He didn't claim that smuggling and illegal immigration had been eradicated in the Rio Grande Valley Sector. But he did say that the Border Patrol in the area caught fewer people floating on inner tubes or scrambling up the riverbank in mass human waves in 2006 than it did a decade before.

We left the command center ten minutes later. Agents had not yet apprehended the group of eight, but they were hot on their trail when we departed. I asked Agent King if he thought the border could ever be secured. "We've done it," he said, holding up the Border Patrol's statistical success in south Texas as an example.

Personnel, technology, and infrastructure. This was the Border Patrol's sacred triad. I would hear it in every office I visited and from every agent and sector chief I interviewed. These three things, agents said, will secure the border. More men and women who can cut for sign to snatch up those who illegally cross. More towers with infrared cameras, more seismic sensors, more command centers, more trucks, more helicopters, and more off-road vehicles. More aluminum fences and barbed wire and steel barricades and concrete.

Personnel, technology, and infrastructure. According to King and his comrades, border security increased up to a certain plateau in direct proportion to the ratio of each element. When it hit that plateau of stability, it meant "success." To King, the Border Patrol is no different than a police force in a large city fighting crime. You will always have someone trying to break the law, and most will be caught. Invariably, a few will get away.

The Border Patrol's estimate of the number of people they fail to catch—what they call the "get-away ratio"—hovers annually between 67 and 75 percent. In other words, for every three or four people who illegally cross into the U.S., agents will only apprehend one of them. On the surface, this would suggest that 3 million people illegally immigrate each year. But because the Border Patrol does not account for individual apprehensions, the get-away ratio is not a scientific metric. The numbers include aliens who are captured two, three, even ten times. After each apprehension, the migrants are released back into Mexico. If they are willing to endure repeated hardship in search of *El Norte*, they will keep trying until they triumph.

King's definition of border security—which was similar to that of almost every veteran Border Patrol agent I met—might be broader than many Americans can accept. In a 2006 Gallup poll, 81 percent of Americans said the U.S. needed more Border Patrol agents. The same year, the federal government authorized the Border Patrol to raise its force to 21,000 by 2010. That percentage of Americans might say that illegal means illegal. They might say that even one smuggler is too many. They might say that any alien left undiscovered could easily be a terrorist. They might even say that Operation Rio Grande—despite the drop in crime and rise in property values for Brownsville—was, for the United States, not much of a success at all.

━━━━━━◆━━━━━━

Exploring the American side of the border would only provide half the story. To find the other, I would need to understand the Mexican perspective, which is not something a gringo—even one who grew up in San Antonio—could do with ease. Going into the Mexican interior might have been interesting, but seeing the capital of Mexico City or the middle-class metropolis of Monterrey would obscure the real questions. What does Mexico look like on the other side of south Texas? Is *la frontera* on the Mexican east coast different than the states south of west Texas, Arizona, or California? Are Mexicans in Matamoros more or less satisfied than those in Nogales? Do they view Americans differently in one place than another? And what do they want from their northern neighbors, both now and in the future?

Not long after my visit with Agent King, I parked my rented Toyota hatchback at a lot next to Texas Southmost College and walked toward the Gateway International Bridge in downtown Brownsville. All normal, noncommercial ports of entry into Mexico from the United States have both a vehicle and pedestrian entrance. Both the U.S. and Mexico charge for driving or walking across the bridges that span the Rio Grande; in 2006, these tolls generated $18 million for Brownsville's Cameron County alone. Of the thirty-seven passenger and commercial crossings along the U.S.-Mexico border, the Rio Grande Valley has eleven. The Texas Department of Transportation has proposed building four more in this frenetically traveled area.

I paid sixty cents and went through a turnstile, passing a heavy-set, bored U.S. Customs agent who glanced at me listlessly. I walked on, ascending the concrete path toward the bridge's apex. To my left was the road for vehicles; cars going to Mexico drifted past and a line of traffic faced toward me in the opposite lane, waiting to enter Texas. The walkway was surrounded by chain link fencing and razor wire, and topped with a vinyl cover for shade.

As determined by treaty, the physical border between Texas and Mexico runs down the middle of the Rio Grande. When I reached the crest of the bridge, I saw a brass plate posted on the wall. The left side said: *Limite de Los Estados Unidos Mexicanos* in gold letters. The right: Boundary of the United States of America. A vertical line separated the words. I passed by it, entered Mexico, and walked downhill to the end of the walkway, where I found a heavyset, bored Mexican Customs agent who waved me on.

I strolled down Álvaro Obregón Avenue toward downtown Matamoros. The scent of fresh tortillas and fajitas wafted through the humid, stagnant air. Signs advertised dentistry, prescription drugs, and *mayoreo y menudeo* (wholesale clothing) on discount. Poor Americans of all ethnicities—white, black, Asian, Hispanic—who live near the border routinely travel south to purchase these daily necessities or find affordable health care. Men standing near taxis perked up; an approaching gringo could mean a payday. A banner hung on a one-story concrete building that said: Welcome Winter Texans–Tourist Information Center.

Álvaro Obregón, whose name was honored on this street, was born to an Irish-Mexican ranching family south of Arizona in the Mexican state of Sonora (the name originated from the Spanish spelling of O'Brien). In 1915, Obregón lost his right arm fighting Pancho Villa, whom he defeated four times on behalf of the Mexican government. Five years later, he led a successful revolt against the man he had supported during the Mexican Revolution. Obregón served a four-year term as president that was marked by increased petroleum exports and, subsequently, good relations with the Americans. He stepped down in 1924 amid a revolt against his chosen successor. In 1928, after Obregón won a tumultuous election to a second presidential term, a Catholic seminary student assassinated him in a restaurant. His surname is now linked to a drug cartel.

Thirty yards from the concrete building advertising tourist assistance, a short, wiry Mexican man approached wearing a white, untucked t-shirt and jeans. He smelled like beer and his eyes were cloudy and bloodshot. A plastic laminated card dangled around his neck from a chain. Underneath his black mustache, he was smiling.

"Hey! Hello! You are visiting here, yes?" he called out.

I nodded.

"Meester, listen to me." The man came closer, lowering his accented voice. "You want girls? I know a place. They are pretty," he said. His bloodshot eyes lit up and he smiled again, turning on his salesman shtick. "Young ones too! $25 for anything you want. $5 mattress rental." He made a dramatic pause. "And a free condom!"

I looked at him and said nothing.

He sobered up and switched tactics. "I am José," he said, lifting the laminated card that hung on his neck. "I work for the Tourism Office. My job is to help visitors."

I exchanged pleasantries and courtesies with José in Spanish, establishing the fact that I spoke a little and not much more. It broke the ice, but left me with a decision: stay and talk, or walk away. I thought that José might be a good "fixer"—a local able to find connections to an interesting story. Now was the time to find out. And in a place as byzantine as the border, sometimes candor is the simplest ruse.

I looked at José. "Can you find me a *coyote*?"

"A *coyote*? Sure!" José's eyes lit up and I could see his brain working calculations while he took my bait. A *coyote*, an illegal alien smuggler, wasn't a cheap commodity. This would be a far better payday, he thought, than a trip to a strip club or whorehouse. He would get something from me and something from the smuggler. "I can find a *coyote* for you, no problem. What, you need to get somebody across?"

"No," I said. "I want to talk with him."

José looked me over. "Why you wanna talk with a *coyote*?"

"I want to interview him. I'm writing a book about the border."

That was the last thing José expected to hear, and his face said so. A bald, beefy white guy speaking little Spanish waltzes into his turf, asks to see a *coyote*, and says he's writing a book. All in twenty seconds. If I'm lying, I might actually be spying for someone that José does not want to upset. If I really am a journalist, then anything he says or does could wind up in print. Either way, I had leveled the playing field.

"When you wanna see a *coyote*?"

"Right now," I said. "Before sunset, if possible."

José stopped. I was probing his connections, a delicate process for both of us. If I wasn't careful, it would look like I was trying to call his bluff; if he tripped up, he would lose face. Unless I had a lot of money and José had some powerful close friends, it was unlikely that a *coyote* would talk to me so quickly. If José started mentioning numbers, he was well-connected and influential (and he would be calling my bluff, because I didn't have enough cash to bribe my way into a *coyote* interview). If he begged for time to set things up, expressing a lot of concern about my safety, he had low street credentials and was poor. I was betting on the latter; no serious player in Matamoros, I thought, would be hawking hookers to passing gringos.

"I dunno. You don't just walk up on a *coyote*, you know? It wouldn't be right. I gotta make sure things are okay," José said. "Make sure they'll talk. I wouldn't want you to get hurt."

"When can you make it happen?" I asked.

"How long will you be in town?"

"Depends."

José paused. "End of the month."

"I'm supposed to leave tomorrow," I said. "But I'd like to learn more about Matamoros. You're a tour guide—want to show me around?"

José's eyes lit up again. He was not important; he knew it and I knew it. But I had allowed him to save face, I had treated him with respect, and I was offering him a chance to earn money. He would tell me how dangerous it was for me to walk around town—especially at night, of course—without him. I would nod thoughtfully. He would say that for $25 he would watch out for me. I would say $10. $20, he countered. $15. "Ah, you pay me whatever's in your heart," José said, smiling and waving his hand. Literary prostitution, fair and square.

For three hours, José Louis de la Fuente Amaro—that was how his name appeared on the official Tourist Guide badge he wore— talked to me about Matamoros, his job, and himself. He said Matamoros used to be much worse, before a drug kingpin named Garcia Obregón was captured and sent to prison several years ago. After that, the city became, according to him, "the safest place on the border." (When José said this, I didn't bring up his earlier comments about needing his protection to walk around town.) Compared to Nuevo Laredo, where drug violence had skyrocketed, Matamoros was, in José's words, a paradise.

"There are actually two cities called Matamoros," José said. "We are in the old city. The new one is several miles away. It came after NAFTA."

I asked José if he thought NAFTA was good. "Of course!" he said. "Look at all the riches. Malls, businesses, tourists—they wouldn't be here without NAFTA." Not everyone shares this attitude on either side of the border, but in Texas and northeastern Mexico, José's enthusiasm for free trade was, in my observation, a standard response.

It started to rain and we were hungry. I asked José where we could find some good fajitas. When I was stationed in Iraq, one of the popular stereotypes that Americans had of Arabs was that nothing important would be discussed without some kind of ritual hospitality—usually drinking several glasses of sweet tea. This was true. But the cultural classes taught, incorrectly, that this kind of phenomena was unique to Arabs. Emotional barriers recede in European coffee houses, minds are opened in Asian power lunches, and deals are made on American golf courses. Hospitality is good business in any culture.

José relaxed as we sipped Tecate and munched on thick, stale corn chips and salsa while we waited for our food. Earlier when we were walking, I had asked him if he had ever been to the United States. He nodded, but was vague and evasive when asked to explain. When did he get across? He laughed and changed the subject.

Our food came—thick, soft chunks of grilled steak, peppers, and onions, a bowl of soupy *frijoles*, and a stack of small corn tortillas. I asked José about his work as a tourist guide. He said he paid $10 a month to a local *jefe* for the license. Most of his clients were American men wanting girls, generic pharmaceuticals, or dental exams. This time of year, he was lucky to meet one tourist a day.

Spring Break was José's peak time. Collegians under twenty-one who had come to South Padre Island would walk across the border where they could drink without looking over their shoulder. Some rented condos on Playa Bagdad and stayed the week. José would act as escort/security/bar authority, telling them where it was "safe" to party. He usually raked in $50 per group, plus kickbacks from the club, bar, or disco where he took the revelers. A few weeks later, I searched fruitlessly through Mexican online databases for the names of the city officials listed on José's tourist guide card.

"How old are you?" I asked.

"Forty-two." He grew up somewhere other than Matamoros and had four brothers and four sisters. His parents lived in the States; he didn't say where.

"You married? Any kids?"

"No way, man," José said. "I have been divorced my whole life."

I confirmed, without mentioning his creative idiom, that José had never been married and (to his knowledge) had no children. He said he had a woman once, but that changed in 1984.

"*Por qué?*" I asked. "Why? What happened?"

By this time, José and I had been talking for a couple of hours. It seemed like it was uncommon for him to meet a white man who showed more interest in his life story than the available local women. But I had already told José my angle, even though he didn't seem to believe it, and we had established some degree of trust.

"I was nineteen and living in Dallas," he said. "I emptied trash at the Galleria Mall and did some construction. Then I got into drugs. I had money, a car. Lots of things. Life was good." José prefaced his accented sentences with: "What I'm a-talkin' about is . . ." and a sip of beer.

"A friend, he took my car one night and totaled it. He never said anything, never paid me back. Nothing. One night we got drunk and started arguing. I told him I wanted my money. He said no. I beat him up. We were both drunk, you know? I was just hitting and kicking him; I didn't know when to stop.

"They charged me with manslaughter. I thought they were going to kill me, but I got twenty years. I learned English at the prison school. They let me out on parole in 1991."

"And then you were deported?"

José nodded, drifting into melancholy. It was unclear exactly how old he was when he and his siblings had first entered illegally, or how long he had been in Dallas before he was arrested after beating his *amigo* to death. His mother had banished him when he had been paroled and deported, saying that he had to stay here in Matamoros and should not try to return to the States. If he came back over and was caught, she feared the whole family would be at risk since he had been in prison. (José's mother had a green card, but not all his siblings did.) She had visited him a year ago and did not stay long.

I asked when he and his family had first come to America. He didn't answer. Instead, José, in slurred, sad speech, described himself as a kind of family leper. He mentioned God a couple of times, as though by staying in the purgatory of Matamoros he was performing penance and, in some mystical way, warding off the curse of *La Migra* from his family. He lived in a one-room shack on a ranch fifteen miles south, he said. He paid rent to the rancher, as well as an electricity and water bill. For a few cents, he took a bus in and out of the city to work.

No tour guide stays sad for long, and José brightened: "But I didn't think I'd be eating in here for dinner tonight! *Gracias, mi amigo.*"

I slapped José's shoulder in response and looked at him with mock seriousness. "*Eres mi cabrón,*" I said, and we both laughed. Depending on the situation, *cabrón* is either an insult or a greeting among friends. Literally, I had called José my castrated goat—something like saying "you're my bitch" to a pal. It was a good way to lighten the mood; we were both tired from him telling me his troubles.

It was getting dark which meant it was time to go. I paid $10 for the food and beer, and José walked back with me toward America. Two hundred yards from the Gateway International Bridge I stopped, shook José's hand, and gave him a twenty.

"I knew you would pay me what was in your heart," he said. "You are a good man. Now I can pay my water bill!" José pulled a piece of paper out of his pocket, waving it triumphantly.

I asked if I could take a picture of the water bill. *Claro,* José said, and held it out for me to shoot. We shook hands and I waved as he ambled off.

José might have just been caught up in the moment. Or he might have decided that he didn't care if I discovered his thirty-peso water bill—about $2.75—was made out to a man with a different name. Perhaps the man, whose name I will not say out of respect, was José's landlord.

My own theory: José Louis de la Fuente Amaro and the man named on the water bill were one and the same. Like the strippers he sells to the sex-hungry, José had a stage name and a real one. So was his entire story a fake? I didn't think so. His jail time, his purgatory, his struggle with shame—I think he used a false name because he didn't want to publicly embarrass his family with his present or his past.

Either way, it was none of my business. José, or whoever he was, had showed me around Matamoros and given me things to think about, especially his affection for NAFTA, which I found mirrored throughout the Rio Grande Valley. Free trade between the North American countries has many critics and skeptics, but few of them seem to live near Brownsville.

As I was walking toward the bridge, another man called out to me. He was sitting down on a brick pavilion and had blue eyes, light skin, a beard, and a Jansport backpack. He was wearing a blue button-down shirt with the sleeves rolled up to his forearms, faded khakis, and white tennis shoes. He looked like a disoriented college freshman who had stumbled into Mexico instead of his 9:00 A.M. psychology class.

"Can you help me?" He asked, eyes begging for attention. "Please, I need help. I've been here a day, and I don't know anyone."

"What do you want?" I asked.

"My wife and kids are in Houston," he said, sounding like a man who was shoved into a deep lake before learning how to swim. "They brought me here yesterday."

"Did you go to Grupo Beta?" I asked, referring to the migrant refugee centers the Mexican government has established in large towns along the border. When U.S. Immigration and Customs Enforcement agents apprehend an illegal alien, the person is interrogated, fingerprinted, flown or bussed to the border, and simply dropped off on the other side like this man who had been in Houston. Grupo Beta's official charter was to provide assistance to the deported, but each station seemed to play by different rules.

"They said they can't help me at all," he said. "I'm from Guadalajara and I've been out of Mexico for too long."

I considered his options. "What do you do to make money?"

"I'm a painter."

"Can you paint here?"

"I don't know anyone," he said. "Who would I work for?"

"Can you go back to Guadalajara? Take your wife and kids home?"

"I haven't been there in years. We don't know anyone there either. And how will they get here? They have no car. And what about our things?"

I tried to put myself in his shoes. Let's say I had entered America at a young age as my great-grandparents did: gotten married, had children, had a clean record, and earned a respectable living. What if someone showed up at my house in the middle of the night, rounded me up, and flew me back to Italy? What would I do if I were snatched from my family and discarded into a place I had never seen? How would I react if my wife and kids were poor, destitute, and depending on me for their survival?

"You could go west a few miles and make a swim for it," I said, remembering the trails that Agent King and I were observing. "Not too much Border Patrol activity out there. Once you get across, a farmer might let you use the phone. Maybe a friend from Houston could pick you up and get you through the checkpoint."

"They said if they caught me again, I would do six months," said the man. "I don't wanna go to jail! I've followed the rules. I did nothing wrong. I work hard!

"What should I do?" He whined.

I was losing sympathy. In fact, I was getting frustrated. Instead of clearing his head and looking for answers, he was begging a random gringo on the street and then telling him reason after reason why he couldn't help himself. It seemed like he wanted me to say: "Sure *hombre*, let me go get my car, drive back over, pick you up, and get you over to Houston for free." He came across spoiled, as though his opportunities had always been handed to him by an elder, a parent, or some other benefactor.

Maybe it was because I have macho issues. I should probably be more compassionate about the fact that he couldn't think straight; that he'd never been shocked so much in his short, poor existence. But I couldn't respect a man who was unwilling to take any risks at

all, who wanted someone else to tell him how to fix his life or protect his family or make his way in this cruel, unfair world. I hoped,
for the sake of their kids, that his wife was made of stronger stuff.

But his immaturity wasn't the main reason I seethed. It was completely fair, in a way, for him to beg for my help. After all, I represented the country that profited from his cheap labor on the
painting crew; that stole whatever shred of manhood he once had by
catching him in the ridiculously criminal act of hard work; and that
tossed him, like a terrified rabbit, back into a home country he had
never known. Since my representatives refused to pass laws to document him, what did my country do? Rip the painter from Guadalajara from his bride and children, cast him into the shadows, and
rhetorically make him—a person, a human being, our own species—
into an "illegal."

At the same time, his homeland was owned by oligarchies that
choked off credit and capital, forcing money overseas and into their
own (narcotics-lined) coffers while preventing their countrymen
from achieving education and success. Because the law means so little in so much of Mexico, my own police officers are often forbidden
from enforcing the existing laws—which include deporting a person
residing illegally in America—thus encouraging him to violate the
law in the hopes of prospering.

I didn't need any special skills to forecast what would happen
next. For the next few days, the painter would scramble around
Matamoros. A drug runner would find the painter and offer him a
couple hundred dollars to pack a load of dope across the river. If he
was lucky, he would take the money, do the run, and make it back to
Houston. If not, he would be prosecuted and locked away for years,
under the theory that prison time would work as "deterrence" to
prevent further misbehavior (such as trying to put beans on his
table). Together, Americans and Mexicans have, through a combination of willful apathy, obtuse ignorance, and rigorous inaction,
enslaved millions of people like this painter in a terrifying and tragic
no-man's land.

"Here's a dollar for some food," I said, pointing to a taco stand.
"There's a man a couple blocks back wearing jeans and a white
t-shirt. He goes by José. Maybe he can help you."

I said goodbye, turned, and walked back into the United States.

**W**hen asked to name the largest cities in Texas, McAllen is usually not on the tip of anyone's tongue. Dallas comes first, followed by Houston, San Antonio, and Austin. Someone eventually remembers El Paso. A transplanted Texophile might toss out Corpus Christi as a guess, or large exurbs like Fort Worth or Galveston. But McAllen? Few Texans, let alone Americans, even know where McAllen is.

Seventy miles west of Brownsville on Highway 83, the McAllen metropolitan area, 700,000 and counting, is the fastest growing region in Texas. Before NAFTA, the city had topped out at 350,000, growing during the 1970s and '80s in proportion with other cities caught up in the boom time. Those years of prosperity—moderate population growth of 10 to 15 percent—resulted from the traditional building blocks of Valley industry: farming, ranching, and oil.

Four years after NAFTA passed in 1998, McAllen was growing at a 36.2 percent rate—the third-fastest in the nation that year behind Las Vegas and northern neighbor Laredo. The NAFTA population boom was caused by the new local economy: international trade. By 2018, if current projections hold, McAllen will leap ahead of El Paso as the state's fifth-largest metro area. By 2020, McAllen will hit 1 million.

Despite the chaotic pace of economic growth and unemployment that hovers at a modest 7 percent, more than 41 percent of McAllen's Hidalgo County population lives below the poverty line. According to the 2000 census, 51 percent of Starr County, which borders Hidalgo to the west, is also legally poor (eerily similar to Mexico's poverty rates). With a per capita income of $7,069 as of 2006, Starr County was both the poorest in Texas, and third poorest—to two counties in South Dakota—in the United States.

Because it does not capture the regional cost of living—food, housing, shopping—the statistical definition of poverty is a complicated metric for measuring the region's overall quality of life. The salaries are low in McAllen, but breakfast is also cheaper. Seen one way, the huge growth and expansive poverty could be viewed as racial oppression: wealthy white and Mexican businessmen are conspiring to keep a generation of new arrivals from Mexico—like the misfortunate painter I met in Matamoros—from obtaining wealth or political power.

But Latinos are not the only ethnic group flooding into McAllen. Big name corporations—Nokia, Panasonic, Sony, Motorola—have forced working-class Anglos to migrate south from the Bible Belt heartland. Both whites and Hispanics are contributing to McAllen's population explosion in their search for the American dream.

City-data.com, a public online forum with almost 200,000 registered users, collects and publishes statistics and information about U.S. cities. Judging from the posts on the user threads, the apparent value of the Web site is not the statistics, many of which can also be found through Wikipedia or local government sites. Many subscribers are potential nomads trolling for up-to-date information about little-known places where the forces of globalization might take them. These searchers include a woman named K. A. Brown, who posted this message on August 24, 2007:

> Moving to McAllen Texas from Indiana:
> I'm wanting to get information about living in the McAllen Texas area. My husband has accepted a position with a company in [the McAllen suburb of] Reynosa. We are from Indiana and have 2 girls who are 12 and 10. My concern is how well we will be accepted especially our blond haired blue eyed children. My husband and I are excited about this opportunity, but don't know if it is a good move for the kids. I don't want to offend anyone, but I know if we move we will be the minority and I don't want my kids to feel lonely and unaccepted.

Mrs. Brown's post generated thirty-five replies from persons claiming to be local residents. "TexasNick" said it would be a bit of a culture shock, but the hospitals and shopping are great. "RGV" provided links to school districts. "Teatime," an Anglo resident of the Valley, advised her not to buy a house and said her middle-school son was often called racial names. "Crbcrbrgv," an Anglo married to a Mexican and fluent in Spanish, bluntly told them not to move to the Valley because the schools were bad. "Grandma 24," an Anglo born and raised in McAllen, said she moved away to Colorado because it was just like living in Mexico.

Just when I thought I wouldn't find anyone who actually enjoyed living in McAllen, I read this from "Dr. Patricia":

> I know how you must feel about being the minority, but don't be afraid of change. I have learned so many things in this period in my life: when I realized that the world is not this little universe around me where everything is perfect. I try to teach my children (mostly my oldest who is 6) that people are different in color, beliefs, customs, etc and that it is ok. I wish you luck and if you decide to live there we can communicate and maybe meet down there. Let me know if I can be of help. Good luck.

⟫〉-◎-〈⟪

The Brown family and others like them are the latest generation of a long line of Anglo colonists to the Rio Grande. Texas—the name comes from a Plains Indian word meaning "friend"—was not fashioned by design, but, like many of the border's developments, evolved through a series of accidents. Anglo-American involvement in Texas began in the fall of 1820, when a southwestern Virginia man named Moses Austin traveled from Missouri to San Antonio and petitioned the King of Spain—as Europeans had done for centuries of New World colonization—for a charter to settle a group of families, the vast majority of Scots-Irish ethnicity, in Texas. Spanish colonial administrators approved, on the condition that the emigrants would surrender their U.S. citizenship and become Spaniards. Austin agreed and returned to Missouri.

At the same time Austin made his request to Spanish authorities, bands of Mexican guerrillas had been fighting for independence from European colonial rule. A latecomer to the revolution was Col. Agustín de Iturbide, a disillusioned, charismatic Spanish officer who fought against the insurgents before switching sides. On July 24, 1821, the Spanish viceroy capitulated, signing away all of Spain's claims in North and Central America to Iturbide, who fancied himself a North American Napoleon. Less than a year later, Iturbide was crowned Emperor Agustín I by a Mexican congress of appointed loyalists.

Moses Austin died a month before Spain's defeat; his oldest son, Stephen, was left in charge of the colonial venture. The younger Austin, who had settled in New Orleans, had been reluctant to join the pioneers, but his father's passing left no other option. Stephen Austin embraced his calling to become a Mexican with gusto, traveling to Mexico City to present his request to the emperor. Austin, a bachelor whom one writer described as "a small, fastidious man, with a head rather large for his body," threw himself into learning Mexican culture and custom, writing letters to Louisiana imploring his younger brother to write and speak Spanish, which, Austin earnestly believed, would be the key to their future success.

But in less than a year, Emperor Agustín, who Austin had initially felt was "a very good man," had bankrupted the nascent Mexican nation. Departing Spaniards were granted exchange for the value of their lands in hard currency, depriving the Mexican treasury of silver and gold. Debts exceeding 2 million pesos had accrued from his frivolity. Agustín was drunk daily, and his wife, the Empress Ana María, was spending hundreds of pesos on chocolate. He was more Nero than Napoleon—all foam and no beer.

Austin, who was still in Mexico City, had been lucky. All laws of the emperor had been voided, and, henceforth, any loyalist of Agustín was a traitor; the emperor, however, had never acted on his colonial grant. In the meantime, Austin had kept busy observing the rise and fall of the Mexican government. It was the first of several revolutions during his years as a Mexican citizen, and the experience left him disillusioned. The corrupt Catholic clergy, the incompetent bureaucracy, and the instability of each succeeding administration—each seemed, like a political *telenovela*, destined to fall in a more operatic drama than the last.

To Austin's frustration, the Mexican inefficiencies seemed to thwart each of the grand opportunities that Texas offered. The American colonists had expected to be doing business with a stable, Spanish bureaucracy that would ensure their freedom and eventual prosperity. Instead, they wound up with a different leader and legislative system each year. They didn't land on Mexico City. Mexico City landed on them.

While Austin recognized the lack of unity between the Anglo and Mexican systems, he had no enthusiasm for secession. Texas, which had been an unsettled northern frontier, was joined as a state with Coahuila in the Mexican Constitution—they were known as the "Twin Sisters." Austin had two main ambitions: to expand the population of Texas through immigration and to make Texas an independent state within Mexico. He accomplished his first goal in April 1823, when, just after the emperor fell, the Mexican Congress approved his petition. Texas could be settled. And the floodgates were opened.

In 1828, a Mexican man named José Sánchez visited the Austin settlement from Matamoros. He thought little of the Anglos—their log cabins and mud plaster and villages lacked order compared to his civilized pueblos and plazas—but something about Austin concerned him. These Texicans, as some called them, didn't wait for central authority to tell them what to do. Energy, ambition, and opportunism drove them, not tradition, custom, and honor. They had mouthed the pledges of allegiance, but in their eyes—and in reality—their fate was in their own hands. Some were Catholics, but they lacked the fervent Mexican devotion to the Church and the clergy. They trusted in God, but helped themselves. "In my judgment," Sánchez wrote, "the spark that will deprive us from Texas will start from this colony."

By now, Austin's original Scots-Irish group of Anglo-American settlers had become known as the Old Three Hundred. As word spread of the land and opportunity that abounded, the human waves grew to 3,000. They built farms and log cabins in east Texas, between the Brazos and Colorado rivers. Some followed Austin to his settlement, an hour north of San Antonio de Bexár. Many brought slaves. In seven years, by 1830, their numbers had swelled to 30,000—twice the number of Mexicans and Indians combined.

Although the colonists were required, like Austin, to forsake their U.S. citizenship and swear allegiance to Mexico, their new mother country found the immigration explosion unsettling. Mexico had outlawed slavery in 1821, granting one Mexican state, Tehuantepec, a legal exemption. Austin asked for and received permission for Texas to also be a Mexican "slave state." In his letters, he expressed moral regret about this, in the same utilitarian, rational vein that the American Founding Fathers did in their own memoirs. According to an 1830 letter, the slavery issue was the main reason, Austin wrote, that he opposed American plans to acquire Texas—either fairly or with force.

Although Mexico City granted the slavery exemption, in 1830— on the heels of yet another revolution—their patience ran out. Laws were passed banning all immigration from the United States. Texas seaports were forced, for four months, to admit only Mexican or European ships, hindering trade with American merchants. American ships were taxed at all Mexican ports. No American could even visit Texas without a visa issued by Mexico City. And all edicts were to be enforced with military power; garrisons were mobilized in Matamoros. It was, for Texans, the equivalent of the Intolerable Acts.

After several intrigues and yet another revolution, the Mexicans turned their loyalties to another pretender to the Napoleonic legend, Gen. Antonio López de Santa Anna. This latest president had helped engineer the fall of the emperor in 1823, repulsed a Spanish assault at Tampico in 1829, and offered his military assistance in one way or another to each new revolutionary leader. At the end of each cycle, Santa Anna would return to his Veracruz ranch, and, like a self-styled Cincinnatus, declare that he was retiring "unless the people need me." In 1833, General Santa Anna's army convinced the Mexican people that they needed him to become the new president.

Tensions in Texas increased. In 1833, Austin traveled to Mexico City to appeal directly to President Santa Anna for an end to the immigration ban and, once again, for division of the "Twin Sisters" state of Coahuila-Texas into separate provinces. But Santa Anna was away from the capital; several southern provinces had rebelled and the president was personally leading his army to put down the revolt. Austin pled his case to numerous congressmen, ministers, officials, and even the vice president. Some were sympathetic, but it went nowhere. Frustrated by the inaction, Austin wrote a tempestuous letter in October 1833 urging the settlers to form their own state government, separate from Coahuila's authority, as soon as possible. "If the people of Texas do not take matters into their own hands," Austin wrote, "that land is lost."

Days after sending the letter, Austin learned that the uprising had been quieted and that Santa Anna would be returning immediately. Suddenly, all was well. In two appointments, the president listened to Austin's requests, formally lifted the ban on immigration, and agreed to bring the question of Texas statehood to a quick resolution in the Mexican Congress. It was everything Austin could have asked for. He sent word back quickly, imploring the colonists to disregard his last message.

But Austin's fiery missive could not be recalled with the push of a button. The town council in San Antonio had made copies of the letter and distributed it for public discussion; the copies had found their way into the hands of Mexican authorities throughout the Twin Sisters state. Austin's call for statehood without the government's approval was an act of sedition, and the town council wanted nothing of it. They mailed a copy of the letter to Mexico's vice president, along with their corporate reply. "It is certainly regrettable," wrote the San Antonio town council, "that you should breathe sentiments so contrary and opposed to those of every good Mexican."

In January 1834, while returning to Texas from Mexico City, Austin was arrested in Saltillo, Coahuila, on charges of treason. In Austin's mind, according to a letter he wrote from prison, the excitement was a misunderstanding. "In a moment of irritation and impatience I wrote an imprudent letter . . . for which I have been arrested and ordered back to Mexico." He asked that there be "no excitement about it" among the people, for he believed he had done nothing wrong. In July 1835, after languishing in various prisons, Austin was released under a general amnesty given to all prisoners from recent civil wars, revolutions, and political uprisings. The frequent turnover had made it difficult to determine who had been jailed for supporting whom, and whether or not they were currently in or out of power.

Events were in motion by September 1835 when Austin returned to Texas. Because of the ongoing civil strife, Santa Anna had suspended local authority and proclaimed martial law in varying degrees throughout Mexico. Although Santa Anna declared assemblies unlawful, Texans began violating this law throughout the state. Gen. Martin Perfecto de Cos, Santa Anna's brother-in-law, anticipated orders to crush the burgeoning rebellion. He was garrisoned in Matamoros, along with several thousand soldiers.

General Cos didn't have to wait long. Uprisings had already begun along the Gulf Coast, and Mexico City ordered him to hunt down, arrest, and execute the ringleaders. Austin's followers pressed the question of assembly to him when he returned. He called for a convention to determine whether the people of Texas wished to remain under Santa Anna's centralized government or establish their own republic. Austin's call for assembly was understood and treated by both sides for what it was: a call to arms. No Texan town council opposed the measure. Much had changed in two years since the San Antonio city leaders had so skittishly decried Austin's "imprudent" letter.

The winter 1835 march that General Cos led into south Texas was a dismal failure. It was not the ritualistic, column-and-file method of warfare the Mexicans had customarily practiced when putting down one of their own rebellions. Over the previous two years, when Santa Anna had been putting down civil wars, he fought them—to some degree—as counterinsurgencies. Unless the people rallied for the rebel, the majority were left alone. If they massed, the army formed and charged. The ringleaders were hunted down and executed. This went on until the president felt the population's loyalty had been retained, and his own honor—and Mexico's—had been preserved.

The Texans were outnumbered, but they shot straighter and fought harder at every siege and skirmish. They borrowed their tactics of stealth, ambush, and deception from Revolutionary War heroes like Francis "Swamp Fox" Marion as well as the Apache, Kiowa, and Comanche raiders who often assailed their homes. They did not seek a fair, honorable fight; their only ambition was to drive the Mexican army from their land.

In the spring of 1836, President Santa Anna arrived and took command of over 10,000 Mexican soldiers. We know what happened next, at places like the Alamo, Goliad, and San Jacinto, involving men named Davy Crockett, Jim Bowie, and Sam Houston. By the summer of 1836, the "Texians," as U.S. President Andrew Jackson referred to them in letters, were free. Texas was an independent nation until 1845, when the republic joined the United States and, in so doing, instigated the Mexican-American War.*

I took this excursion into the complexities of Texas history in an effort to illustrate one important point: the relationship between Texas and Mexico differs from that of other border states. In south Texas, I discovered genuine affection and admiration for the Mexicans among the Valley's denizens, even those who were dyed-in-the-wool Texans. I also saw that outlook reciprocated in northeastern Mexico toward Texas by Mexicans. Both reminded me that Gen. Ignacio Zaragoza, who led the Mexican Army in defeating a French invasion of Mexico on May 5, 1862—a date now celebrated as Cinco de Mayo—was born a Texan in Goliad. In the Valley, Texans and Mexicans don't grudgingly tolerate. They like each other.

This melting pot was not something I saw in Arizona—a territory the Mexicans parted with after losing the war with the Americans—where visitors and residents were invariably forced to pick sides. In the Valley and along the border, Texas is to Mexico as New England is to Great Britain. Their attitude toward the old motherland is that of an adult who long ago outgrew an overbearing, myopic parent: awareness, affection, and hope for growth and renewal despite the divisions of the past.

In Texas, the cultural traditions behind each of the six flags that have flown over the territory (French, Spanish, Mexican, Texan, Confederate, and American) have joined with the traditions of Scots-Irish ancestors, imprinting their cultural chromosomes inside the state's collective DNA in ways that are not easily grasped by other Americans. George W. Bush learned this the hard way when he failed to persuade the American public to accept the laissez-faire immigration

---

* The Mexican-American War was one of only five wars in American history where U.S. troops were sent to a foreign land under a Congressional declaration of war. The others were the War of 1812, Spanish-American War, World War I, and World War II. All other American military actions, including the wars in Afghanistan and Iraq, have either been intra-territorial (Revolution, Civil War, Indian Wars) or were not officially declared by Congress.

philosophy he first explored while governor of Texas. The volumes of trade versus passenger traffic are higher in the Texan corridors than anywhere else on the border. Resistance to a fence is, by far, at its strongest near the Rio Grande. And the same pursuits of happiness that caused Moses Austin to migrate have called out to a new generation of colonists seeking opportunity and fortune in McAllen.

⟶⟶⟶⟶⟶◆◆◆⟵⟵⟵

Isaac Guerra is the thirty-one-year-old owner of McAllen's España Mediterranean Cuisine. He is a throwback to a rugged, simple era of capitalism, a Renaissance man of the Rio Grande. He looks like a rock star: long, curly black hair, a scruffy goatee, silver jewelry, a black t-shirt, jeans, and a tennis-style sweatband pulled onto his forearm. "I haven't owned a business card my entire life," Isaac said. It's not the appearance and attitude you'd expect from one of the most successful businessmen in McAllen.

Isaac Guerra grew up in Premont, a blink-and-you-miss-it hamlet of ranchers two hours north of the border. At age fourteen, when kids hailing from suburbia start mowing lawns, flipping burgers, selling clothes, or rolling joints to make extra cash, Isaac began trading cattle. In a few months, he had made enough money to go away to school—high school—in San Antonio. As a fifteen-year-old freshman at St. Anthony Catholic Seminary and High School, he rented his own apartment, paid his tuition, and started a wine collection after securing a fake identification card. Unable to leverage parental forces against his independent spirit, the St. Anthony administration asked Guerra to leave his junior year. He finished high school at Texas Military Institute, ran a landscaping business, and hosted weekend parties.

Isaac had no interest in college. Instead of pouring his time into fraternities and extracurricular clubs, he moved to McAllen and worked with his sister, who, along with her husband, owned six Dairy Queens throughout the Valley. A year later, Isaac secured a lien on a decrepit building on Main and 15th Street. He worked with friends, hired hands, and his five siblings to fix it up. They redesigned the structure into an adobe plaza that blended Texan, Mediterranean,

and Mexican themes. In October 1996, the owner of España Mediterranean Cuisine opened his restaurant to positive reviews. He had just
turned twenty-one.

Isaac is the kind of self-made artisan who mothers either court for
marriage to their daughters or proposition for themselves. Some try to
do both at the same time; Isaac has that kind of magnetism. In the
lobby of a swanky Marriott hotel, I saw him greet the U.S. District
Judge as though he were a lifelong relative. His house is filled with
books, musical instruments, wine, antiques, state-of-the-art technology,
and top-of-the-line appliances. Beyond his entrepreneurial success,
Isaac counts the time he saved a choking friend's life at a party with
the Heimlich maneuver as one of his most notable accomplishments.

The first time I met Isaac Guerra was at a *pachanga*. The driving
force in south Texas politics, a *pachanga* is a cross between a picnic
and a town meeting. Local politicians or those seeking office sponsor a barbeque, cookout, or potluck to strategize with supporters,
attract new voters, and take the pulse of the community on issues of
the day. Depending on the occasion, a *pachanga* will range from
informal to exotic. Some are advertised with handbills, but knowledge of most, like the one where I met Isaac, is spread by word of
mouth. Any interested citizen is welcome to attend. According to the
magazine *Texas Monthly*, attending a Rio Grande Valley *pachanga* is
one of the fifty things you should do "if you're a real Texan."

This *pachanga* was at the Cine El Rey, a Spanish movie theater on
the National Register of Historic Places that Isaac had leased with an
option to buy. After it was built in 1947, the Cine El Rey, with its Span-
ish-only cinematic focus, became the dynamic heart of McAllen's Hispanic community. Profits waned over time, which led to Isaac's
operational takeover in May 2007. He planned to change Cine El
Rey's focus from cinema to live entertainment.

In the meantime, Isaac had rented out the Cine El Rey for the
evening to help Don Medina—a garrulous, fleshy, clean-shaven Hispanic—who was running for McAllen city commissioner. Wearing a
straw hat, "Vote Medina" t-shirt, and long blue shorts, Medina had
campaigned as a populist. He had received support from police and
firefighters unions, as well as young, wealthy locals like Isaac Guerra
who oppose the construction of a border fence. Medina's supporters
had brought cold cuts and chips, and Guerra had some paella

behind the ticket counter from the restaurant that he distributed as he saw fit.

There was little energy at the *pachanga*; it looked like Medina was going to lose the election. The endorsements had come too late, and Medina's opponent—a white incumbent—had already secured a wide margin of write-in votes from the "snowbirds," wealthy winter Texans, mostly also white, who lived in McAllen seasonally and were vested on many levels in maintaining the status quo.

All of this made the *pachanga* venue of Cine El Rey oddly appropriate. The city of McAllen—and much of the surrounding Rio Grande Valley—grew up as a result of the Bracero Program that developed when demand for agricultural labor increased during World War II. The name comes from the word *brazo*, meaning arm in Spanish, which was Mexican slang for "hired arms," or farm workers. During World War II, many white-owned businesses in Texas, including theaters, had refused service to the *braceros*; Spanish-language films were only shown after midnight or not at all.

McAllen's would-be city commissioner understood better than most what the *braceros* had endured. During the 1860s, Don Medina's descendents settled as sharecroppers in Waco, Texas. In 1931, after the Dust Bowl forced his grandparents from the land they worked, they went south, planning to move back to Mexico. They made it to Pharr, a town near McAllen. Soon, they figured out a crop rotation where they would always have seasonal work.

Each year, Grandpa Medina got a crew. Some were legal; many were not. It wasn't important. In early spring, they drove to Indiana to plant tomatoes. Then they went to Michigan to pick cherries. Then to North Dakota to hoe beets. Then back to Indiana to pick the tomatoes they had planted in the spring. And then down to west Texas to pick cotton until December. That was nine months of work. Grandpa Medina did it for forty-four years.

After telling me that story, Don Medina left to mingle with election supporters, leaving me to chew on Isaac's paella and ruminate over the migrant life. Sometimes, I imagined, his grandfather and father had decent food and a comfortable place—a barn, perhaps—to sleep. But they also had more than a few nights with the earth as their pillow and the rain from summer thunderstorms as their blankets. Grandpa Medina was an American citizen, but to his employers, he was no different than the *braceros*; just another *mojado*, or "wetback," they needed for work.

The Cine El Rey isn't the only place Isaac's artistic streak is on display. The walls of his house are covered with sketches and paintings. He did some of them himself; others were the work of a friend named Hector Aristo, whom he called his artistic soul mate. The pair of them could sit in the same room and paint for hours, Isaac said, without saying a word. Hector was the finest artist that Isaac had ever known. Isaac hasn't seen Hector in over two years. A day later, I would learn why.

⟺⟺⟺⟺

I came to know the Cine El Rey, Don Medina, and Isaac Guerra through Eric Ellman, a free-spirited athlete who ran Los Caminos Del Rio—a state-sponsored organization dedicated to the Rio Grande Valley's heritage—from his downtown McAllen home. Ellman, who might best be described as a socially responsible libertarian, is passionate about environmental causes, fitness, cultural preservation, and healthy living. A former travel writer and Manhattan cabbie, Eric organizes kayaking trips on the Rio Grande through Los Caminos Del Rio to encourage athleticism and the exploration of border culture. He is thin, muscular, bald, white, and looked twenty-five even though he is fifty.

Ellman seemed to be a "with-it" guy in the Valley, particularly for someone who hadn't grown up in the area. He owned a one-story house where he lived with a yellow lab, Buster, and an occasional animal he rescued from becoming roadkill on behalf of the SPCA and his own conscience. He spent several years cycling through Mexico, learning Spanish along the way and co-authoring a 1990 guidebook, *Bicycling Mexico*, about his journeys. Although the names of roads, hotels, and restaurants may have changed since Ellman crisscrossed Mexico two decades ago, the cultural mores of the region have not. That Eric Ellman was included in Isaac Guerra's friendly circle indicated that his vagabonding worked to his advantage—at least in McAllen—once he wanted to put down roots.

Two days after the ride-along with Agent Walter King, I spent an afternoon with Eric kayaking the Rio Grande. We loaded up at a gas station/taco stand with barbacoa, chorizo-and-egg, Tecate beer, and a mango/cherry/jalapeño frozen dessert—a sweet, spicy Italian ice—that tasted better than it might sound. Buster, the yellow lab, came along as well. He wore a canine life jacket and rode in the back of Eric's flatbed pickup along with three orange kayaks, climbing on top of the plastic shells as if they were surfboards. I thought Buster might get thrown from the truck, but with the wind in his ecstatic face and an uncanny sense of balance, he was in doggie heaven.

As we wended north along Highway 83 and the dirt roads paralleling the river, Eric gave me his own Valley version of a ride-along, uncensored and politically charged. Our first stops were at *resacas*— calm, hidden lakes formed when the river swelled and receded over millennia. They were great places to take the blind for bird-listening tours, which Eric helped organize, and to kayak with kids during summer camps. The riparian habitats that surrounded the *resacas* had been protected for decades by the federal government, under the Fish and Wildlife Service.

But for Eric, the government's ownership of the land adjacent to the river might be a double-edged sword. Because the land belongs to the feds, it is the first place they can build a fence. That infrastructure could threaten Los Caminos del Rio, the cultural preservation organization that Eric runs under a charter from the Texas Historical Commission. "There are thirty species of birds here that don't exist anywhere else in America," Eric said. "The government won't even have to file an environmental impact statement because this is federal land." Los Caminos del Rio had hoped to develop the river areas into public campgrounds. A fence would make that impossible.

"A Border Patrol agent told us they want to put two fences here, 150 yards apart with a road in between," Eric said. "Then they can drive fifty miles an hour up and down to patrol."

We drove on—past the Los Ebaños Ferry, a hand-drawn barge that held six cars and was the only legal port of entry into the United States of its kind; past San Benito, home of the alligator gar, the second-largest freshwater fish in North America; past a billboard featuring a San Antonio Spurs basketball player that advertised the benefits of a local cell phone company—until we arrived at our launch location. It was a privately owned picnicking spot half a mile from a border shantytown and ten miles south of Falcon Dam, a reservoir and state park. On a handshake agreement that we would lock up and clean up, the owner gave us the keys to the cattle gate blocking the entrance. We gave him two six-packs of Tecate.

I asked Eric if there was any health concern about the river's water quality. He said that Los Caminos del Rio tests water samples regularly and has not found significant amounts of toxins. "That's the biggest problem we face," he said, referring to his efforts to get more Valley residents to use the river for recreation. "People who lived here their whole lives think the river is unsafe," he said. "But really, there's nothing dangerous about kayaking or even swimming in this part of the Rio Grande."

We put in and paddled upriver a third of a mile. Recent rainfall meant that the dam was open, the river was high and swift, and the pull against the stream was vigorous. We went upriver twice, coming back downstream with paddles in the air to ride the rapids. Buster also joined us on the water, taking the front seat in Eric's boat, although he didn't seem to appreciate taking a dip after Eric intentionally tipped his kayak. Even near the riverbank, the current was too strong for Buster, who frantically swam to the shore. Believing Eric was in trouble, he did not stop barking or looking for help until his master was out of the water.

It was a picturesque day on the Rio Grande. The sun was shining, the kayaks were drying out, Buster was napping on his back. We had worked up a healthy appetite for the barbacoa, chorizo, and *cerveza*. A picnic table, bench, and gazebo offered some shade. We sat and talked about the border.

"Legal activities can displace illegal ones," said Eric, referring again to his belief that the efforts of Los Caminos del Rio to develop the river into a destination for outdoor tourism would reduce the incentives offered by the underground smuggling industry. "You can see how poor these people are. Why wouldn't they take money for smuggling? But if we could really build up this place. . . ." His voice trailed off.

Eric said that from a standpoint of national sovereignty he did not understand the political obsession with building a fence. "The international border runs down the river," he said. "Why do we want to give the entire river and the shoreline to Mexico?" To him, fortifying the border would be a waste of an opportunity.

But then, to my surprise, Eric said that he understood the perspective of immigration opponents. "They have a right to be amazed at how porous the border is," he said. "I heard of a guy near Roma who takes up to thirty people a night for $20 per person. When we do our trips, sometimes we see a group on the Mexican side. We wave, they wave. They wait until we're downriver, and then they go in."

Eric went on, saying that when volunteers from Los Caminos Del Rio do cleanups of the riverbanks, the item most often discovered is two water jugs tied together at the handles. "They put one gallon under one arm and then the other, and use them as 'water wings' when they come across," Eric said. "They don't know how to swim."

This brought the conversation to Hector Aristo, Isaac Guerra's artistic soul mate. As it turned out, Hector had also designed Eric's living room floor and painted several of the pictures in his house. But one day, Hector wrote a bad check. Collectors found that he had overstayed a tourist visa and was living illegally in McAllen. Hector was arrested by Immigration and Customs Enforcement agents and deported to Reynosa.

During the summers, the city of McAllen sponsors Artwalk, a free, public event held downtown on the first Friday evening of each month. Shortly after he was deported, Hector's work was selected by patrons for display at the exposition. Hector had made a name for himself among the wealthy winter Texans by teaching art classes at the community college. The snowbirds did not know that Hector was an illegal.

My cynical side figured that nobody as wealthy as Isaac could make it on the border without being involved in smuggling. So I was surprised when Eric told me that it took a couple of phone calls for Isaac to track down someone who knew a *coyote* that would make sure Hector was present for his own Artwalk event. On the Friday of Artwalk, Hector Aristo was smuggled across the Rio Grande in a raft, picked up at a safe house, taken to his own art exhibition in McAllen, and then returned to Mexico before sunrise. Had he been caught by the Border Patrol, he would have faced up to fifteen years in prison.

I told Eric that he made illegally crossing the border sound like a teenager sneaking out of mom and dad's house for an evening out. "Yeah," he said, "with parents who don't really follow through on punishment." Years ago in Tijuana, Eric said, Latino youth gone wild used to jump the fence for Journey concerts and then go back home the next day. For residents of border towns, an illegal crossing often had nothing to do with fleeing oppression in search of a better life. It was practically a recreational sport.

Later, I talked with Isaac about the Artwalk caper. Hector, according to Isaac, had not told anyone that he was illegally in McAllen. (Admittedly, his friends thought it better not to ask.) Being a money man, Isaac thought that bouncing a check was the worst possible way to get caught. And although Isaac will party all night at any club in McAllen, he takes fierce pride at having made his fortune honorably. Hector had forced him to choose loyalty over the law, which, had the operation been unsuccessful, could have left Isaac in a compromised position.

It also could have shaded Isaac's reputation enough that outside observers would want to know if there was more to his money than appearances showed. After I asked if he had ever been involved in smuggling, Isaac shook his head. Realizing that his denials may not be sufficient, he whipped out his Palm Treo, called his mother, and said I was welcome to ask her anything I wanted. Mrs. Guerra and I chatted for a few minutes, and she told me that her son had always been honest and independent. Isaac encouraged me to question all of McAllen to confirm that he had no smuggling ties. I kept getting the same answers: a determined, fair businessmen and a kind, decent rock-n-roll rogue. An artist and cuisine merchant, not a smuggler.

Isaac felt the most frustration with McAllen's wealthy elites. It was their children, he said, who benefited from Hector's art lessons. They admired his paintings and applauded his presentations, while forcing him to hide his life in the shadows by passing laws that tied check-bouncing to immigration in an interminable war against the illegals. Hector, who left on his own for Mexico City after his illegal crossing for the Artwalk, has not contacted anyone in McAllen in two years. Isaac doubts he will ever hear from him again.

Perhaps this was why people as diverse as Agent Walter King and Eric Ellman resisted an aggressive increase in fortifications. Both were gringos, both spoke Spanish, and both saw an interest in creating a better way of life on each side of the boundary. For King, it was through his belief as a constable on patrol that enforcing the law would make both countries safer. For Ellman, his "alternative version of the border" meant using the river for something that would bring vigor and vibrancy to a poor people.

It seemed that both men found most border traffic in the Valley to be either legitimate (thousands working in one country while living in another) or benignly illegal (Hector's art show attendance). Both opposed narcotics, disdained the exploitation of the poor by smugglers, and empathized with the migrants themselves. And King and Ellman both thought that counterterrorism, not migrant control, was the Border Patrol's most important job.

I decided that Walter King and Eric Ellman and many other residents of the Rio Grande Valley I met understood a truth that Americans not living on the border often ignore: Mexico's problems are our problems, too. Like Siamese twins, both nations fight to be rid of each other, but remain bound despite their individuality. Perhaps others can't see that reality because they lack geographical knowledge, or maybe they refuse to accept it because of that truth's inconvenience.

Dr. Patricia, who wrote to Mrs. K. A. Brown on city-data.com reminding her not to fear change, understood that connection from living in McAllen and Monterrey. Apparently Mr. Brown did as well. A month after she asked for advice, Mrs. Brown posted a note to the thread. She said her husband was enjoying the work and excited about their new opportunity. She remained concerned about the girls being a minority, but she also seemed hopeful about making the adjustment to a different reality.

⸺⸺≫-◦-≪⸺⸺

Driving north towards Laredo along Highway 83 north toward Laredo, I stopped near the town of Zapata and walked into a seafood diner. When I entered, I was greeted by a woman who spoke no English. She smiled and pointed to a stool facing the road; I sat down. A man came out, handed me a menu, and asked me, in English, what I wanted. They had obviously judged my appearance, I thought, and concluded that I couldn't carry myself in their native tongue. I didn't sense any prejudice from them. They just wanted to serve a paying customer.

Determined to breach the cultural barrier, I asked in broken Spanish about the alligator gar, the scaly, huge freshwater fish native to the Rio Grande. The waiter told me, in English, that it was meaty, like halibut. I wasn't sure if he replied to me in English because I was a gringo or because my Spanish was much worse than I had thought. I hoped for the former, but feared the latter. He walked away and said, again in English, that he had to check on their stock.

*Muchas gracias*, I said, rolling the "r," softening the "ch," and accenting the proper syllables.

The waiter came back: "We're out of the gar. You want anything else?" He didn't speak a single Latin syllable. I gave up and, in English, ordered the seafood combo. It seemed I wouldn't be shedding my gringo skin anytime soon.

So when did this smuggling take place?, I wondered, munching on a fried scallop. How did it happen? What did it look like? The Border Patrol wasn't able to show me, and Isaac had long ago ditched his smuggling contact. The best option left in McAllen, I decided, was to find out for myself.

A trustworthy source with the local paper confirmed that the Roma Bluffs were a popular nighttime smuggling spot. Founded in 1760 by Spanish ranchers, the town of San Pedro de Roma was divided after Texas gained independence from Mexico in 1836. South of Falcon Dam on the International Falcon Reservoir—a flood control/hydroelectric project built in 1952 and named for the city it flooded out, not for the bird species—Roma marks the Rio Grande Valley's western perimeter. By day, Roma is headquarters for the World Birding Center, where ducks, pigeons, and robins are often seen and heard along the sandstone cliffs that run up from the riverbank. Once a port for Rio Grande steamboats, Roma's plaza has been designated a national historic landmark, and the suspension bridge connecting the city with its southern neighbor, Miguel Alemán, is the only one of its kind on the river.

I went to the bluffs at 9 P.M. on a clear Friday night. I wore what had become my border research uniform: jeans, a short-sleeve button down, and cheap hiking boots I had picked up at Wal-Mart. I carried a small digital camera in one back pocket, a notepad in the other, and an energy drink to keep me awake. The waxing gibbous moon was two days from full and the Rio Grande shimmered. Lights from the suspension bridge reflected off the water's surface. Fireflies twinkled, darting through tall grass along the sandstone cliffs. Bullfrog croaks punctuated the humid air.

My plan was to look for a hiding place, sit for a few hours, and see what I could find. I didn't want to trip any Border Patrol sensors or encounter any agents without an explanation, and being a writer doing research didn't seem like a good one. If I came across anyone official, I would say I was a security consultant for a group of wealthy Canadian birdwatchers who had hired me to scout the area before investing in a trip. Blackwater Birding. Not the greatest alibi.

The paved road leading to the Roma bluffs, which was north of the suspension bridge, stopped at the edge of the cliffs. On top, there were two permanent pavilions; one had benches and was quite open, the other was in disrepair. Between the pavilions and the bridge were steel stairs. Reeds and grass had grown over the steps, and mesquite trees cast shadows while I clattered and clanged down in the dark. Mosquitoes feasted on my scalp. I kicked myself for forgetting both insect repellent and a hat, and for the noise I was making as I descended. I was sure the Border Patrol would find me in seconds. Some scout I was.

I made it to the bottom of the stairs and looked around. At the base of the cliffs was a road running from the bridge to a water treatment plant. Not seeing any agents, I walked down the trail and took a seat below the plant's concrete wall. I had a good view of the river and was hidden from the road. On the Mexican side, two roads went from Miguel Alemán to a train network and what looked like a boat ramp. I sipped on my energy drink and settled in, listening to nature's voices chattering from the shadows and the rhythmic bouncing of cars and trucks crossing the bridge.

I had almost drained the can of syrupy caffeine when, suddenly, on the Mexican riverbank, a four-door sedan started its engine, turned on its headlights, and drove away. Since I didn't see anyone get in or out, I thought it might have been a pair of teenage lovers. Or perhaps a call for a pickup further down or up river. A few minutes afterward, dogs barked to the north.

An hour later, I stood, walked, and climbed back up the stairs to find a better stakeout position. A unit of floodlights was turned on that had been off before; either they were on a timer or someone had flipped a switch. Sitting up on the bluffs near a pavilion, I saw more of the river. It looked about seventy yards wide.

Twenty minutes after I sat down, a Border Patrol Suburban approached on the road, apparently on a routine patrol. I hid behind the adobe and brick, and the Suburban sped off without noticing me. This would be my only encounter with *La Migra* that night in Roma, which I found surprising. The bluffs seemed like an ideal place for the "virtual fencing" of detection sensors and cameras so often mentioned in border security articles. I thought I would have set something off and the Border Patrol would come running.

If virtual fencing had been in place that night, it wouldn't have stopped anyone. Of course, actual fencing would not have provided any greater deterrence. Only a young couple and their elementary school son had noticed me on the pavilion. They had waved to me, but didn't stay and chat. I waved back, and returned to my observation post.

Ten minutes later, I saw what looked like the same sedan return down to the Mexican riverbank. A car door opened and someone got out. It might have been more than one person; I couldn't tell. The car stayed thirty seconds and then revved, heading up the hill. I heard female voices in a normal tone of voice, and then nothing. Five minutes later, just as before, the dogs had started barking.

In another ten minutes, the car was back. Only this time the driver cut the headlights and stayed at the top of the hill. Nobody got in or out. To the north, the dogs yapped. They were not barking continuously; it was only for a few moments at intervals, the way a dog might bark when a stranger passes their house.

The moon went behind a cloud. Upriver, I heard splashing.

The timing was interesting. If there was any smuggling happening tonight near Roma Bluffs, it wasn't here. But it did seem like *coyotes* were herding their alien flocks to a spot upriver. The would-be illegals would climb onto their water wings, slip into the current (terrified because they had never been swimming), and, if they were lucky, survive the float over to the United States. Their destination: a private, *coyote*-owned safe house on the American side of the river, not far from Roma's sandstone birdwatching paradise.

It was after 1 A.M. and the car remained parked. A pair of trucks slipped onto the suspension bridge, growled, and raced each other toward Mexico. The bullfrogs and mosquitoes ignored the chaos and did their thing. The moonlight twinkled on the water.

I called it a night. Maybe what I didn't see was more important than what I did. Four hours sitting on the border, and zero contact with a single Border Patrol agent. Some suspicious noises, but no visuals of any migrants. It makes sense. If a *coyote* is going to stay in business, they shouldn't be easy enough for a curious gringo to spot while hiding next to a well-lit suspension bridge. After all, I could have been *Migra*. But after what I saw on the bluffs, I'd give the advantage—in Roma, at least—to the *coyotes*.

I hit a gas station, wolfed a microwave burrito, and made it back to my hotel around three. I flipped on the television and watched a FOX News report about the criminal illegal invasion. The report was ominous, shrill, and annoying. Something that seemed falsely dramatic to me was apparently happening over 1,000 miles away in Nogales, Arizona.

Also, Congressman Tom Tancredo of Colorado was upset. Chief Carlos Carrillo, head of the Laredo Sector, had allegedly said that the Border Patrol's main mission was to stop terrorists and terror weapons, not illegal immigrants. The Border Patrol on its own, he said, could not end the immigration problem. I saw nothing wrong with Carrillo's statement, but Tancredo did, and demanded his immediate resignation.

Congressman Tancredo droned on, thumping war drums against the illegal invasion and calling for Chief Carrillo's head on a platter. I shut off the tube and fell asleep.

# 3

On November 14, 1956, a team of engineers gathered in Topeka, Kansas, for a ribbon-cutting ceremony. The governor was there, along with a junior U.S. senator, several federal administrators, and a handful of local bureaucrats. The engineers had just completed the first step in building what unbeknownst to the VIPs, would become the largest man-made structure in the world. No major metropolitan newspaper, radio broadcaster, or television station showed up to cover the story. The next day, buried in the middle of the *Topeka State Journal*, a six-inch column announced the dedication: the Kansas State Highway Department had completed the first eight miles of the U.S. Interstate Highway System.

Over forty years, the network of ramps and roads sprawled into 41,000 miles of steel, concrete, and asphalt. It took four times as long to complete as planned. Road builders moved enough earth to cover the entire state of Connecticut in three feet of dirt. Renamed the Dwight D. Eisenhower System of Interstate and Defense Highways in 1991, the American grid is the largest public works project ever completed for infrastructure development by any government in recorded human history. It is ten times the size of the Great Wall of China, the world's second-largest, man-made structure.

As one way of appending their signatures, U.S. authorities designed a clear pattern of road numbering that could bring order to the nation's infrastructure. Abbreviated with the letter "I," all north-south interstates would end in odd numbers. The smallest number would classify the highway on the West Coast, I-5, that would connect San Diego with Seattle. Each major route would increase by ten as roads progressed: I-15, I-25, and so on. They would terminate with

I-95 on the East Coast, which would run from Miami to Maine. High-ways running from east to west would be even, and would follow the same pattern: I-10 would slice through the southern states, and above that would be I-20, I-30, until I-90 united the north.

Interstate 35, a highway planned to bisect the center of the country, had two distinctive features that would shape the nation in ways that transportation committees and road planners never anticipated. It was the easternmost interstate connecting the U.S. with Mexico and it was one of three interstates that crossed every major east-west highway in the nation. In three decades, I-35 would change the face of Laredo, Texas, the highway's southern terminus, creating a network that forms the lifeblood of America's physical web of commerce.

Laredo was founded in 1755 by Spanish colonists and ranchers who established the original community on the north side of the Rio Grande. After Indian raids threatened the town's survival, the village divided in 1771—200 years before I-35's arrival. Believing the river would help their defenses, the majority wished to move south into Nuevo Laredo. The split was controversial; instead of relinquishing their valuable land, several families chose to forsake the collective security of the ranches by remaining north of the river. When Interstate 35 opened in 1971, Laredo had a population of 75,000. Like other border towns, the city was a modest draw for shoppers seeking good deals and tourists looking for a good time.

But after I-35 arrived, one multinational corporation after another established their warehouses and transportation hubs around this once-humble border crossing. Eighteen-wheelers, big rigs, double-drops, wide loads—the road monsters all found their way north through Laredo. Like the Mississippi River once connected the Ohio, Missouri, and Arkansas with steamboats and barges, I-35 carves a path down the spine of Middle America where tributaries branch out today like tentacles. Its asphalt arteries empty one cargo container after another into the stream of commerce, sustained by capillaries of gas stations, fast food restaurants, coffee houses, vending machines, motels, bars, strip clubs. They go north, depositing pallets of clothing, carburetors, or chocolate. A day or two later, the tide of whirring tires pulls them back to Laredo, from whence they came.

The Eisenhower Highway System is a case study in the law of unintended consequences. Fifty years ago, when the network was designed, no engineer on the planet would have predicted that Laredo would become the busiest port of entry for trucks in the world, and the second-busiest for all transported cargo in the United States. On average, 10,000 trucks pass through Laredo each day. Thanks to the fortunes of free trade, 40 percent of Mexico's imports to the U.S. roll north through the I-35 corridor, as well as all Mexican imports to eastern Canada. Transport companies like Old Dominion, Yellow, and Roadway have made Laredo to rolling freight as Chicago, St. Louis, and Dodge City were to cattle.

The volume of traffic on I-35 is so immense that Texas has pleaded for a second interstate to handle the burden. With the numerical sequence exhausted, Laredo has urged immediate construction of the mammoth I-69—the controversial "NAFTA Superhighway" that would parallel I-35 from Laredo to Duluth, Minnesota—as soon as possible. Conservative activists object to a new road, saying that the highway would lead to the tyranny of a North American Union. But they have offered no alternative solution to the transportation boom. In the meantime, the trucks move in and out of Laredo like a swelling tide of geese, migrating to and fro at the call from a freight boss or a logistics company.

—————

Laredo, in East Coast comparisons, is a blend of Boston and Vermont: historical, gentrified, independent, spirited, and working-class gritty. Since I-35 opened, Laredo's population has quadrupled to 300,000. "By the end of the twenty-first century," a community leader named Blas Castañeda boasted, with earnest sincerity, "we will be as big as Manhattan."

Hope notwithstanding, it seems unlikely that Laredo will match the cultural or economic significance of New York anytime soon. Even the most generous population projections put the combined tally of Brownsville, Laredo, and McAllen at only 5 million by 2100—barely a third of the Big Apple's projected metropolitan growth. But stranger things have happened, and, at the very least, this blossoming trio of towns in south Texas is poised to match the industrial might that Cincinnati, Cleveland, and Pittsburgh wielded in past generations. "We are the new pioneers," Castañeda said. Conestoga wagons have become Mack trucks.

Pioneering is a longstanding Laredo dream. In 1840, after Texas had seceded and won independence, Laredo became a magnet for Texans and northeastern Mexicans who wanted to keep the good times rolling. After several years of local lobbying, Antonio Canales, a Mexican lawyer and part-time general, proclaimed the Rio Grande itself an independent republic. The national boundaries were vague, but the general concept was that the border—the Rio and surrounding municipalities—should not be sovereign to either Texas or Mexico. On this rallying cry, Canales enlisted almost 200 Texans who were recently demobilized from the army. The Texans fought, as one historian put it, "for the simple joy of fighting."

But soon after they volunteered, the Texan commander, Col. S. W. Jordan, discovered a pair of treacherous colonels who were planning to betray the Texan volunteers to the federal Mexican army. Colonel Jordan confronted the Mexican officers, who denied the conspiracy and angrily accused him of injuring their honor. Jordan backed off.

Days later, the colonel and his men narrowly escaped being ambushed in a canyon; a lieutenant reportedly warned Colonel Jordan that something didn't feel right. The Mexican army had been tipped off by the officers inside the rebellion. The Texans found cover in a *hacienda* on high ground, fought off the ambush, and promptly quit the army. The Rio Grande returned to normal, and Laredo became known as the only city in Texas where seven flags, not six, have flown. The mayor, Raul Salinas, brings this up from time to time when talking about resistance to a border fence, threatening (somewhat hollowly) that if the federal government acts against Laredo's will, the Rio Grande Republic will rise again.

It's been said, especially as a military cliché, that amateurs in any profession talk about tactics, while the real professionals discuss logistics. There's no absence of talk about logistics in Laredo, whose unemployment rate averaged below 5 percent in 2007. "Everyone

**Gulf of Mexico: Boca Chica, Texas** PHOTO BY ROBIN BHATTY

**View into Playa Bagdad, Mexico: Boca Chica, Texas** PHOTO BY ROBIN BHATTY

Rio Grande:
Brownsville, Texas
PHOTO BY ROBIN BHATTY

Brownsville Station
Command Center:
Rio Grande Valley
Sector, Texas
PHOTO BY ROBIN BHATTY

Agent Walter King:
Rio Grande Valley
Sector, Texas
PHOTO BY ROBIN BHATTY

Levee roadway and farm: Brownsville, Texas PHOTO BY ROBIN BHATTY

Unidentified reconnaissance team: Matamoros, Tamaulipas
PHOTO BY ROBIN BHATTY

Camera tower: Rio Grande Valley Sector PHOTO BY ROBIN BHATTY

Smuggler's ditch: Brownsville, Texas PHOTO BY ROBIN BHATTY

Gateway International Bridge: Brownsville, Texas PHOTO BY ROBIN BHATTY

Ferry/international port of entry: Los Ebaños, Texas/Diaz Ordaz, Tamaulipas
PHOTO BY ROBIN BHATTY

Eric Ellman, with
Buster: south of
Falcon Dam, Texas
PHOTO BY ROBIN BHATTY

Isaac Guerra:
McAllen, Texas
PHOTO BY ROBIN BHATTY

Don Medina:
McAllen, Texas
PHOTO BY ROBIN BHATTY

Juárez-Lincoln Bridge: Laredo, Texas PHOTO BY ROBIN BHATTY

Chief Carlos Carrillo:
Laredo, Texas
PHOTO BY ROBIN BHATTY

Downtown: Laredo, Texas PHOTO BY THE AUTHOR

Gateway to the
Americas Bridge:
Nuevo Laredo,
Tamaulipas
PHOTO BY THE AUTHOR

Mayor Chad Foster:
Eagle Pass, Texas PHOTO
BY ROBIN BHATTY

Agent Randy Clark:
Eagle Pass, Texas PHOTO
BY ROBIN BHATTY

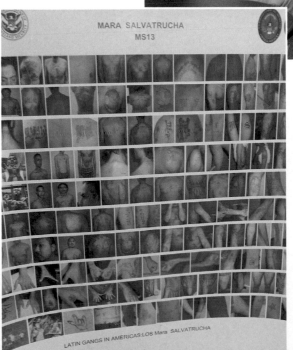

Poster displayed in
Eagle Pass Station:
Del Rio Sector, Texas
PHOTO BY THE AUTHOR

Pecos River: east of Langtry, Texas PHOTO BY ROBIN BHATTY

Rio Grande: Langtry, Texas PHOTO BY THE AUTHOR

Jersey Lilly: Langtry,
Texas PHOTO BY ROBIN
BHATTY

Restaurant: Study
Butte/Terlingua, Texas
PHOTO BY THE AUTHOR

Pete Billings: Langtry,
Texas PHOTO BY THE AUTHOR

Highway 90: east of Alpine, Texas PHOTO BY THE AUTHOR

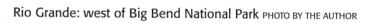

Rio Grande: west of Big Bend National Park PHOTO BY THE AUTHOR

Army National Guard
observation post:
Marfa Sector, Texas
PHOTO BY ROBIN BHATTY

Army National Guard
observation post:
Marfa Sector, Texas
PHOTO BY ROBIN BHATTY

Soldier, Army National
Guard: Marfa Sector,
Texas PHOTO BY ROBIN
BHATTY

Neely's Crossing, Texas PHOTO BY THE AUTHOR

Entrance from the Santa Fe/Stanton Street International Bridge:
El Paso, Texas PHOTO BY THE AUTHOR

Migrant: El Paso, Texas PHOTO BY THE AUTHOR

Near the international line: El Paso, Texas PHOTO BY THE AUTHOR

Segundo Barrio mural: El Paso, Texas PHOTO BY THE AUTHOR

Monument One:
north of Segundo
Barrio, Texas
PHOTO BY THE AUTHOR

who wants to work is working," said Bob Zachariah, president of the Laredo Hotels and Lodging Association. And they are carving out unusual niches in Laredo. This once-humble border town is now home to a thriving Mexican-American industry: the family-owned international logistics company.

Veronica Reyes, thirty-six, a bilingual, buoyant, full-figured single mother of two, is the general manager of B&V Logistics. Her initial resume is not traditional: after graduating from high school in Laredo, she took a job for a large, established transportation company. Trucking and transportation, Veronica said, was a man's business. It wasn't easy for a woman to find a path for advancement in the Laredo trucking network. She worked at junior levels for a few years, but she started looking for something more challenging.

In 1995, Veronica enlisted in the Marine Corps and shipped off for Parris Island. Two weeks before finishing boot camp, Recruit Veronica Reyes was bit by a fire ant and suffered a severe allergic reaction. Her days with the Marines were over, and she returned to Laredo and her old company. The experience stuck with Veronica; she didn't hesitate to offer a vigorous "hoorah" greeting to me and share this story the first time we spoke on the phone. It disappointed her not to advance beyond the lowly rank of recruit, but Veronica said that her training gave her confidence to try new things. God has a plan for everything, she said.

While Veronica was enduring drill instructors and sand fleas on Parris Island, her mother, Bertha, was an investigator for the Laredo Police Department—another tough arena for women to succeed. In 2000, after Bertha retired from the force, she and Veronica made a plan: combine Bertha's local connections with Veronica's transportation knowledge. Although logistics services exist all over the world, the labyrinth of customs regulations that suppliers must navigate in Laredo means that local, bilingual companies are in especially high demand. Thus, B&V Logistics was born.

Logistics companies are different than trucking agencies. They act as middlemen between railroads, ships, airplanes, courier vans, or eighteen-wheelers to deliver products to their destination. In Laredo, B&V Logistics signs contracts with suppliers to coordinate the pickup and delivery of international cargo. Usually, B&V subcontracts the shipments to a Mexican trucker, a freight forwarder, and an American trucker. The Mexican truck hauls the container to the freight forwarder. They prepare a *pedimento*—a customs form— detailing the rig's contents. All containers are subject to inspection while the freight forwarder processes the paperwork. This happens randomly; many containers are shipped on without the seals being broken. Freight forwarders assume responsibility, and if the contents don't exactly match the list on the *pedimento*, the forwarder pays a large fine. Once the cargo is cleared, an American trucker links up with the container at the warehouse and delivers the freight to its destination.

In an unscientific study of a telephone book, I found several hundred logistics companies and freight forwarders in Laredo. I found more logistics companies, transport companies, trucking associations, freight forwarders, and truck drivers advertised here than I did in any other city on the border. Although B&V Logistics was hardly about to dethrone the supply powerhouses, they had established a strong, dependable reputation among their clients. Because nobody in logistics—or in Laredo, it seemed—was hurting for work, B&V could stay as small or as large as it wished.

What seems like a routine nine-to-five job is actually a competitive, risky business. Manufacturers and factories, Veronica said, pay more for delivery of freight directly to production lines than to warehouses. Suppliers move parts and expect them to arrive within a certain window—they call it "Just in Time" delivery. But if a logistician contracts for Just in Time services, companies can assess penalty fees of $10,000 for every minute the load is late. Earthquakes, fires, hurricanes, traffic accidents—it doesn't matter; the logistics company is left holding the bag.

Take the case of the refrigerated shipment of chocolate bars. Landstar Carrier Group, a transportation and logistics company, had assumed responsibility for moving a shipment of chocolate heading north. The container was left at the freight forwarder on a Friday, but the trucker forgot to set the timer that controlled the refrigeration unit. It sat in Laredo over the weekend. "On Monday, it looked like Willy Wonka and the Chocolate Factory," Veronica said. Landstar had to pay for the driver's mistake.

Two years after they went in business, two significant things happened in the life of B&V Logistics. First, Bertha fell ill and had a stroke. Many people in the community were praying for her, especially the congregation of a small Pentecostal church called Castillo Del Rey. Bertha recovered. Although Veronica had been raised Catholic, the experience was too powerful for her to ignore. The family enthusiastically embraced Castillo Del Rey and the Pentecostal faith. They also dedicated any future success of B&V Logistics to God. "We have been blessed," Veronica told me, "Without God, we wouldn't be where we are today."

And then, soon after Bertha returned to work, they had a breakthrough with their biggest client. When Veronica had first called on Mitsubishi, their senior logistics specialist, Janet Casagrande, had not sounded enthusiastic. "Most of the *maquilas* in Mexico that make the auto parts are owned by the Japanese," Veronica said. "And you know what they think about women. So Janet was tough on me at first because she didn't think I could handle the pressure." One botched delivery and B&V Logistics was done.

One day, Mitsubishi needed to import a specific part of a radiator. The part was for a presentation the company was giving to General Motors on their climate-controlled vehicles. It was a small part—it could fit in the back seat of a car—but it was fragile. At the time Veronica took the call from Janet, the part was in Ramos Arizpe, a city of *maquilas* four hours south of Laredo. According to Veronica, there are so many *maquilas* in Ramos Arizpe that manufacture auto parts, the city is now called "Little Detroit." Less than twenty hours from the time Veronica took the call, the radiator component had to be in Indiana.

Veronica and Bertha didn't take any chances. They drove to Ramos Arizpe in their own sedan, picked up the part, filled out the *pedimento*, and lined up for three hours on the World Trade Center Bridge; they were the only passenger car in several lines of eighteen wheelers. It caused a scene at the customs house and with the freight forwarder—international trade just wasn't done this way!—but the radiator arrived. Just in time. Janet Casagrande was impressed. B&V Logistics landed Mitsubishi as a full-time client, and Veronica and Janet became friends. Because of Veronica's success with Mitsubishi,

75 percent of B&V's business is with auto manufacturers. She still says that none of this would have happened without God, and the B&V Logistics Web page also affirms their belief that faith is what matters.

When I was staying at the La Quinta in Laredo, I met Roy Biegay, a divorced man from Houston who was in town as a recruiter for O'Reilly Auto Parts. Roy was engaged to Gloria, a thirty-eight-year-old woman from Honduras who came into the U.S. illegally. They met on the sidelines at a soccer game. Gloria has to be home—she lives in her older brother's house—by 10 P.M. each night. Her younger brother was recently smuggled across the border inside the dashboard of a minivan and is now living in New York. According to Roy, she has never had "relations" with a man. If she did so before marriage, she would risk permanent rejection from her family.

I asked Roy what he preferred about the new Latin culture he had discovered. "On Sunday, nobody in your family invites you over after church," he said. "You're just expected to go." His own white relatives, he said, would be surprised if he stopped by for a visit without calling ahead. Family businesses are more common, and faith and tradition are more central to the culture than selfish pursuits.

Veronica Reyes, like Roy's fianceé and many Latinos I met on the border, places equally strong emphasis on faith and family. B&V Logistics started out of Bertha Reyes's kitchen, but today the entire house is an office and the family resides elsewhere. They employ six people, and even though all but two are family, Veronica puts all of them, even herself, on a time card. The house/office also includes a transport company—GIO Transport—owned by Veronica's brother-in-law, George Gonzalez. At least once a week, one of George's ten rigs makes a run for B&V Logistics.

Because truckers are the grunts of the logistics industry, they are a separate caste in the transport culture. America has truck stops, trucker-themed restaurants, anthems, and bands dedicated to the triumphs and tribulations of trucking. Advertised in the pages of *Overdrive*, the magazine that serves as "the voice of American truckers," are agencies that claim to speed a load to an owner-operator overnight, lawyers who expedite speeding ticket removal, and even dating services for the single trucker. The annual National Truck Driver's Championship—competing drivers must select equipment, properly navigate a virtual course, and take a written exam—was held in Minneapolis in 2007, three weeks after the collapse of the 35-W bridge.

Drivers often own their rigs, contracting their services to transport companies (who, themselves, are typically contracted out to logistics companies). Owner-operators, as such drivers are called, are reimbursed for fuel but pay for maintenance and upkeep. Because long-haul driving is rigorous, trucks are typically owned and operated in pairs. In Laredo, the teams are mainly brothers, friends, cousins, father-son, or mother-daughter. One drives through the night while the other sleeps on a mattress behind the seats. The rigs are decorated with pictures, postcards, and sentiments of home; many also have microwaves and mini-DVD players installed for convenience and comfort. The cabs feel like a chromed family kitchen inside a fighter pilot's cockpit.

Not all rigs are owned by teams of drivers. Some operators claim to drive in tandem but actually roll solo. For long-haul trips that happen under a certain period of time—say, a forty-hour drive from Laredo to New Jersey—this is against the law. But sometimes a solo operator will claim to be two people in order to collect the check for both. Other times the companies turn a blind eye to the violations, knowing that the truckers will "modify" the driver's logs once the job is finished.

I learned more at Coyote Creek, a trucker-friendly cantina minutes from the international bridge, where a former owner-operator told me how things really happened on the road. Coyote Creek was the kind of smoky, country/tejano cantina where fajitas and margaritas are served alongside barbecue and chicken fried steak. Bilingual music videos flitted on a flat screen mounted behind an empty karaoke stage. Overweight waitresses wore skin-tight shirts. The televisions were tuned, respectively, to CNN's Anderson Cooper, Major League Baseball, and a Mexican dating show called "12 Corazones" that seemed to be playing at all hours.

A trucker from Houma, Louisiana, was sipping Budweiser at the Coyote Creek's bar and chasing his brew with shots of Jim Beam while I waited for a steak fajita platter. The trucker was thin, his short, brown hair was greasy, and his brown eyes sunk behind a thick mustache and stubble that covered his tanned, weathered skin. He wore Wranglers, a short-sleeved blue-and-white pinstriped work shirt with his name on a patch, and a watch with a brown leather band and a gold face.

The trucker, who spoke with a Cajun drawl, had a profile that might raise a criminal psychologist's eyebrows. "I'm a loner," he said. He had no family: both parents were dead, not married, no children. No brothers, sisters, aunts, uncles, or cousins. No friends. "I don't make them very well," he said, without regret. "I'm a loner," he repeated. It appeared that Bud and Jim were his only long-term companions.

He had no interest in social chatter and came off as a sociopath—until I asked him about life on the road. Then he perked up. "I drove 1,140,000 miles in six and a half years," he said. "I've been to all forty-eight states. I would go on the road for three months and then be back home for five days. $1,400 a week. Best money I ever made."

The key for him was the per diem. His company paid their long-haul drivers a rate of thirty-five cents/mile. On paper, he only drove about 2,000 miles/week, which came out to $700. But drivers often traveled much further to deliver loads, exceeding the legal driving limits but shipping the freight on time. Instead of paying the mileage, which would have been flagged as excessive on a driver's log, his company paid him in per diem for his "travel expenses." The per diem, which often came to another $700 or more, was tax free— a bonus for performance and an incentive to keep delivering.

The U.S. government publishes a safety handbook—a thick, multivolume green manual that is updated quarterly—and all owner-operators are supposed to follow the guidelines. The handbook imposes limits and restrictions on transport carriers for mileage, weight, and time. If a driver is caught breaking the rules, the liability can fall on the transport or logistics company. Professionals like Veronica Reyes have to choose between slowing down their drivers and preventing a timely delivery, or ignoring the rules and paying the price.

So how does B&V Logistics handle safety? Veronica told me that she tried to avoid contracting for "just in time" freight whenever possible, delivering loads for manufacturers to warehouses instead of assembly lines. She sniffed out ruses by taking the cell phone numbers of both drivers in the truck, calling one or the other on the road, and then asking them to put their partner on the line. If she caught a team of drivers lying, she stopped doing business with the trucking company they represented. She refused to cut corners. "I have a reputation as a mean bitch," she said, admitting that she wore it, in her male-dominated profession, as a badge of honor.

That isn't to say Veronica hasn't sometimes bent the rules herself. "All companies have their magic drivers," she said telling me that B&V Logistics had, to her knowledge, only a single wayward incident. One day, she found out an important client needed a container delivered to New Jersey within forty-eight hours. She called a friend, Rudy, who promised to take a team immediately. Forty hours later, he called from Newark after dropping off the load and said that he had gone alone. All of Rudy's other drivers were on the road, and he hadn't wanted to lose her business. He apologized to Veronica for not telling her. "I didn't want to lose your trust," he said. "I wanted you to know I'd always come through for you."

The trucker I met at Coyote Creek was with a company where everyone was a magic driver, and, because almost half the money that he made was under the table, it was a terrific carpet ride. But he got tired of the months on the road, so he took a job as a safety supervisor for a trucking company. His duties, on paper, were to ensure that all safety standards—minimum driver mileage, for example—were rigorously upheld. His real job was to make sure no safety violations were ever reported outside the company.

The man wanted to know why I was so interested in his work on trucks. Was I looking for a job? I told him I wasn't, that I was just passing through. I was working on my own project. He nodded, satisfied. Being a loner, he went back to his beer. I paid my tab and left.

The cuisine at Coyote Creek pales in comparison to Taco Palenque, home of the best Mexican fast food on the south Texas border. Open twenty-four hours, the Palenque, as it's locally known, is a border icon. Kiosks inside the restaurant hawk phone cards, cellular accessories, and electronic bling. You pay for combinations of meat, tortillas, and beans (or eggs, potatoes, and chorizo), but chips, salsa, and a healthy spread of veggies, dressings, and fixins are available for free. Taco Palenque, with its large selection of free food, has served meals at midnight to more than one hungry migrant. During the day, the restaurant is a common destination for businessmen catching lunch or mothers feeding children. At night, truckers passing through mingle with Border Patrol agents finishing their shift.

The first time I pulled up to the Palenque's drive-thru, I was greeted in Spanish. With the teller unable to see that I was white, I managed to complete the entire order without switching over. It was one small step for a gringo; one giant leap towards bicultural appreciation.

And both times that I sat down to eat inside at Palenque, the television was tuned to the ubiquitous "12 Corazones." Filmed in Los Angeles, "12 Corazones" ("*Doce Corazones*" or "twelve hearts") airs on Telemundo throughout the U.S., Mexico, and Central America; it is also transmitted to Colombia, Peru, Panama, Honduras, and Guatemala via local stations. The show's hostess, the brazen, beautiful Penelope Menchaca, teases and advises four boys and eight girls looking to mate—think Salma Hayek meets Orly the Matchmaker. Each contestant represents a different zodiac sign and is drawn from one of several Latin countries. They revolve through two rounds of games and flirtations, the boys and girls take turns, voting to eliminate one or two from the opposite gender. The remainders get to pick their favorites, hoping the affections are reciprocated. The host tells the girls and boys which zodiacs go together, and why. If she gets stumped, Edward'O, the resident astrological advisor, acts as her oracle.

The rapid growth and syndication of "12 Corazones" illustrates an important aspect to me about Latin culture. Although some contestants are eliminated, it isn't a competitive program, looking to crown the survivor, coronate the idol, or exterminate the weakest link. Americans seek victory from their game shows, but the popularity and entertainment in the Latin world seems to come from the rituals—the coy glances, the prancing and posturing, the *mamacita* irreverently holding court, the divining for the signs and stars to reveal the lucky one. The victor is less important than the game itself, which demonstrates, to me anyway, a fatalism that exalt the journey above the destination.

Perhaps there is a cultural aspect to crossing the border illegally. Opportunity is certainly no guarantee; there are far more who fail to convert the chance than succeed, winding up in debt to drug lords or *coyotes*. But what would you do if given a choice between the rich land of *el norte* or a dusty village? I'd be making a run for the border too. Like love, some risks are always worth a shot. It's better to try and fail, I suppose, than spend the rest of your life wondering what could have been. At least you're on the road.

———————◆○◆———————

As I walked out on the streets of Laredo, I couldn't shake the feeling that I must be a terrible journalist. Laredo, after all, is supposed to be famous for violence—the drug and murder capital of southwest Texas, according to some hyperbole. I'm sure there is a seamy underbelly in Laredo, but I couldn't find it. The overt anarchy was south of the Rio Grande.

"Laredo is the best-kept secret in the Border Patrol," Chief Carlos Carrillo told me. "The violence is almost entirely on the Mexican side. The overall quality of life here is much higher than people think."

Carlos Carrillo, chief of the Laredo Sector, was the man who had sent Congressman Tom Tancredo into fulminations after being quoted as saying the Border Patrol's primary mission was counterterrorism, not enforcing illegal immigration. He was also one of the reasons why lawlessness stayed south of the Laredo border.

Born in Calexico, Carrillo had served on the force for twenty-five years before his appointment as sector chief.[*] Before taking over as Laredo Sector chief, he was the deputy commander of BORTAC, the Border Patrol's little-known special operations unit/SWAT team. BORTAC is the Border Patrol's version of the SEALs or Delta Force. Carrillo served in counternarcotics missions in Bolivia (the Border Patrol was in Bolivia?) and several other drug-related hotspots. In Bolivia, Carrillo's BORTAC unit worked alongside the DEA, private

_____

[*] A sector chief in the Border Patrol—especially one of the nine chiefs on the southwestern border—is something like a two-star commanding general in the Army or the Marines

contractors, and military Special Forces. In April 2000, BORTAC achieved some notoriety after carrying out Attorney General Janet Reno's orders to seize Elián González in Miami and return the boy to his Cuban father.

Carrillo also served in the San Diego and El Paso sectors as an agent, but it's clear that his worldview and mindset were sculpted primarily through his time with BORTAC. The chief has brown eyes, a narrow face, a spotless uniform, a trim physique, and a sharp, angular mustache. He feels passionate about the official Border Patrol motto: Honor First.

For Carrillo, who comports himself with the dignity and bearing of a nobleman, a good Border Patrol agent has more in common with an exceptional Marine than with a local sheriff. The Border Patrol, in Carrillo's view, is a band of warriors; brothers and sisters responsible for defending Americans from evil. They are the sheep-dogs who protect innocent lambs from ravenous wolves. They guard America's boundaries and put their honor first. Carrillo's eyes communicated intensity about this motto. He took it to heart.

The first time I spoke with Carrillo, I wanted to understand why illegal aliens were trafficked across the border in Arizona at a rate exceeding that in south Texas by several orders of magnitude. The total number of migrants apprehended each year at any one of the eight stations of the Tucson Sector—a 250-mile stretch in Arizona that accounted for half of all illegal crossings in America—amounted to the same as the total haul in Laredo's entire sector. Carrillo felt that deterrence, especially through the use of permanent check-points on major roads coming to and from the border, was keeping down Laredo's illegal alien traffic.

"Smugglers and narcotics traffickers make the decision where they are going to cross long before they get to the border," Carrillo said. "They want to find the most cost-effective place to move across. There are six permanent checkpoints in Laredo that have been operating for many years. This sends a strong message to the criminal element."

The permanent checkpoints were important, Carrillo said, because smugglers knew that negotiating them increased the risk of capture. This meant they were likely to avoid those routes and move through areas where Border Patrol agents would either be staked out or screening traffic. Agents used computer databases with fingerprint and biometric identification technology at the checkpoints, enabling them to identify criminal suspects. Carrillo referred to this as "defense-in-depth," a military term that, although reasonably self-explanatory, was not something I heard any other Border Patrol agent use during an interview.

Tucson Sector, where Carrillo had also served, was the only stretch of border in the country that had no permanent checkpoints. Why? He said it had to do with local Arizona politics. Carrillo believed that the level of violence and illegal activity was much higher in the Tucson Sector because a local congressman, now retired, had thwarted the Border Patrol's efforts to install permanent checkpoints on the roads leading north from the border. I made a note to follow up on this in Arizona.

I asked about the fence in Laredo. At first, Carrillo expanded what I had called the Border Patrol Triad into a new name—the National Security for Border Strategy—with flashier adjectives for familiar nouns: "Well-trained personnel . . . detection technology . . . tactical infrastructure." Carrillo told me that the Rio Grande in Laredo provided a physical barrier—tactical infrastructure—that was better than a fence.

The problem, he said, was the carrizo cane. Imported to Texas from the Mediterranean in the sixteenth century as roofing material for New World haciendas, the tall, dense, bamboolike reeds have taken over the riverbanks like verdant vines that climb historic brownstones. The noxious, nonnative weed is a nuisance for the Border Patrol, and it's also a problem for farmers, city officials, and environmentalists. As it sprawls, carrizo consumes increasing quantities of the river and chokes out existing species. It offers cover for smugglers and reduces the mobility and visibility of agents. Carrizo removal, the chief said, was his number one priority on the river.

Efforts to remove the plant are not moving fast enough for anyone. It's been burned, mowed, sprayed, mulched, and napalmed. It keeps coming back. Also, carrizo leaves secrete a chemical that scare away most local herbivores. One possible solution is a type of wasp, fly, or scale insect native to Spain or Portugal that preys on the plant.

In 2007, John Goolsby, a McAllen-based biologist, traveled to the Mediterranean coast armed with a grant from the Department of Homeland Security to collect samples. The Portuguese and Spanish insects have been quarantined. It will take up to three years for the bugs to be vetted for environmental impact. In 2010, we should know more. In the meantime, the carrizo proliferates.

I understood why law-abiding citizens clamored for a fence—politicians and activists had bamboozled them into believing an illusion that such a structure would stabilize the border. But it was obvious to me in Laredo that imposing this monstrous edifice along the Rio Grande would create even more challenges for the city, and the nation, than the Eisenhower Highway System. Tactically, building a fence on top of the carrizo would be ludicrous. Smugglers could cut holes in a fence that the carrizo would conceal; adding swaths of fencing to the plant growth would actually make it more difficult for agents to find and apprehend illegal crossers.

And current cost estimates were hardly accounting for the law of unintended consequences. After all, the Interstates were supposed to be finished in twelve years at a cost of a mere $25 billion. The system took almost four times as long to build (forty years), and cost over four times as much as predicted ($114 billion). The highway, like many of the U.S. government's ambitions, is both a testament to the American spirit and a cautionary tale for any citizen listening to a border charlatan promising a simplistic solution with a quick fix.

I left my two-hour interview with Chief Carlos Carrillo thinking that he was a pretty good guy. He seemed tough, fair, and polished. A poster Patrolman. He also embraced the warrior ethos of service, courage, and self-sacrifice to a degree that I had found uncommon within the Border Patrol agents I had met thus far. I didn't like him because he was friendly. I liked him because he had adopted a set of values for himself that I respected and identified with. I'm sure he has flaws, like we all do. But my initial impression was that Carlos Carrillo was one of the most professional veterans on the border.

On August 15, 2007, at a Laredo town meeting, Chief Carlos Carrillo addressed the Border Patrol's priorities to the public. As a professional, he felt his primary duty was to keep terrorists and their weapons from entering the country. That was the Border Patrol's number one mission. Of course, agents would also encounter narcotics and migrants. But, Carrillo said, the Border Patrol alone could not solve the problems of illicit drugs and illegal immigration. Their first priority, he said, was homeland security.

The next day, a journalist from the *Laredo Morning Times* quoted Carrillo as saying that Border Patrol agents don't have the responsibility of apprehending illegal immigrants. "Senior Agent Surrenders Laredo" was the headline throughout the anti-immigration blogosphere. This didn't sound like the Carrillo I knew. But I was basing my judgment on the rapport we had developed, and the kind of person I had decided Carrillo was. Perhaps I had too strong an affinity for my interview subject.

A correction to the original story ran in the *Laredo Morning Times* the following morning; apparently the editor had run the wrong quote. "The Border Patrol is not equipped to stop illegal immigration," Carrillo had actually said. "Illegal immigration is obviously much bigger than the Border Patrol. The Border Patrol's mission is to stop terrorists and terrorist weapons from entering the country. During the course of doing that, we will encounter illegal aliens and we will encounter narcotics."

The correction didn't matter to Congressman Tom Tancredo, who continued to call for Carrillo's firing weeks after the furor had subsided. It also didn't seem to matter to T. J. Bonner, president of the National Border Patrol Council, the Border Patrol union. Bonner used the opportunity to condemn Chief Carrillo, as well as everyone else in the chain of command: Chief David Aguilar (the senior agent in the U.S.), Customs and Border Protection Commissioner Ralph Basham, and Homeland Security Secretary Michael Chertoff.

Yes, Border Patrol agents have a union. The National Border Patrol Council represents 12,000 members of the Border Patrol who have not reached supervisory rank. Like all civilian employees of the federal government, patrolmen cannot strike. But they do have the legal right to assemble and have representatives seek redress for grievances. Union president T. J. Bonner, an agent himself, had no qualms about condemning senior Border Patrol agents in a manner that made him sound more like a cynical politician than an "Honor First" soldier for freedom. I made a note to contact Bonner. Perhaps he could explain this discrepancy.

By the way, I have nothing against unions. My late grandfather, Joe Danelo, was a member of the International Brotherhood of Teamsters in Spokane, Washington, and my uncle and cousins from San Pedro, California are with chapters of the International Long-shore and Warehouse Union (both cities have the same working-class spirit I saw in Laredo). The union men I've known possess a fierce devotion to honest, hard work in exchange for fair treatment. Electricians, welders, farmers, and all other union professionals—even writers, athletes, and entertainers—deserve a square deal. The workers rate equality and management needs checks and balances to prevent abuse of power.

It's one thing for a truck driver, carpenter, or dock worker to have an us-against-them attitude toward senior management. But it's entirely different for uniformed defenders of a nation to be rent with this kind of provincialism. On the one hand, Border Patrol agents operate under a paramilitary structure: a chain of command, a warrior ethos, a mission to defend the public. At the same time, the agents have an alliance with public advocates who take great effort to undermine the leadership they are supposed to obey. It doesn't seem very useful or efficient.

My grandfather wasn't just a union man. Grandpa Joe also spent two decades in the Navy and fought in World War II. In the military, if an enlisted man or woman has a grievance with an officer that can't be worked out face-to-face, they deal with senior noncoms—gunnies, first sergeants, or chiefs—to address the problem. Issues arise, of course, but airing dirty laundry outside the unit is considered bad form by all concerned. It's tactless. It just isn't done. Can you imagine the dysfunction that would occur in a battalion or on a ship if privates, lance corporals, or sailors could mutiny whenever they saw fit? I know at least one retired boatswain's mate who would be rolling in his grave.

Despite the rhetoric about being modern-day centurions, few patrollers I met in south Texas actually saw themselves as warriors. In this region, I observed the workday grind of a postal employee, not the yearning for action of a soldier or Marine. (In contrast, I would find an abundance of aggressive zeal in Arizona.) The agents I met in south Texas were decent people who were proud of their jobs, their paramilitary training, and their teamwork. They cut sign, drove the lines, and sat on their Xs. The seasoned vets had a handful of high-adrenaline stories of dangerous encounters with aliens. But not many I spoke with had ever been in a firefight.

That's not necessarily a bad thing. After all, the national border should be a stable divide, one where mutual prosperity and respect for the law on both sides reduces smuggling to a trickle. An agent's schedule should theoretically be as hectic as the Maytag repairman.

But that lack of action in Laredo is a dreadful illusion of security. Laredo may have appeared safer than other border cities, but that didn't mean it was free of illegal activity. A terrifying war and prosperous narcotics trade was happening right across the river, practically under the Border Patrol's noses. And they could do nothing to stop it.

<hr/>

In addition to the 10,000 freight trucks that enter daily, another 10,000 passenger cars and trucks line up in Laredo to pass through the gateway to I-35 and the interior United States. Dogs sniff the autos, trucks, and big rigs when they enter, but full searches are random and rare. The volume of traffic makes it impossible to search every vehicle, or even every tenth vehicle. From my observation, and according to both Customs and Border Patrol agents, 90 to 95 percent of the trucks entering the U.S. in Laredo are never searched at all.

The drug cartels call the port cities "plazas"—sprawling border exchange areas where the black market trade flows both ways. More than just a city, a plaza is a network of operatives that consists of a few people at the right places or times: an agent that looks the other way, a customs inspector inside your camp, a freight forwarder to clear your cargo for travel north into America, a crooked police chief. Smugglers bring narcotics into the United States in exchange for cash payments and weapons, which are delivered to Mexico.

Some plazas don't need any double agents. All it takes is the right *pedimento*, the correct cargo container, or the proper deception ploys to fool the dogs. A fence wouldn't eliminate the Laredo plaza; after all, the vehicles carrying their illicit cargo drive unmolested over the bridge and legally through the port of entry. Plazas bear no resemblance to the dusty, worn paths that migrants traverse in the Arizona desert, or the ditches where piles of water bottles and canned food are discovered daily. Either trucks or cars can be used to smuggle marijuana, heroin, crystal meth, or cocaine.

In all cases, plazas represent meeting points for groups of violent men loyal to crime bosses. Until 2003—when the United States went to war in Iraq, reducing its special forces in Latin America to the lowest point since the early 1980s—the Gulf Cartel, which was commanded by Osiel Cardenas Guillen, had a lock on the entire Nuevo Laredo plaza. Assisted by their enforcers, a cadre of commandos called Los Zetas, the Gulf Cartel's operations were stable.

Then two things happened. First, Mexican police arrested Osiel Guillen, sending him to a maximum security prison and creating a leadership vacuum. That perceived weakness gave the Sinaloa Cartel an opportunity to push their operations east, and touched off a cartel war that continues today—and it may not end for awhile.

Unlike the Gulf Cartel, the Sinaloa Federation evolved into a decentralized franchise instead of a hierarchical pyramid organization. Originating in western Mexico, south of Arizona, the Sinaloan leader, Joaquin "El Chapo" Guzmán, has used his cartel as an umbrella for dozens of plazas and smuggling operations. (Most *coyotes* on the Sinaloa turf who traffic migrants are linked to the cartel.) Widely known in Mexico by his nickname, "Shorty" in Spanish, Guzmán escaped from a maximum security prison in 2001 by hiding in a laundry van, reportedly shelling out over $500,000 in bribes to dozens of guards and police officers.

In August 2003, Guzmán threw down the gauntlet. His senior lieutenants took 200 men into Nuevo Laredo and started seizing control of territory. They killed the mayor. The Gulf Cartel responded by sending a squad of Zetas to Acapulco, a beachfront resort city deep inside the Sinaloan realm. Assassinations, bombings, kidnappings, extortions, and gunfights became the norm in these two east and west Mexican cities.

Terror gripped Nuevo Laredo in 2005. No one would become the police chief—the title sentenced the office holder to a choice between *plata o plomo*: silver (taking a bribe) or lead (taking a bullet). Finally, a businessman named Alejandro Dominguez decided enough was enough. Dominguez volunteered for the job, publicly vowing to crush both warring cartels and drive their forces away. "My duty is to the citizenry," he said. "I think those who should be afraid are those who have been compromised."

On June 8, 2005, Alejandro Dominguez was sworn in as Nuevo Laredo's first police chief since the war had started. Nine hours later, as Dominguez was climbing into his Ford pickup outside the chamber of commerce, he was gunned down by a hit squad. The killing continued.

Two days after Dominguez was murdered, President Vicente Fox ordered the Mexican Army into Nuevo Laredo. The military took over the police department, but they could not halt the violence. Both cartels outspent and outgunned the army. Nuevo Laredo's plaza was the crown jewel for eastern Mexico's narcotics traffic, and neither side was willing to back down. In January 2006, Fox sent troops into Acapulco and received the same results.

Days after taking office in December 2006, President Felipe Calderón, Vicente Fox's successor, deployed 24,000 soldiers to the border. The next month, Calderón took the extraordinary action of extraditing fifteen drug lords to the United States, including Osiel Cárdenas Guillen, the Gulf Cartel kingpin captured in 2003. Sending so many narcotics godfathers to the United States was unprecedented. In the past, Mexican smugglers had simply run their businesses from prison—before his 2001 escape, "Shorty" Guzmán of the Sinaloa Cartel had a wine collection and a rotation of prostitutes in his cell (he preferred brunettes). By extraditing Guillen to the States, Calderón was sending his own message: the old days are over.

But it still wasn't enough. The cartels fought both the government and each other, and, in classic guerrilla strategy, worked to outdo each other in apparent acts of benevolence and community relations. La Familia, the Gulf Cartel's most feared faction (enemies of La Familia have been found beheaded), made a show of refusing to deal in methamphetamines. Their published rhetoric about the "scourge" of crystal meth brought to mind the *Godfather* scene when Don Corleone calls for a moratorium on narcotics trading.

Not to be outdone, in early 2007—soon after Calderón had shipped away his rival to face charges in America and extradited another seventy-nine drug bosses to the U.S.—El Chapo Guzmán walked into a Nuevo Laredo diner with several dozen bodyguards, confiscated the cell phones of every patron, and sat down to eat. After leaving, he returned the phones to the restaurant owner and paid the entire cantina's tab. Shorty left a few hundred dollar bills as a tip.

I didn't know about the Zetas, Calderón, or Shorty Guzmán when I went across a Laredo bridge one sunny May afternoon. But I knew things were bad in Nuevo Laredo, and I wanted to find out why. A colleague who lived in Nuevo Laredo guided me around the city. Over half of the stores and restaurants were shuttered, graffi-tied, and dilapidated. Across from the bridge, in the city plaza—a real, actual plaza—I strolled on pavement where a policeman had been gunned down the night before. City workers had scrubbed most of the blood from the concrete, but a slight dark stain was still visible on the asphalt.

My friend introduced me to a sixty-year-old merchant. After the 9/11 attacks, fewer Americans ventured south of the border for week-ends or holidays, the shopkeeper said. It was a small decrease, but not a devastating one. Businesses cut their hours back, but they stayed open. Then, the Iraq war also created another small drop in activity. All of that was nothing compared to the drug wars.

The Calderón government appears to be serious about fighting organized crime. Since taking office, Calderón has spent $3 billion and deployed 30,000 Mexican troops to combat the estimated 70,000 gangsters and *narcotraficantes* in Mexico. In 2007, Mexican officials asked the U.S. to support the Merida Initiative—a three-year, $1.4 billion counterdrug investment in technology and information-shar-ing funded by the United States for Mexico. As part of the Merida

Initiative, Mexican leaders requested a provision that would send U.S. Special Forces to train, equip, and support the Mexican military. "This is for our own self-interest," said U.S. Representative Henry Cuellar (D-Laredo) in August 2007, who helped negotiate the agreement. "Helping Mexico will address issues that spill over onto the U.S. side."

That might be the position of the Mexican government, but what about the mayors and police? Given the long history of municipal corruption, any U.S.-Mexico federal agreements seem easy prey for the *mordida* at all levels. But city leaders, particularly in northeastern Mexico, are voicing their agreement with the plan for U.S. forces to provide assistance. "As long as it goes through the proper channels," said Héctor Cantú, mayor of Marín, a city 200 miles south of Nuevo Laredo, "the aid is welcome."

Meanwhile back in Nuevo Laredo, residents like the shopkeeper remained in despair. "This city is becoming a ghost town," he said. "If this menace remains, there will be nothing left." For two decades, his business had brought in an average of $50,000 each year in profit. But now, he faced bleak economic prospects, courtesy of the Sinaloa–Gulf Cartel war. He said that if I mentioned his name, he might be killed.

Nuevo Laredo's citizens are not the only Mexicans with this opinion. In a 2004 poll taken in Mexico City, 86 percent said they would support government restrictions on civil liberties in order to dismantle organized crime. Another 67 percent believed that militarizing the police force was the only way this could be accomplished.

"Why are the Americans in Iraq? They should be here instead," insisted the Mexican merchant. Last year the Bush administration sent 6,000 National Guard troops to assist the Border Patrol on the American side of the boundary. This desolate shopkeeper agreed with the Mexican government: the U.S. military should help bring law and order to Mexico as well. "If the U.S. does nothing, then Mexico will look like Colombia. Is this what America wants?"

**4**

North of Laredo, the horizon widens. The humidity of the Rio Grande Valley evaporates. Mesquite wafts along a stiff, dry breeze, blowing tumbleweeds in from the north and west. The air smells deceptively peaceful, like it could erupt at any moment into a tornado or furious thunderstorm. You haven't yet arrived at the rugged, jagged desolation of west Texas, but you can glimpse it further ahead, north-by-northwest. The riverbanks are sandy, shallow, and thick with the carrizo that is sucking the river dry. A bucking cowboy on a billboard announces: "Welcome to Eagle Pass, Where Yee-hah meets Olé."

At just under 25,000, Eagle Pass is the largest village on the Texas-Mexico border. According to local history, the United States established the settlement in 1849 as a staging ground for prospectors heading west for the California Gold Rush. It was the first city founded by the Americans on the Rio Grande once Texas became part of the United States. After the Treaty of Guadalupe Hidalgo in 1848, Camp Eagle Pass, as it was called, subsequently spawned Fort Duncan. Like most bases along the Rio Grande, Fort Duncan was named after a Mexican-American war hero. In total, the Army Corps of Engineers built thirty-five forts along the Rio Grande after the war. A West Point graduate named Robert E. Lee commanded the construction project.

In 1855, the Governor of Texas granted a man named James Callahan permission to recapture runaway slaves. Callahan used Fort Duncan as a base to raid neighboring Piedras Negras, burning the Mexican town in the process. His unauthorized invasion of Mexico touched off a diplomatic row, and Fort Duncan was soon abandoned. It was garrisoned by the Confederacy, abandoned again, and then re-garrisoned by U.S. soldiers fighting the Indian wars. The base was decommissioned in the 1930s and is now a city park.

Piedras Negras, the Mexican city of 140,000 opposite Eagle Pass, means "black rocks." The town's name pays homage to the coal deposits that have fueled the economy, which has now evolved, like most border cities, to include the post-NAFTA staples of manufacturing and trade. A regional bastion of education, Piedras Negras sports eight colleges and three hospitals. Less well known is its status as the birthplace of a snack food popular in America: the nacho.

In 1943, a dozen U.S. Army wives—Fort Duncan had been reopened during World War II as an officer's club for pilots stationed at Eagle Pass Army Air Field—were shopping in Piedras Negras and stopped by a diner for a meal. The restaurant was closed for the afternoon *siesta*, but the chef, Ignacio "Nacho" Anaya, didn't want to look rude and disappoint the hungry women. He carved up some tostados, grated a block of Wisconsin cheese, and threw the pile in the broiler, topping the creation with sliced jalapeños. The wives loved the meal—what was it called? Anaya smiled and said, "*Nachos Especiales*"—Nacho's Specialty. By the 1950s, nachos were known throughout Texas, and the rest is culinary history.

Most Eagle Pass residents have a foot on each side of the river, and no one embodies this cultural paradox more than Mayor Chad Foster. Elected to his second term in 2006, Foster grins, drawls, and strides like an old Texas cowboy. With a bushy, neatly trimmed salt-and-pepper mustache, Foster stands at 6'3" and chats with a small toothpick in his mouth if he isn't smoking a cigarette. He wears boots, jeans, white long-sleeve shirts with silver buttons, and a spotless ten-gallon hat fixed atop his cranium like a permanent toupee.

When we spoke at his Foster & Associates Real Estate office, my impression was that the mayor liked to see himself as the kind of fellow who could bring warring parties together, forge a compromise, and make all sides believe they had emerged as the victor—an impressive skill for a man of both Scots-Irish and Cherokee descent. His wall sports many hunting trophies and community service awards. He speaks fluent Spanish and is a member of the National Association of Hispanic Real Estate Professionals. Jesus Mario Flores

Garza, the mayor of Piedras Negras complimented Foster by saying that he was more Mexican than most Mexicans. (He's also more Texan than most Texans.) After the first of two interviews, Foster told me that he genuinely likes talking with journalists. I think he genuinely likes talking to everyone.

Mayor Foster meanders when telling stories, illustrating fact and opinion in a sequential order that is determined as much by his own agenda as the interests of his interlocutor. With each joke or anecdote, Foster builds a case for the various interests and positions of the border like a salesman, lawyer, or politician. But there's nothing offensive about his manner; Foster is logical, rational, and interested in other observations and views. I thought that Foster wanted to engage with me for two reasons: he sincerely enjoyed the discourse, and he strongly believed in the positive future that the binationalism of the border could bring to America. Mayor Foster liked to sell things, especially things that he believed in.

When we met in 2007, Mayor Foster was the chairman of the Texas Border Coalition, an alliance of mayors, judges, and county officials that represent the 6 million Texans who live in the border communities along the Rio Grande. The chairmanship rotated from city to city every two years, similar to the presidency of the European Union or temporary seats on the United Nations Security Council. Politicians and border activists from all sides had sought out the Texas Border Coalition for their observations and views, which meant a meeting with Mayor Foster. In the past year, Foster had met Senator John McCain, former Vice President Al Gore, and a dozen other luminaries from each party. Mayor Chad Foster is not so important, but if Chairman Chad Foster phones the offices of U.S. Senators John Cornyn or Kay Bailey Hutchison, the dignitaries who represent Texas will personally call him back.

In January 2005, Foster's city council unanimously passed a resolution opposing any new construction of any walls or fences within the city of Eagle Pass. A few days later, Border Patrol agents representing the Eagle Pass station, Del Rio Sector, approached the council with a request. Using Department of Homeland Security funds, the Border Patrol wanted city approval to destroy a mile of carrizo cane on the river south of a municipal golf course that had become a major smuggling area. The Border Patrol also wanted to pave a road on top of the existing cart path that paralleled the river, install sixteen light towers north of the golf course, and erect a "decorative" fence between each of the towers. (It was called decorative because, unlike a tactical fence, there would be no barbed wire running along the top.)

The Eagle Pass City Council has five voting members: four council representatives and the mayor. The council told the Border Patrol they would not approve the project as long it included the decorative fence. Through their Del Rio superiors, Eagle Pass asked headquarters in Washington to delete the fencing requirement from the project. Washington agreed. The resolution passed on a 3-2 vote, which surprised Mayor Foster. After all, with the clause about the fence removed, the construction was essentially a golf course improvement project that Eagle Pass would get for free. He asked the two dissenters why they voted no. "We don't trust them," they said, referring to the federal government, and, tangentially, to the Border Patrol.

The council's lack of trust stemmed from the mention of any barrier whatsoever, decorative or not, being placed north of local land. When Congress passed the Secure Fence Act of 2006, they allocated $1.2 billion to build 700 miles of fence in urban areas along the border. Federal government planners apparently assumed that the fences would be placed along the Rio Grande. This would effectively cede the Rio Grande to Mexico, a fact that appeared to disturb border communities, the state of Texas, and environmentally conscious river activists far more than U.S. Homeland Security officials.

Because the carrizo has overwhelmed the riverbanks, any double fence that would be installed along the Rio Grande would have to be set back from the river. As maps of the twenty-one prospective fencing sites trickled into local communities, it seemed to Foster and his fellow mayors that the mysterious legions of homeland security bureaucrats who had drafted the proposed barriers did not account for local considerations on their maps. Brownsville's planned fence would lop off several buildings from a community college. Laredo would lose several acres downtown. And Eagle Pass? Say *adios* to that golf course, *compadres*.

Or maybe the bureaucrats looked at the map, but they didn't care. The U.S. government has wielded the power of eminent domain over its subjects—the right of the state to take private property for public use—to construct railroads, public utilities, and, more recently, the Eisenhower Interstate Highway System. The Fifth Amendment to the Constitution required only that the state pay "just compensation" to the owners of seized property, a term whose definition often skews toward the state's advantage. Beyond the meager hopes that an injunction from another federal organization—such as the Bureau of Land Management or the Environmental Protection Agency—would prevent construction, the only legal recourses private citizens could use to halt the expropriation of several thousand acres were their negotiation skills, votes, and voices of protest.

So the border cities raised their voices high and loud. "Why are we building a wall when we've already got a moat?" Foster asked. Their practical objection to the U.S. Congress and Department of Homeland Security in general (and to the Border Patrol in particular) was that everyone on the border knew that building a fence on the Rio Grande was neither smart nor effective, but no bureaucrat or politician would take a stand against Washington. Each section of fencing would effectively give hundreds of square miles of Texas— parts of cities, access to the river, private property and large sections of state parks—to Mexico. Did the government want to give away the country?

And who would be left with the bill for upkeep? Congressional auditors estimated that the 700 miles of fence would cost $49 billion to maintain for twenty-five years. That figure did not account for carrizo removal. The Rio Grande fence was a cheap political ploy, the Texas Border Coalition said, that would discriminate against border communities while giving Americans a false sense of security.

⋙⊶⊙⊷⋘

By January 2005, when Agent Randy Clark went before the Eagle Pass City Council about the public land surrounding the golf course, things had gotten out of control for the Border Patrol. Agent Clark, who also grew up in Eagle Pass, has short brown hair, blue eyes, a closely trimmed mustache, and the ruddy, expressionless face of a veteran. Along with another agent, Clark told me about what had caused their portion of the border to become overwhelmed, and what they had done to fix it.

Because of geography, most migrants from Latin American countries other than Mexico—Guatemala, Honduras, El Salvador, and so on—illegally cross near Brownsville or McAllen. The Border Patrol refers to all non-Mexican aliens they capture as OTMs, for "other than Mexicans." But shortly after 9/11, *coyotes* specializing in Central American smuggling discovered a bureaucratic loophole in Eagle Pass. By February 2005, the small station was capturing over 7,000 illegal aliens per month. Over 90 percent were OTMs.

The Eagle Pass golf course had become the busiest crossing point in the Del Rio Sector, and one of the most active in the nation. It was also unlike any other in the country: agents were not hunting and chasing illegal aliens. The migrants were walking up to the agents and asking to be arrested. Groups of 30, 50, or 100 would stand in line patiently to be apprehended and detained. During the day, migrants would stroll across the sand traps and putting greens and approach golfers, thinking they were agents. Caddies would point, directing them to a *Migra* vehicle. At night, if an agent turned on their flashlight, illegal aliens would pop out of the carrizo and head for them like the Pied Piper. It was an OTM assembly line: an efficient, well-planned surrender operation.

When Mexican citizens are apprehended illegally crossing the border, they are fingerprinted, processed, interrogated, and returned to Mexico via the closest port of entry. They never face a federal judge; they are simply caught and released. But it wasn't so easy to send someone from Eagle Pass back to Nicaragua, Venezuela, or Uruguay—especially if they had asked to see a U.S. immigration judge to plead for asylum, a request the Border Patrol had to grant. The closest federal courthouse was two hours away in Del Rio.

In the meantime, Eagle Pass didn't have enough space to put the detainees. So since there was no place to keep them, the customs authorities had little choice. Aliens were issued a *permiso*—a thirty-day official U.S. government travel visa—along with a "Notice to Appear" at a certain time and place before the immigration judge. In the meantime, they could go wherever they wanted. The travel visa allowed them to board any bus or airplane and travel freely within the United States. Mixed in with the migrants were members of Mara Salvatrucha, or MS-13, the infamous street gang that originated in Central America but blossomed in Latino urbana, particularly Los Angeles. It was like being freed on bail, only better—they paid nothing for their release. Few returned for their court date.

So things were a mess in 2005 for the Eagle Pass station. Scores of agents spent their entire workdays screening and shuttling Central Americans from fingerprinting stations to cellblocks to courthouses. They restocked freezers with microwave burritos by the hour. They filled and emptied Gatorade tanks of water. They handed out forms and filled out truckloads of paperwork. They did very little patrolling.

The solution to the problem, Border Patrol agents argued, was to enforce the law. The best way to end the caper was to charge all captured illegal aliens in federal court with the misdemeanor crime of entry without inspection, and send them to jail for 15 to 180 days. It didn't matter who or why. Zero tolerance would discourage illegal crossing. But enforcing the law was easier said than done.

This was not because of corrupt constabulary, government conspiracy, or recalcitrant bureaucracy. It was a simple matter of logistics. The courthouse in Del Rio could only hold so many people in the main chambers. There were only so many attorneys. There were only so many jail spaces. There were only so many busses, and drivers, and so on. Operation Streamline II, as it became known, required the Border Patrol to work with the Federal Bureau of Prisons, the U.S. District Attorney, the Immigration and Customs Enforcement, the Department of Homeland Security, and the U.S. Marshals. (It was called Streamline II in recognition of a previous attempt at "streamlining" that had not been as thoroughly coordinated.)

Streamline II started in December 2005. Aliens were herded into courthouses and stuffed into rooms for hearings—up to 200 at a time. One by one, they entered guilty pleas, donned orange jumpsuits, and served their jail terms. When space ran out in Eagle Pass and Del Rio, prisoners were bussed as far north as Waco—an eight-hour ride through San Antonio and Austin traffic. Each illegal alien cost about $90 a day to keep in jail.

One year later, apprehensions in the Del Rio Sector were down by 66 percent. Agents patrolled. Golfers played golf. Things were back to normal. The Yuma Sector, in western Arizona, coordinated with federal agencies and adopted the same strategy. They had the same results. A year later, the Laredo Sector also incorporated streamlining.

Illegal immigration cases have surpassed narcotics as the single-largest category of federal prosecutions in the country, jumping 85 percent in two years. But as of December 2007, only three of the nine Border Patrol Sectors—Yuma, Del Rio, and Laredo—had adopted the zero tolerance policy. This amounts to 499 miles of the 1,952 that comprise the southwestern border. Other sectors cannot muster the funds, manpower, or coordination to implement full-scale prosecution. Along 1,452 miles, catch-and-release—either dropping arrested aliens off into Mexico, or granting asylum to OTMs for an immigration hearing—remains operational policy.

In June 2007, a local news source reported that Agent Clark had gone north to Del Rio to discuss improvement projects with the city council. Clark wanted the city to allow the Border Patrol to landscape forty acres of riverfront into a park. Although lighting and decorative fences would be included, Clark's basic idea was to encourage Del Rio to make the land more accessible to the public. Bike paths and walking trails would be included. "The more people there are in legitimate activities down there," Clark said, "the more hesitant other people will be to engage in illegitimate activities." Agent Clark probably didn't intend to, but he sounded almost word for word like Eric Ellman, the McAllen-based river activist.

—————◆◇◆—————

When I told Mayor Chad Foster that, according to an Eagle Pass Border Patrol agent, some of the OTMs had been stealing items from the golf course, he laughed out loud. "Those aren't OTMs!" he said. "Those are kids from Piedras Negras." The mayor said that Piedras teenagers had a running underground contest to see who could swim across the river and steal the flag from the eighteenth hole without getting caught (something like American teens with street signs). The flag theft had occurred frequently enough that the clubhouse had started using a piece of carrizo cane for the marker. "What the hell would an OTM want with a bag of golf clubs? What's he gonna do—carry them across the country?"

Mayor Foster supported Operation Streamline II and the end of catch-and-release—"Eagle Pass fully believes in upholding the law"— but he resisted attempts to draw any connection between his city and the broader immigration debate. Before Operation Streamline was implemented, Foster said that OTMs benignly strolled through the city, *permisos* in hand, getting directions from locals to restaurants or the bus stop. According to Foster, they posed no threat to public safety. "Illegal immigration is not an issue in the city of Eagle Pass," said the mayor. "Migrants pass through here on their way to other places."

Foster was a good salesman, and he didn't have to twist my arm to make me believe that a fence on the Rio Grande was a bad idea. A wall? A massive concrete fortification? None of this made sense. Walls can be climbed and fences can be cut, especially when tall, thick reeds make illegal entry that much easier to conceal. Months later, the Texas Border Coalition supported a plan by the Brownsville and Laredo mayors to widen the Rio Grande by digging out the riverbank. It won't be possible without removing the carrizo that's draining the river, but a wider waterway that agents patrol using boats would be more valuable for riverfront security than a pile of barbed wire in the middle of a thicket.

The mayor's next pitch didn't come off quite as well. I understood what Foster said about the border needing a guest worker program. The mayor told me about a melon farmer from the Rio Grande Valley who had lost 400 acres of cantaloupe in 2006 because he couldn't find anyone to pick his crops after the immigration crackdown. (The farmer responded by leasing his land in Texas and moving his operations to Mexico.) But I wondered just how easily Mayor Foster could relate to Americans who didn't live on the border—or in a stable, friendly border town like Eagle Pass.

When Americans unfamiliar with the border hear politicians talk about a guest worker program, they often think or say very aggressive things. Those illegals are taking our jobs. Those illegals aren't paying taxes. A guest worker program would just give the illegals amnesty for breaking the law. If the illegals come in and take these jobs for nothing then the carpenters are out of work. The electricians are out of work. The painters and plumbers and Teamsters are out of work. Although I was drawn to Mayor Foster's tolerance for two cultures, I was unconvinced that he could export that attitude to an unwilling audience.

But like anyone wanting to close a deal, Foster sensed my ambivalence and launched into another anecdote. Lonnie "Bo" Pilgrim, founder of Pilgrim's Pride Chicken, had been the featured speaker at the Texas Border Coalition's 2007 Annual Conference in Austin. Bo Pilgrim was born northeast of Dallas in Pine, Texas (pop: 100). When he was in high school, Bo drove feed trucks for his older brother Aubrey who owned a chicken farm in nearby Pittsburg. After Aubrey died in 1966, Bo took over what had become a medium-sized poultry company. In 2007, with a workforce of 56,000 and annual revenues of $7.4 billion, Pilgrim's Pride was the largest chicken company in the United States and the second-largest in Mexico. It is the main supplier of Wendy's, Wal-Mart, and Kentucky Fried Chicken.

In his 2005 memoir *One Pilgrim's Progress*, Bo talked about the role that faith played in his business. At age ten, two months after his father died, he walked down the aisle at a revival and didn't look back. He has been a member of First Baptist Church in Pittsburg, where he has attended Sunday services—morning and evening— with his wife since the 1950s. After his brother died, Pilgrim believed that his calling was to be a Christian businessman. Pilgrim extolled the entrepreneurial spirit, but read his Bible daily; he had the work ethic of Isaac Guerra and the passion of Billy Graham.

Mayor Foster didn't tell me all those details about Bo Pilgrim. What he talked about was Pilgrim's speech at the conference, where he told stories about giving testimony before the Texas state congressional hearings on immigration. At Pilgrim's Pride Chicken hatcheries throughout the southeastern United States and Mexico, 9 million chicks peck out of their shells seven days a week. The instant the baby bird emerges and begins its brief, processed life, someone has to lean over, lift the chick up, inspect it, and stand the ball of fuff upright on its feet. That's an average of 104 chicks per second.

For several years, an inability to find laborers willing to dedicate ten hours a day to this task for meager pay has been Bo Pilgrim's biggest challenge. "How many parents today are teaching their children to be farmers?" Pilgrim asked in testimony, according to Mayor Foster's account. The company pays well for grunt work—$10 an hour—but that is still little incentive. "We work a hard day," Pilgrim had said, "and I want my workers paid a fair wage." Plant managers have gone to homeless shelters, halfway houses, temp agencies, and even college campuses. No one wanted to pick up chicks.

In subsequent research, I learned how Pilgrim's Pride might have made up for the labor deficiency. All the workers they hired were legal and documented, but many used the methods of Joel Garibay-Urbina of De Queen, Arkansas. Originally from Guadalajara, Garibay-Urbina legally crossed the border in 1995 at Laredo on a six-month visitor's visa. For six years, Garibay-Urbina lived and worked in the States. In January 2001, after arriving in Arkansas, he rented the birth certificate and Social Security card of Juan Rodriguez for $800. Assuming the name of Juan Rodriguez, Garibay-Urbina landed a job with Pilgrim's Pride. He also used those documents to buy a gun. After getting a job, Garibay-Urbina obtained an Arkansas ID card in his own name, and used it to buy a house for his wife and three children. He had a mortgage when he was arrested.

Pilgrim's Pride didn't know who Juan Rodriguez was until January 22, 2007, when Garibay-Urbina's wife, Guillermina, went to the courthouse and told the police that her husband had beaten her and was threatening to kill himself. Upon questioning, Joel Garibay-Urbina admitted that he had falsified documents in order to obtain employment. He was convicted for violating a law prohibiting illegal immigrants from owning a gun, sent to prison for a year, and then deported to Mexico. Had Garibay-Urbina not been accused of domestic battery—a crime for which he was not convicted—his real identity would never have been discovered.

According to a 2000 report from the U.S. Department of Health and Human Services Inspector General, birth certificate fraud is seldom prosecuted unless it can be linked by an employer to large monetary losses or another punishable crime. In a 2007 fourth quarter report, Pilgrim's Pride admitted this reality. In an outline of factors that could affect its forecasted performance, Pilgrim's Pride listed "new immigration legislation, or increased enforcement efforts in connection with existing legislation" as an event that would disrupt operations, increase costs, and cause it to change the way it did business. This struck me as an uncharacteristically honest and audacious statement for an employer of illegal aliens to make. Pilgrim's Pride did not return my call asking for comment.

It seems reasonable to assume that Joel Garibay-Urbina is not the only Juan Rodriguez working at a chicken plant. A Pilgrim's Pride employee with the United Food and Commercial Workers union said that in his seventeen years, the industry has gone from being 95 percent African American to 80 percent Hispanic. For poultry companies—and for every American who likes to dine on their products—their lack of legality is an awkward truth that most would rather avoid or ignore. The visa inspected when he legally crosses the border into America: Jorge Gonzalez. The name on her birth certificate when she legally applies for the job: Leticia Garcia. Everything checks out in the database, but neither was the name they were born with south of the border. In many cases, migrants will simply maintain their new identities until the day they die. Their employers will never know the difference. And they like it that way.

———————————⟫⟩·◦·⟨⟪———————————

I hadn't planned to talk about chicks with Mayor Chad Foster, but he had strong feelings about the U.S. needing a guest worker program, and I figured I should try to understand why. His views on the border fence and immigration issues were interesting, but what impressed me most about Mayor Foster was his ability to disregard partisanship and cultivate the team spirit within the border communities. Three weeks before I met Foster, a tornado had started in Mexico, hit Piedras Negras, crossed the border, and sliced through Eagle Pass. The disaster killed eleven people in both cities and destroyed numerous homes, schools, and businesses. After responding to their own citizens, Eagle Pass firefighters crossed over to Piedras Negras with chainsaws and generators. Neighbors and friends needed help. Nationality wasn't relevant.

And Mexico reciprocated. The governor of Coahuila, the Mexican state bordering Eagle Pass, had his entire cabinet on the stricken ground within two hours. Once the governor was satisfied with the response, he called Mayor Foster and asked how he could help. Backhoes, front-end loaders, and trucks were shuttled from Piedras Negras to Eagle Pass in short order, along with 100 men to help with cleanup. Mayor Garza of Piedras Negras, coordinated relief work with Mayor Foster by cell phone until the job was finished in both cities to their satisfaction or ability. Four days later, when FEMA finally arrived on scene, the major tasks were complete. Their partners across the border had mattered more to Eagle Pass in time of need than their own federal government.

Foster argued his case with statistic after statistic, bragging on his neighbors and asserting that their growth will bring a prosperous future to each side. Within the next ten years, he said, 40 percent of Mexico's population—40 million people—will live in a border state. The greatest proportional growth is expected to occur in Coahuila. With a current population of 2.5 million, 25 percent of Mexico's new jobs in the next decade, Foster says, will be created in Coahuila. The Mexican state is primed to explode.

The biggest anticipated economic catalyst for Coahuila, Piedras Negras, and Eagle Pass will come with a twist of lime. Fifteen minutes south of Piedras Negras, the manufacturers of Corona beer (among several labels), are building what could become the largest brewery in the world. If the first phase of construction is finished in 2010 as planned, Corona makers Grupo Modelo will be exporting 8.5 million barrels of beer each year from the plant. Once fully complete, the brewery will pump out 25 million barrels. The rate would surpass the annual facility production of the current king, Coors, which brews 20 million barrels annually at a single brewery in Golden, Colorado.* The Grupo Modelo brewery will bring 8,000 new jobs to Piedras Negras (and, presumably, lots of nachos).

To Mayor Foster, the border is intimately tied to Mexico's success in a way that the rest of the United States either does not appreciate or refuses to accept. It is difficult for men like Foster to understand why so many people are angered by men and women accused of

---

* Anheuser-Busch uses twenty-seven breweries to annually produce 122 million barrels of beer. Anheuser-Busch is the largest beer manufacturer in the U.S. and fourth largest worldwide, but the company does not own a brewery larger than the Coors plant.

"breaking and entering" when he sees so much work that needs to get done. Though he is not about to back down from his goals, Foster admitted as much to me when talking about a letter he mailed to President Bush as chairman of the Texas Border Coalition. "I'm just an old yay-hoo from Eagle Pass," he said. "What am I doing here writing a letter to the president of the United States and debating national issues with senators?" There was an amazed, Mr.-Smith-Goes-to-Washington tone in his voice.

Mayor Foster wanted me to stay longer and walk around Piedras Negras with him. I was interested, but it was late in the afternoon and I had hoped to explore Del Rio, the town an hour north of Eagle Pass. Del Rio was directly west of San Antonio and boasted two major highways, an Air Force base, and Amistad Lake, a man-made reservoir which claimed to offer the best bass fishing in the state. The mayor chuckled and told me that Del Rio wouldn't be nearly as interesting as I wished. I took this as some kind of border town rivalry.

Then he said that Ciudad Acuña, the border town across from Del Rio that inspired the George Strait song, "Blame It on Mexico," was the real hidden treasure. *Desperado*, the western starring Antonio Banderas and Salma Hayek, was filmed in Acuña's Corona Club, as was its prequel, *El Mariachi*, and several scenes from *Kill Bill Vol. 2*. But Acuña wasn't Del Rio, Foster said. If I felt strongly about going north, he told me I should at least cross *la frontera* and take the hour's drive along the Mexican side of the Rio Grande on Mexico Highway 2. Foster wasn't sure where I could stay in Acuña, but he believed the drive would give me a better sense of the differences between the towns. How? "Trust me," he said. "You'll see."

I got lost in Piedras Negras. That's almost impossible to do, but I pulled it off. I wasn't using a global positioning system, but that wouldn't have mattered. I would have gotten lost anyway. At any rate, I felt there was something artificial about taking a GPS on an exploratory road trip. Sometimes getting lost is an important part of the story.

But not today. I had wanted to get north before sunset and see this beautiful road the mayor had raved about, so driving aimlessly through the *mercado* felt like an annoyance. I thought I'd find my way out of the town—how hard can it be to find the only highway heading north?—but I discovered a dead end at every turn. Eventually, I pulled over next to a house and rolled down my window.

"*Donde esta Calle 2?*" I asked a man standing on his lawn. Blank stare. I repeated myself, hoping that *calle*, Spanish for street, would translate. It didn't.

He smiled and shrugged. "I don't speek English."

I drove ahead and pulled over at a PEMEX gas station. PEMEX is Mexico's national petroleum company. They own and operate all gas stations in Mexico.

Two Mexican men were sitting in a garage, adjacent to the pumps. One of them walked over to me as I lowered the glass.

"*Donde esta Calle 2?*"

He glanced at me, waved for his *amigo* to come over, and walked back to the garage.

"Where do you need to go?"

Chagrined, I asked for directions. He pointed to an exit, and then a right turn two blocks ahead. I still don't know how to say "highway" in Spanish.

As I drove north on Mexico's Highway 2 feeling culturally defeated, I remembered someone important to Eagle Pass who I'd forgotten to ask the mayor about: Grupo Modelo's owner, María Asunción Aramburuzabala. Known in Mexico as simply Maríasun, her Basque grandfather was penniless when he came from Spain to Mexico and founded the company that her father, Pablo, turned into Mexico's largest brewer. In 1995, Maríasun's father died and left the company to Maríasun and her mother and sister. A divorced mother of two, Maríasun took control of the company and earned a reputation as a tough, fair, competent manager. In 2007, Maríasun, who has a net worth of over $2 billion, was ranked by Forbes as the 382nd richest person in the world. She is the wealthiest individual woman in Latin America; a celebrity in her home country who, when not called by her nickname, is known as "the beer heiress."

In the fall of 2004, Maríasun quietly started dating Tony Garza, the United States ambassador to Mexico. Garza grew up in Brownsville and befriended President George W. Bush in 1988, six years before he was elected as the Texas governor. After Bush defeated Governor Ann

Richards in 1994, he appointed Garza as Texas Secretary of State. Garza oversaw elections and mediated issues along the Texas-Mexico border. Despite Garza's lack of experience in the national diplomatic corps, Bush appointed him to the ambassadorship in 2002 based on his popularity in Texas and his reputation as a rising Latino star. According to a *Texas Monthly* profile, Garza is humble, intellectually curious, and well-liked by his staff.

After meeting each other at a dinner party, Garza and Maríasun discreetly began exchanging e-mails, then phone calls and lunch dates. One restless October 2004 evening, the love-struck ambassador snuck past the Marines who guarded his Mexico City residence to meet Maríasun for an evening out. Their surprise engagement was, for a time, the hottest gossip in Mexico. Would Maríasun become a U.S. citizen? Would Ambassador Garza admit that his newfound wealth created a political conflict of interest and resign? First Lady Laura Bush and Mexican billionaire Carlos Slim Helú were honored guests at their April 2005 wedding. Maríasun did not become a U.S. citizen, Garza did not resign, and the drama surrounding their nuptials eventually subsided.

In 2005, as the war between the Gulf Cartel and Sinaloa Federation raged, Ambassador Garza had sent several strongly worded warnings to Mexico about the kidnapping of U.S. citizens in Nuevo Laredo. For the first week of August in 2005, Garza shut down a U.S. consular office in Nuevo Laredo because of the violence. On August 16, eight days after reopening the consulate, Garza commented on his decision. "Some have said that I ordered the shutdown to punish the Mexican government for its failure to control violence in the region," he said, "and in a sense, that's true." The decision and statement caused uproar among Mexican diplomats, who rebuked his remarks as "unfortunate" and "typical of the Bush administration."

Despite the media reports about Garza's modesty and border savvy, there was something that rubbed me wrong about his remark. Who exactly was he punishing by closing down the consulate? The cartels? The Mexican government? The American drug addicts that the Mexican pushers were fighting for the right to supply? No. The people whom he punished were the same ones who had already lost everything else in the interminable war: civilian shopkeepers like the one I had met. Closing down the consulate only drove the knife further into the very hearts and minds of those they were trying to reach.

The shopkeeper in Nuevo Laredo had taken me aback when he pleaded for America to "do something" about the violence in his town. "Tell Ambassador Garza that we need more men!" he had said. "Tell President Bush! If they cannot make this safe like it was before," he emphasized, "they should close the border!" I had pondered the value of sending U.S. troops down to the border in response to the American people's demands, but I hadn't expected a Mexican to be begging me for troops to enforce the law on his own side. It was the first time, as a civilian, that I had fielded this kind of request.

But it wasn't my first time in the situation. I had seen this happen in Iraq, with equally frustrating results. I thought about the dozens of Iraqi men I had met during my tour in 2004 and as a journalist in 2006. Some were wrapped in billowing one-piece garments called *dishdashus*, clothes that U.S. soldiers and Marines referred to as man-dresses. Others were dressed like I was today, in blue jeans and a shirt. Some were wearing fresh military or police uniforms. They all had ideas, requests, and passions. They all wanted America to do something.

And just then, I hated a lot of people, including Ambassador Tony Garza. I hated him and his wife and the drug smugglers and the dope smokers and the crack dealers and the addicts, the politicians, the voters, and everyone in between. I hated every American who had never seen someone believe in our nation's omniscient ability to save them from imminent suffering. The foreigner's begging eyes are different than those of a wino or street addict asking for a handout. Men like that shopkeeper just want to feed their families and make them proud. Can you understand his misery, Garza? Or are you too busy conducting affairs of state to notice?

All the anger I felt was irrational, unfair, and unjustifiable. If I ever met Ambassador Garza or his wife or anyone else I'd hated at that instant, I would have to apologize and I would sincerely mean it. I want to believe that they are decent folks who truly care about the shopkeeper's plight. But at that moment, for no specific or intelligent reason, I hated them all.

The sun was setting when I arrived at Acuña. Because reentry into the U.S. was more complicated with a car, I had dawdled too long in Piedras Negras to explore. But driving into Del Rio, I understood what Mayor Foster meant. Unlike Eagle Pass, where downtown was less than 1,000 yards from the river, the town of Del Rio sat five miles back from the carrizo-infested shoreline. At Eagle Pass, Yee-hah met Olé with a full *abrazo*. At Del Rio, Yee-hah stood at arm's length, shook hands, and nodded respectfully. Del Rio was a truck stop, military outpost, and railroad station. After that, it was a border town.

I ate at a local steakhouse and pulled into a Ramada Inn. The next morning, I didn't feel like exploring Laughlin Air Force Base or the Amistad National Recreation Area. I wasn't taking this journey for fighter pilots or fishing. I wanted to learn about the border: its essence, its people, its soul. And in this respect, Del Rio—in comparison to Brownsville, McAllen, Laredo, and Eagle Pass—appeared to be more of the same, only in definitively smaller increments.

After glancing around and finding nothing significant to report, I wished Del Rio well, slipped out of town, and drove west on Highway 90 towards the Pecos River.

To understand the Pecos River country in West Texas, it's important to first become familiar with the history of a Mexican War veteran from California named Joshua Bean. After the Mexican-American War ended in 1848, the pueblo of San Diego, California, became home to hundreds of disgruntled American soldiers. The U.S. Army had fought for and acquired a number of forts in Baja California, but the Treaty of Guadalupe Hidalgo forced them to surrender their conquests to Mexico.

By 1850, Joshua Bean was an important person in town, but San Diego remained under U.S. military occupation. The sinewy, Scots-Irishman from Shelbyville, Kentucky, had leveraged his distinguished wartime record into political muscle. By virtue of his connections, Bean was appointed *alcalde* of the San Diego pueblo.[*]

Soon after Bean's appointment, San Diego was incorporated as a city. Joshua Bean was voted in as its inaugural mayor. In 1851, after being appointed major general of the California state militia, Bean resigned as mayor, left San Diego, and bought a saloon and general store in San Gabriel. He wanted to have closer geographic ties to Los Angeles, the most important base in the region for the militia.

A couple of years earlier, Joshua's youngest brother, Phantly, also left Shelbyville seeking western fame and fortune. He drove a team of oxen from Independence, Missouri, to Santa Fe, New Mexico, then on to Chihuahua, Mexico. The same year that Joshua Bean was placed in charge of the state militia, Phantly arrived in San Diego and called on his brother. Joshua asked Phantly, who at the time was about eighteen, to run the store and saloon.

---

[*] *Alcalde* is a Spanish title for the chief civil administrator of a town. It is derived from an Arabic word for judge.

Phantly R. Bean was known as a gambler, cock fighter, horse racer, and playboy. He had black hair, a fair complexion, and was as "handsome as an Adonis." He wore a colorful cotton *poncho* and *sombrero* like a Mexican—common in San Diego for the upper class—and carried two revolvers and a bowie knife. Since his father had the same first name—and because Phantly was not a manly moniker in the West—he usually went by his middle name, Roy.

In February of 1852, Roy Bean's name appeared in the newspaper for the first of what would become many times. Roy had caused a stir in San Diego: a crowd had watched him duel a man named John Collins on horseback. Collins fired twice, but both shots missed his mark; then Bean hit Collins in the leg and blasted his horse. Hubbub ensued. Arrests were made.

Two months later, both men were arraigned before the county judge, charged with assault with intent to kill, and freed on bail. Legend has it that Roy Bean never posted bond. Instead, he escaped from prison after receiving a package of tamales from a Mexican lover; enfolded in the cornhusks were knives that he used to dig out of his cell. Like many tales involving Roy Bean, fact and fiction are undoubtedly intertwined.

In November 1852, Gen. Joshua Bean was killed near Los Angeles. One source says Joshua Bean was murdered by "Mexican ruffians"; others say he was shot by a romantic rival. Regardless, Roy inherited Joshua's store and saloon in San Gabriel. But in 1853, Roy got into a knife fight and had to flee California. He went to New Mexico, where his brother Samuel was a sheriff. Having been indicted in California under the name Phantly, and perhaps not being fond of it anyway, Roy Bean never again used his given name in public.

After the Civil War started in 1861, Roy headed for Texas. Samuel may have come with him to San Antonio for a time, but he eventually returned to being a sheriff in New Mexico. In 1866, Roy, who was about thirty-two, married fifteen-year-old Virginia Chavez. In time they had four children, and the place they lived in San Antonio was called Beanville. Roy ran a general store in Beanville, selling staples, merchandise, and whiskey. He was known for thinning his milk with creek water, and then blaming the cows for "bad digestion" when his customers discovered minnows in the bottles.

Around 1880, Roy Bean abandoned his family and headed west with several rickety wagons toward the arid Chihuahua Desert, where the Pecos River meets the Rio Grande. About 3,000 men were building the second transcontinental railroad—the Galveston, Harrisburg, and San Antonio Railroad crews were pushing west, while the Southern Pacific Railroad track worked east. The main obstacle to completion was the Pecos, where two tunnels would need to be designed, dynamited, and built underneath the waterway. Camps of thirsty roughnecks emerged on both sides of the Pecos, and Bean opened a tent saloon about three miles from the river. Business wasn't bad, but his competition was better networked. Bean often drank alone.

Over time, reputable Texans decided they had enough of the railroad men, whom they saw as "roughs, robbers, and pickpockets." Letters were written to officials asking for a lawman to be sent out west. One man was already available for the job. No one knows exactly why, but on August 2, 1882, Precinct No. 6, Pecos County, appointed Roy Bean—knave, reprobate, scoundrel, and con man—as justice of the peace. Thus was born a Texas legend.

The Pecos River trumpets through west Texas like a tuba in a symphony. After meandering from its source in New Mexico, twittering south and pausing at three hydroelectric dams, the Pecos slices through the rolling plateau north of Del Rio, carving miles of canyons before dumping into the Rio Grande. Yucca, agave, ocotillo, and prickly pear dot the limestone cliffs that rise 200 feet above the water. You can almost hear the ancient murmurs of the Apache, Comanche, and Kiowa on the breeze. The scent of wild oregano freshens the evening air, and—as thousands of Indians, pioneers, backpackers, and paddlers have discovered—adds a fine flavor to a meal cooked over a fire or camp stove.

As the southern transcontinental railroad neared completion, the aesthetic pleasure of paddling past wild oregano was not on the mind of a railroad engineer named George Langtry. Along with others on his design team, Langtry focused on the details of constructing the only tunnel system that would exist on the line. After the system was finished in 1882, the east and west lines were joined on January 12, 1883, about three miles west of the Pecos; the event was marked with a ceremonial photo and silver spike. The railroad line, which ran from Houston to Los Angeles, was the first to connect the Gulf of Mexico with the Pacific Ocean. Before the railroad was built in 1883, the first town west of the line was named Eagle's Nest. But soon after the railroad opened, the Southern Pacific wanted to pay tribute to George Langtry's work on the railroad and system. So the railroad rechristened Eagle's Nest—the first whistle stop across the Pecos—in his honor.[*]

When he was in San Antonio, Judge Roy Bean had developed an infatuation with Lillie Langtry, an actress from Jersey, an English Channel island near the French coast of Normandy. Nominally wed to an Irish landowner, Lillie Langtry was best known for charming her way into high society through the beds of British royalty. In 1879, one of her lovers, Albert, the Prince of Wales (who was also married, and would become King Edward VII) disapproved of her expensive tastes. "I've spent enough on you to buy a battleship," the prince complained. Lillie quieted him with her reply: "And you've spent enough in me to float one."

This was Judge Roy Bean's kind of girl. He moved his saloon/courthouse to Langtry, called it The Jersey Lilly in her honor, and told all who would listen—and they had to; he was The Law West of the Pecos—that he had named the town after the beauty across the ocean who would soon come to visit. It wasn't true, but Judge Roy never let the truth get in the way of a good story. Or a good show.

For twenty years, Judge Roy Bean ruled this desolate, unforgiving land with a theatrically legislative flair that was more P. T. Barnum than Wyatt Earp. Ostensibly, Judge Roy referred to a single law manual in his rulings—the 1879 edition of the *Revised Statutes of Texas*—but he didn't let the book stop him from creating his own rules as well. Most courtroom exercises were comedic antics that mingled greed with entertainment and common sense. For example, if Judge Roy was in a cranky mood, he would amuse himself at the expense of railroad passengers on a whistle stop, whom he

---

[*] Ten years later, the railroad company completed a bridge, replacing the tunnels as the main route across the Pecos. The tunnels are no longer in use today.

would fine for swearing in public after his barkeeper withheld their change as they rushed to catch their departing train. Jurors and sergeants-at-arms were selected from among his clientele (or fined on the spot for disrespect) and participated in the trials. If the judge got too drunk during court, one of his deputies would step in. Beyond that, anything went.

One afternoon, a railroad hobo rode into town and claimed to be a cripple. His act solicited both compassion and money from the Jersey Lilly's patrons. It was a farce. After the tramp left the saloon, Judge Roy learned of the ruse and became furious. He deputized a posse, picked a jury, and had the "cripple" brought in for questioning. Quickly extracting a confession, the judge made the hobo return the money he had received for charity. Then he moved directly to sentencing.

Criminals were not sent to jail in Langtry. They were either fined, chained to a tree (the Pecos equivalent of the pillory), or chased out of town. As his ruling, Judge Roy ordered the tramp's leg cut off as punishment. "We'll make you a real cripple now," he said. An old, rusty saw emerged, and a carpenter produced a blue construction pencil. First, he marked the hobo's leg at the ankle. No, said the judge. Higher. Kneecap. Mid-thigh. Just as the bailiff was about to saw the limb, Judge Roy called the jury to the bar for a drink. One of the deputies whispered "run away" in the hobo's ear. The man was never seen in Langtry again.

In 1896, Judge Roy Bean gained international fame from the sports world for outsmarting the lawmen of two nations. A year earlier, the U.S. Congress had banned prizefighting throughout all American states and territories. Before the Congressional ban, Dallas-based promoter Dan Stuart had pledged a $10,000 purse to the winner of a bout between Robert Fitzsimmons and Peter Maher. Stuart had also said the pugilists would split the take if he could not organize the fight. After the U.S. ban was announced, Fitzsimmons and Maher started training in El Paso, anticipating a fight somewhere in Mexico. Then the state government of Chihuahua also banned boxing. Stuart would lose a lot of money if he couldn't find a venue.

How Judge Roy Bean learned of Dan Stuart's dilemma is not known. But sometime in January 1896, Judge Roy told the promoter that he could handle the fight. At 3:30 P.M. on February 22, a train carrying Fitzsimmons, Maher, Dan Stuart, 200 boxing fans, a score of reporters, and twenty-six Texas Rangers arrived in Langtry from El Paso. Judge Roy had run a bridge across the Rio Grande and built a boxing ring on a sandbar. Because the fight was not in the United States, the Rangers could do nothing to stop it.

The bout was anticlimactic. Ninety seconds into the first round, Fitzsimmons knocked out Maher. But the Jersey Lilly had never shone brighter, and Judge Roy was in his elemental glory as reporters surrounded the Law West of the Pecos for interview after interview.

Judge Roy Bean died in 1903 of a heartattack, most likely brought on by an evening of drinking in Del Rio. It was a fitting end to a tempestuous life. A year later, when Lillie Langtry was traveling from New Orleans to San Francisco on the Southern Pacific, she finally arrived for her long-awaited visit. The town welcomed her with fanfare, presenting Lillie with a Langtry-formal "welcoming committee" (including a pet bear), one of Judge Roy's pistols, and some poker chips from the Jersey Lilly. She kept all the gifts until her death, and wrote fondly of Langtry in her autobiography, grateful for the man whom she believed had honored her.

Langtry reached its zenith after World War I, when the railroad made the city a boom town. Southern Pacific had built a water pump for the trains; the spring water was clear, clean, and, for the locals, free. Ranchers watered flocks, and about 250 people lived in town. The city even fielded a baseball team. But progress threatened, and in 1926, the railroad moved to a new depot a mile north of the city. The Jersey Lilly was abandoned, and in 1929 the rails that ran through Langtry were removed.

Langtry should have become a ghost town. Instead it lives on, thanks to the Texas Highway Department and State Historical Commission. In 1939, the Texas Highway Department paved a spur from Highway 90 into Langtry, restored the abandoned Jersey Lilly, and turned the Law West of the Pecos into a tourist attraction. Langtry still has a post office and general store, although the saloon no longer serves as a bar or legal dispensary.

Fifteen people still live in Langtry, making it the border's smallest settlement. The old-timers—Torres, Skiles, Billings—either grew up and returned, or have never left. Before 2006, the population was twelve. Then a Border Patrol agent moved back to his home community with his wife and child, and Robbie Dudley, who works at the Judge Roy Bean visitor's center, rented out the guest house that Pete Billings had remodeled for his kids. An unknown number of Mexican migrants live in an abandoned house and work in a rock quarry. They aren't counted as population—don't ask, don't tell. Nobody bothers the migrants, unless they play their music too loud.

———◆◇◆———

Pete Billings, one of Langtry's seventeen residents, turned ninety in 2007, a few months before we met. Pete has white hair, smiles easily, and is a man of deliberate words and actions. He wears simple, functional clothes: jeans, work shoes, a hat, and a long-sleeved button-down shirt. Pete has worked his entire life: on the river with his dad, on a crew for the Texas Highway Department, and, most enthusiastically, on the railroad as an engineer for the Southern Pacific.

Aaron and Lizzie Billings, Pete's parents, were married in 1904; Lizzie was eighteen and had come to Langtry qualified to teach school, but Aaron changed her plans. In June 1907, eight sections—about 5,000 acres—opened up on the Pecos for homesteading. Aaron and Lizzie staked their claim and set out to achieve the American dream.

The first three years were the hardest. Lumber is not plentiful in Pecos River country, so Aaron and Lizzie lived in a cave abetting the river bluffs. The floor of their home was caliche, a soft, pungent variant of limestone. They ate fish three times a day and scrounged for turnip greens to support their diet. Lizzie gave birth to their first child, Pete's older brother, in their cavernous natural abode.

Times improved, and Aaron and Lizzie built a house. For nine years, the couple worked the fledgling goat ranch, but the unusually bitter winter of 1916 ended their homesteading dreams. One morning, Aaron awoke to find all 500 goats frozen to death. He rounded up the family, moved back into Langtry, and became a butcher. Pete was born the next year.

Pete's eyes brightened when I asked what it was like growing up in a bustling Langtry, and he seemed to grow eighty years younger in his mind's eye. "It was a boy's paradise," he said. He hunted deer and javelina, fished for bass and gar, and built turtle and coon traps.

He swam in Pump Canyon's watering holes, discovered thousands of arrowheads embedded in silt and caliche, and hiked through *vegas* and *arroyos* with the other boys from the town. The river was his playground and an empty ranch in Mexico was his backyard.

I have spent enough time in the wilderness to know that the religious magic of nature can, at times, be overrated by the casual gawker. When I looked around at the majestic nothingness of Pete's neighborhood, I saw more than his idyllic memories. I saw scorching droughts, fierce thunderstorms, and frigid winters bearing down on the plains. As I glimpsed the hazards of rattlers, scorpions, and bobcats in my mind's eye, I remembered the many outlaws, past and present, who have taken refuge amid the sand and scrub. The Pecos is beautiful, but callous. It could mercilessly crush an aspiration as quickly or randomly as it might nurture one.

Pete's sense of manhood was cultivated by necessity on one of the nation's harshest frontiers, by a set of parents who had tamed the untamable with fortitude, intellect, and instinct. This was the inheritance that Pete's parents bequeathed him, and he expressed pride—not with words, but in the inflections and tones in his eyes— at passing on these values of self-reliance to his own children. Although outdoor hobbies may provide challenge for many Americans, no mere sport can replicate the education given by a mother and father who hewed their uninhibited existence out of a cave.

Pete took that legacy of self-confidence and invested it in a life running iron horses. For thirty-six years, Pete ran the Southern Pacific's West Texas lines from Del Rio to El Paso, retiring in 1978 to a house near Laughlin Air Force Base. During the 1990s, he noticed a disturbing change in Del Rio. Fluent in what he called "border Spanish," Pete had always enjoyed his Mexican neighbors—and often hunted for free at their ranch across the river. But the new crowd was different. They were younger, louder, and tougher. They raced cars, blasted music, and made themselves a nuisance. Pete bought land in Langtry along the Rio Grande and built his own homestead. His wife of sixty-three years, Dorothy Louise, had said it was her dream home. She died in 2002.

Pete finally had to give up hunting last year—he didn't trust his eyes anymore—but he still lives with greater vigor than many men half his age. One of his daughters, Linda, keeps an eye on him in

Langtry, but Pete's mind is strong and his voice is youthfully effervescent. One day, Pete was sitting with me on his back porch and talking about the sewage tank and sump pump that he had installed. I asked where he had gone to rent the backhoe to dig the hole—Comstock? Del Rio? Pete laughed. He had used a wheelbarrow, pick, and shovel. Twelve feet deep, and just as wide, through the resilient, rocky soil. At the time, he was in his mid-eighties.

As far as Langtry, Pete's only lament has been the loss of his beloved river. When the Amistad Dam was built in 1969, the reservoir that resulted between Del Rio and the Pecos drained much of the water that had once poured into the arroyos and canyons. Silt filled the river bottom, slowing the flow and increasing the spread of the ubiquitous carrizo. Simultaneously, a new dam was built north on the Río Conchos, the Mexican river that drains into the Rio Grande. "They took away my river!" Pete said in mock horror.

I asked Pete if he was still upset or angry about the loss of the river. He shook his head, shrugged and waved his hand. "You can't stay mad about that sort of thing," he said. "Things change. I miss the river and the way things were. Change is tough. But you just have to move on and get used to the new way."

━━━━━◈━━━━━

The river may ebb and flow, but the land west of the Pecos feels fixed and eternal. To inhabitants of this unchanging vastness between Del Rio and El Paso, the county where you live is more important than the city. The county seat is the most significant town in the area. It's the place where people go to fetch supplies, see a movie, or exchange gossip. Of the eight Texas counties west of the Pecos that bump into the border, only two have county seats with a population of more than 10,000.* Sandwiched among these comparative giants are Terrell, Brewster, Jeff Davis, Presidio, Culberson, and Hudspeth counties. These six barren boroughs are almost twice the size of Maryland, but with only 25,000 people—less than one-half of one percent of Maryland's population of 5.6 million.

---

* Del Rio is Val Verde County's seat, which covers both sides of the Pecos. El Paso governs its namesake county.

West of Langtry, Terrell County's gentle rolls are a harbinger of the miles of mountains that will emerge even farther west and south. The plateaus are sprinkled with mesquite, yucca, and creosote. Spanish explorers called this region *la tierra despoblada*: the land without people. Unless you possess the rawboned toughness of Pete Billings, you shouldn't stay too long. This is no country for men of any age.

The rugged individualism of American myth emanates from the soil as you walk caliche-strewn trails, navigate empty roads, and listen for the hum of iron wheels gliding along steel tracks. City dwellers shun this as flyover country, but remote places like the Pecos forged the core of the American ethos. The land undulates, plunging deeper into the wild with every earthen wave. Hardy souls from the southern side also populate this part of the border, as *vaqueros* come north from Coahuila or Chihuahua to work with cowpunchers in obscure ranches near Sanderson or Alpine.

Brewster County is the biggest of these vacant spaces. At 6,200 square miles, Brewster is the largest county in Texas. The county's southeastern line begins where the Rio Grande tips south, extending 182 miles along the river's big bend. The railroad runs through the north, stopping in Alpine, the county seat. Prior to 1959, when Alaska moved from territory to state, Alpine's 6,000 citizens could truthfully boast that they lived in the largest city, in the largest county, in the largest state in the Union.

Campers, hikers, and mountain bikers are drawn to the trails that wind through the Chihuahuan Desert and Chisos Mountains in the southern crown of Brewster County's Big Bend National Park. River runners ramble down the Rio Grande's canyons. As 300,000 tourists come and go through Big Bend each year, small enclaves of societal castaways have homesteaded west of the park, where they indulge in spiritual and carnal curiosities.

The most publicly prosperous of these appears to be Marfa, which is neighboring Presidio County's seat. In 1971, Donald Judd, a New York City artist, escaped Gotham to seek inspiration for his minimalist style. Marfa was it. Over twenty years, Judd purchased several buildings, two warehouses, a 60,000-acre ranch, and a decommissioned U.S. Army fort. He restored the buildings and used them to display his paintings, sketches, and sculptures. Judd believed that art was not something that should be interpreted or represented; it should stand on its own and simply exist. Judd died in 1994 and left his mark on Marfa through an endowment.

Today, Marfa has the highest per capita concentration of bookstores, cafes, and yoga studios west of the Pecos. Judd's stylistic convictions have endured as well. The most publicly accessible mark of his legacy is a fully restored Prada store sitting on the side of the highway miles from town. Racks of expensive shoes have been locked away here, sealed off from humanity since there is no handle on the door. Besides art, Marfa is also a magnet for UFO buffs, who claim that the unexplained appearance of lights several miles south of the city each year is caused by paranormal phenomena.

South of Marfa, a triangle of communities—Terlingua, Study Butte, and Lajitas—has formed its own eclectic, libertarian civilization. If Marfa is the Upper East Side in west Texas, these three villages are the equivalent of Greenwich, SoHo, and TriBeCa. About 1,500 hippies, loners, and self-described freethinkers live in cars, buses, and shacks made from corrugated metal, tires, and stones. They have embraced political minimalism: beyond the county sheriff, they answer to no authority.

In the 1850s, prospectors discovered one of the three largest veins of mercury in the United States on the Rio Grande's bend. At the turn of the twentieth century, W. L. Study ("Stoo-dee") staked a claim, calling it Study Butte. The ore was high grade, and Study made a fortune on his quicksilver lode, selling his mine in 1903 for $6,000 to the Big Bend Cinnabar Mining Company. During both world wars, mercury was important for mass production of thermometers, barometers, and electronic equipment. The mercury mines became less significant during longer stretches of peace, and the last owner, Diamond Shamrock, closed the mine in 1973. Most quicksilver mines remaining in North America are in Mexico, and the world's largest producer is now China.

Study Butte is now a ghost town, home to squatters, RV compounds, and peculiar restaurants like Kathy's Kosmic Kowgirl Kafe. The alliterative vendor serves burgers and barbeque out of a florescent pink trailer—diners sit around a campfire, eating on picnic benches and folding chairs. Kosmic Kathy hosts a flea market on the second Saturday of each month, and her restaurant also doubles as an outdoor theater for independent movies.

Another place that outgrew mercury mining is neighboring Terlingua, the world's largest producer of international cook-offs. Terlingua means "three languages," a reference to the Spanish, English, and Indian tongues spoken historically in the land. Today, the language most often spoken in Terlingua is that of chili. Like races that qualify runners for the Boston Marathon, chili lovers compete in 500 preliminary cook-offs throughout the world, vying for one of the 340 slots available for Terlingua's annual main event.

Since 1967, the year that the war of words between Texas and New York writers evolved into a culinary duel, Terlingua has hosted the annual International Chili Championship on the first weekend of each November. About 15,000 attend the festival, which also includes a splinter competition called the Original Terlingua Cookoff run by a rival camp. (At one point, both sides were in court over the spicy schism.) Proceeds, which are reportedly donated to charity, run into the millions.

The three-day festival's opening acts—think Woodstock for Harley-riding, RV-driving food lovers—include contests for barbequed wings, brisket, beans, ribs, black-eyed peas, ugly hats, and margarita mixes. There's an unofficial competition requiring women to parade naked from the waist up. The sheriffs make a handful of arrests each year, mostly for disorderly conduct and, if things get too wild, indecent exposure. "We plan all year for this," said Sheriff Ronny Dodson in an article, adding that he thought the cook-offs were great for the area.

When not occupied with riotous chili consumption, Sheriff Dodson's jurisdiction includes Lajitas, which is west of Terlingua. If Sheriff Dodson passes through Lajitas, he often stops for a beer with one of his drinking buddies, Mayor Clay Henry III. The mayor is not the biological descendent of Clay Henry I or II, but that has not diminished his ability to govern or drink. Mayor Clay Henry III, who has held office since 2000, is literally a beer-chugging goat.

The mammalian political monopoly started as a backlash in the 1970s against Walter Mischer, a wealthy Houston mogul. Mischer had purchased the land on Lajitas, built a resort, and had a friend elected as mayor. Angered at his imposition, Lajitas residents rejected Mischer's candidate, voting in an actual goat, Clay Henry I, to prove their point.*

Soon, Clay Henry became famous. He appeared on The Tonight Show with Johnny Carson. Willie Nelson partied with him. For more than thirty years, the mayor's office has been a cage outside the Lajitas Trading Post. A posted sign reads: "Office Hours: 24 Hours a Day, 7 Days a Week. Bribes Accepted."

And since his election in 2000, the Lajitas magistrate's administration has indeed been embroiled in scandal. That same year, Steve Smith, an Austin-based millionaire, purchased Lajitas. Smith poured $100 million into the resort, expanding it into a five-star hotel and calling it "the ultimate hideout." He also began using Clay Henry as a marketing tool, serving "Clay Henry Queso" at his restaurant and naming his bar "The Thirsty Goat."

On a Sunday in November 2001, Steve Smith was escorting a VIP guest, actress Anne Archer (*Fatal Attraction, Clear and Present Danger*). Sitting among a bricklaying crew was Jim Bob Hargrove, forty-one, of Del Rio. Texas law restricts the sale of alcohol on Sundays, but Hargrove had a cooler with bottles of suds. Smith asked Hargrove for a bottle and then handed it to Archer. The actress gave the beer to Mayor Clay Henry, who happily quaffed the beverage.

But Hargrove became angry. He felt insulted that his beer had been given to the goat by those "rich people" and their "rich friends." He told others on the crew that he was going to castrate the goat. The next morning, Mayor Clay Henry III was found lying in a pool of blood without his testicles. A dull paring knife was nearby.

Lajitas was outraged. Hargrove was arrested in Del Rio, extradited to Brewster County, and charged with felony animal cruelty. The charges could have imprisoned Hargrove for ten years and led to a $10,000 fine. Residents openly discussed a lynching. Hargrove posted bail, hired an attorney, and pled not guilty.

Because goat castration is common practice on ranches, jurors acquitted him on an 8–4 vote in August 2002. "It was serious," said Sheriff Ronny Dodson, referring to the trial. "Clay Henry is one of

---

* Lajitas is not the only town in the United States to elect a mammal to higher office. Other known American communities who elected animal mayors include Florissant, Colorado (Paco Bell, donkey); Rabbit Hash, Kentucky (Goofy, dog); and Anza, California (Opie, goat).

the icons of our community." The mayor recovered from the assault, but some say that he drinks more now than he did prior to his emasculation. Hargrove's fate is unknown.

---

Every small-town sheriff knows that the best place for a speed trap is less than ten miles on either side of the city limits, which is why I should have learned the location of every county seat before driving through west Texas. The worst places to be caught speeding are near small towns, where ambitious journeymen contribute a lion's share to the city or county coffers. I know this from experience. In several thousand lifetime road miles, including nine trips that ran coast-to-coast, I have been pulled over at least twenty times.

Although a radar detector is the most proactive approach, I've learned that the best defense if stopped is to smile, treat officers with respect, and sport a Marine Corps decal. More often than not, I am given a warning; former servicemen and women are prevalent in law enforcement, and they are usually generous with their own. My worst luck came in 1999, when I was flagged down near Winnemucca, Nevada, by a humorless sheriff for exceeding 100 in a 70 mph zone. He gave me an option: pay a $605 fine or spend the night in jail. I wrote the check.

The back roads of west Texas beckon the lead-footed. Posted speed limits rarely dip below 70 mph, and 80 is the common threshold on the interstates. From Marathon to Alpine, Highway 90 is a wide two-lane highway that, while not as straight as the salt flats, rarely meanders from its course. It appeared to be a comfortable place to do 90. Or better.

Drumming absentmindedly on the steering wheel as I drove toward Alpine, I crested a curve and spotted an oversized white Ford F-350 sitting 300 yards ahead on the opposite shoulder. Red lights were mounted on the roof. I hit the brakes, but it was too late. The siren was already wailing by the time I passed the Ford. I thought I saw a wolfish grin on the officer's face as he wheeled behind me.

I moved into the breakdown lane and stopped my rented Toyota hatchback ahead of the menacing crimson flickers. A six-foot-four, 220-pound man wearing jeans, boots, a Stetson, and a short-sleeved uniform shirt with a silver star above his left pocket stepped out of the truck and walked up to my window. He was built like someone who wrestled stallions in his free time.

"License and registration," the officer said, sizing me up. "Before you slowed down, I had you at ninety-two."

"Yessir," I said to Sheriff Ronny Dodson, who had nabbed me. "I was trying to make some time."

"You in the service?"

"Yes, officer. I was in the Marines."

Sheriff Dodson wasn't interested in my answer. Either this wasn't my lucky day, or it was the start of a legal kabuki dance that Judge Roy Bean would have relished.

"What brings you out here?"

"I'm writing a book about the border."

This wasn't my first encounter with the law on this journey. I had been mildly interrogated at twenty Border Patrol checkpoints, and screened at ports of entry from Mexico at least half a dozen times. If they asked what I was doing, which they always did, I told them. The port of entry officials could care less, but the Border Patrol agents had appeared genuinely interested. Some of them would offer research tips before waving me along.

"Really? So you're one of them media types. What kinda book are you writing? Who you been talking to?"

My first mistake was not being alert for Sheriff Dodson's speed trap. That was a minor tactical error compared to the faux pas I was about to commit.

"I've talked to everyone," I said. "Mayors, truckers, restaurant owners. You name it."

"You mean like the Border Patrol?"

"Of course, officer. I've spent plenty of time with the Border Patrol. In fact—"

Abruptly, the sheriff's eyes narrowed. "Yeah, that's what I thought," he said, turning away. "I'll be right back."

In addition to arresting drunken rogues and goat castrators, Sheriff Ronny Dodson presided over 182 miles of border, a greater amount of frontage than both Border Patrol sectors in California combined. I didn't know that when I met him. If I had, I also would have known that Sheriff Dodson was a charter member of the Texas

Border Sheriff's Coalition, a force as politically significant as Mayor Chad Foster's civilian border alliance in Eagle Pass.

In 2005, Sigifredo Gonzalez, the sheriff of Zapata County (south of Laredo), sent a letter to the sheriffs of the sixteen Texas counties bordering the Rio Grande. In the past decade, Gonzalez wrote, smuggling and crime had increased stratospherically in the border counties. Things had gotten beyond their ability to control. The federal government wasn't doing enough.

After the meeting, the sheriffs formed the Texas Border Sheriff's Coalition and, as a single voice, delivered this pointed testimony to state and federal authorities: the border is more violent now than at any point we have seen in our lifetime. You need to do something about it.

In response, Texas implemented a program in September 2005 called Operation Linebacker. The stated objective was to create a "second layer of defense" in support of the Border Patrol's theoretical first line. The Texas Rangers designated four "rapid deployment teams" of fifty officers that would be available for quick reaction and support. New officers would be hired for the border counties.

Five months after Operation Linebacker's start, the Laredo Police Department executed a joint federal/local search warrant on January 27, 2006, on an ordinary house. They were joined by extraordinary company: agents from the FBI, Immigration and Customs Enforcement, and Bureau of Alcohol, Tobacco, Firearms and Explosives. The search revealed two completed improvised explosive devices (IEDs), 300 primers, 1,280 rounds of ammunition, fifteen AK-47 assault rifles, five grenade shells, nine pipes with end caps, twenty-six grenade triggers, nineteen black powder casings, and unreported quantities of cocaine, methamphetamines, and cash. And enough explosives to make thirty-three more IEDs.

Throughout 2006, the Texas Border Sheriff's Coalition testified at hearing after hearing, including appearances at the U.S. House and Senate Judiciary Committees. Sheriff Gonzalez made it clear that the issue of the border coalition was not race or ethnicity. "We believe that many persons have entered our country with intentions of harming us," he said. "Terrorists have expressed a desire to exploit the existing vulnerabilities in our border security to attack the United States." An Arizona paper reported that if the twenty-five counties along the U.S.-Mexico border were compiled into the fifty-first state, it would rank first in federal crimes. Seeking to strengthen their voice the sheriffs expanded their coalition in 2007 to include New Mexico, Arizona, and California counties. It has been renamed the Southwest Border Sheriff's Coalition.

I didn't know about the coalition when Sheriff Ronny Dodson stopped me for speeding, but it was clear that I had annoyed him when I said that I had learned about the border from the Border Patrol. The sheriff stepped out of his truck and returned to deliver my verdict. My driver's license was clipped to his aluminum clipboard, along with the pink and green copies of a traffic citation. Sheriff Dodson looked at me severely.

"So you've been talkin' to the Border Patrol for your book?"

I was frustrated. Not too long ago as a Marine, I was the guy making stops, running checkpoints, and issuing orders. My eyes narrowed and I stared back. He might ticket me, but I wouldn't let him do so while treading on my journalistic honor.

"Sheriff," I said, "I've talked to everybody who will talk to me. I've called local police departments that haven't called me back. I've gotten the runaround from public affairs officers. I've heard stories from Josés, Jorges, and Javiers. You wanna talk to me? Hell, I'd like to talk with you too. Right now. Tell me sheriff, what don't I already know about the border?"

Sheriff Dodson blinked. Two more seconds passed.

"You know, them Border Patrol boys just drive around like they own the place," the sheriff said. "They'll blow down this road doing 100, 110."

"Those bastards," I said.

"I don't know what they told you," the sheriff said. He had lowered the aluminum clipboard to his side. "It's easy as hell to cross. We see it all the time."

"I thought Border Patrol agents were deputized in some counties as local law."

"Not here they ain't," Sheriff Dodson said proudly. "And not anywhere in Texas that I know of."

"Damn right." My notebook and pen were in hand.

Instead of waiting for another question, the sheriff launched a preemptive strike. "Last week, one of my eight deputies found a pair of drug mules," he said, referring to hikers carrying loads of marijuana. "The mules had been on foot for eight days in the mountains." He stopped and shook his head. "Were you in Iraq?"

I nodded.

"Well, no disrespect, but these boys are probably tougher than you," he said. "They don't carry much food out on the trail and they find their own water. I hiked around for half a day in those mountains, and it whooped my ass." Sheriff Dodson was an athletic man. "I don't think you could keep up with them."

The sheriff wasn't trying to impugn my manhood. His point was that the drug mules survive because they don't have a choice. They're called mules for a reason. If they make money, it might pay off a debt or keep a family member out of trouble. Or maybe they were just kidnapped from a poor village and enslaved into servitude. If they get caught, someone back home might pay the price. Whatever it is, their reward for evading their hunters and delivering their supplies is much higher than the Border Patrol's incentive to catch them.

I asked about illegal aliens. "We see 'em all the time," he said. "Most are on their way to Midland or Odessa to work in the oil fields." He pronounced the word monosyllabically as Texans do— "ool" instead of "oye-al." He said that some travel back and forth from the villages near Big Bend for temporary work. To him, these migrants caused no trouble.

He brought up the drug mules again. Their strength appeared to disturb him. After all, the cartels were the ones responsible for the IEDs. If they can't be stopped, the sheriff rhetorically asked, how could a terrorist? How would you even know the difference?

Then Dodson switched topics and mentioned his frustration with the feds opening up a courthouse in Alpine. The move was in response to the lessons learned from Operation Streamline, but the influx of well-paid federal workers meant that his small town ranchers couldn't keep up with the higher rent and grocery bills. The carefree, bucolic innocence of his empty border had been violated by Shorty Guzmán's Sinaloa Federation on the one hand and Washington D.C.'s Department of Homeland Security on the other.

This took about ten minutes. Finally, Sheriff Dodson said he had to go. He invited me to call him again and visit anytime. Said I was welcome to go out in the field with him or his eight deputies. Said that he had taken the FBI into Mexico and back a few months ago, just to show them how easy it was to do. He told me to look into the Sheriff's Coalition. Then he shook my hand with a grip that could strangle a python.

"Slow down from now on," he said, granting me amnesty. "You just talked your way out of a ticket."

⟫⟩◇⟨⟪

I have not brought up Mexico since Piedras Negras and Ciudad Acuña. There isn't much to mention. Between Del Rio and El Paso, the only official crossing into Mexico from Texas is west of Brewster County and the big bend: Presidio into Ojinaga. Prior to 9/11, Mexican boys had operated rowboat ferries at Boquillas del Carmen, a town across from the national park, and at Paso Lajitas, south of Mayor Clay Henry's city. They ran tourists, visitors, and citizens back and forth for $2 per person.

But in early 2002, the Border Patrol cracked down on these illicit crossings which the agents referred to as Class B ports of entry. They arrested the ferry operators, impounded their rowboats, and jailed them in El Paso for a month. Almost overnight, the Mexican towns shut down, infuriating the hermetic denizens of Brewster County who were not accustomed to the government meddling in their affairs, legal or otherwise.

At Presidio/Ojinaga, a river from Mexico, the Río Conchos, meets the Rio Grande. For centuries the Jumano Indians, believed to be cousins of the Tigua tribe, lived in a pueblo at the confluence of the rivers. When Spanish explorers arrived in the sixteenth century, they named the pueblo La Junta, which means "the meeting."

In his 1954 epic *Great River*, a four-volume history of the Rio Grande, Paul Horgan describes a Spaniard following the Rio Grande south from Taos, New Mexico. North of the Conchos, the Rio Grande flowed seasonally, sporadically, and intermittently. "Where the river reappeared," Horgan writes, "it was brought back to life by the never-failing, full, and clear green water of the Río Conchos out of Mexico."

In most official literature, the Río Conchos is defined as a tributary of the Rio Grande. While ostensibly accurate, this description is a misnomer. It implies that the Rio Grande is a river whose full source originates comfortably in the United States. But that's not correct. From a hydrological standpoint, the Río Conchos *is* the Rio Grande—at least, the Rio Grande we have seen up to this point. If cartographers and geographers were to precisely describe the water's source, they would say that the body of water north of Presidio is actually a tributary of the river running east from the Sierra Madres in northwestern Mexico.

The headwaters of the Río Conchos lie in the Sierra Madre Occidental mountain range in western Chihuahua, which is, by rough geologic approximation, a southern extension of the Rockies. From its source, the river flows down the mountains to the east, picking up runoff from tributaries to the north and south in the same pattern as South America's Amazon River. Were it not for the national boundary, the thick blue line on the map would run east through Mexico into Texas—not south through Colorado, New Mexico, and west Texas—before emptying into the Gulf of Mexico at Boca Chica.

In a 1944 treaty, Mexico and the United States agreed that the U.S. (specifically, the Rio Grande Valley in Texas) was entitled to a third of the total volume of water that reached the confluence of the two rivers from the Río Conchos and its tributaries (about 350,000 acre-feet of water per year, or 11.5 billion gallons).[*] Without this water from Mexico, farmlands in the Rio Grande Valley would disappear. In exchange, the U.S. is supposed to release about 1.5 million acre-feet into western Mexico from the Colorado River. The 1944 treaty grants Mexico an exception clause during periods of "extraordinary drought." What constituted an extraordinary drought was not clearly defined in the treaty.

From 1992–2002, this vagueness infuriated officials from the Brownsville and McAllen irrigation districts. Mexican ranches, farms, and businesses violated the treaty, they said, by using the seven dams along the Río Conchos and its tributaries to hoard over 1 million acre-feet of water. Mexico countered, saying that years of extreme drought along the Río Conchos had prevented them from keeping their commitment. Texas responded with satellite images of the reservoirs, as well as statistical evidence saying that Mexico's

---

[*] An acre-foot is about 326,000 gallons.

exports of fruits and vegetables grown in the Conchos irrigation areas had doubled during the "drought."

By 2002, the mouth of the Rio Grande at Boca Chica had become a sandbar. Border Patrol agents were sent to man the unexpected gap. Privately, Homeland Security officials questioned whether Mexico was further siphoning the flow of water as retaliation for the post-9/11 crackdown on illegal immigration.

In 2004, three Rio Grande Valley counties, with support from the state of Texas, threatened to sue the Mexican government for $500 million under a NAFTA arbitration treaty if Mexico failed to reimburse the water. The following April, Mexico agreed to release 400,000 acre-feet from the Conchos for the next three growing seasons. This would replenish the reservoirs in the Rio Grande Valley and return the river to the normal, pre-drought flow.

After learning this, I understood why the Rio Grande had been moving so swiftly when I was kayaking with Eric Ellman near McAllen. It had little to do, per se, with the flow of water released from Falcon Dam near Roma. That was because the water level at Falcon Dam, like the water level of the Amistad Dam near Del Rio, was affected by the seven dams that slow the Río Conchos and her tributaries as she runs east toward Presidio.

Since the Río Conchos is the main source of the Rio Grande, the river that separates Texas and Mexico north from Presidio is not grand at all. This part of the Rio Grande is ugly and uncouth. In most places, it's barely a creek. I wondered if the names of the rivers that join at this juncture had somehow been accidentally switched, perhaps after the War of Texas Independence or the Mexican-American War. In English, Río Conchos means Crude River. I found no evidence to support my theory, but the bottom line remains: the Río Conchos is the actual Rio Grande. For this reason, and to distinguish its own characteristics, I will refer to the river that runs south from Colorado to Presidio, Texas, as the Northern Rio Grande.[*]

---

[*] Archaeologists and historians say that in the sixteenth century, Spanish explorers described the Rio Grande as two separate rivers: Río Bravo (south of La Junta) and Río Grande del Norte. Eventually, Mexico amalgamated both names into the Río Bravo del Norte; however, the reason why the names merged—beyond the necessity after Texas independence and the Mexican-American War—is unclear. The original description was more accurate

In the 1980s, the simplicity of crossing the Northern Rio Grande made Presidio/Ojinaga a citadel for Mexico's Pablo Acosta, a drug lord who brought more wealth to this remote border than any legal enterprise had ever accomplished. In west Texas, he is also known as the lover of Mimi Webb-Miller, a former debutante and niece by marriage of the late Senator John Tower. At the same time that she was seeing Acosta, Mimi also dated the former head of the U.S. Customs counternarcotics unit. At one point, she introduced the pair on a ranch she owned near Paso Lajitas, Mexico.

In 1987, Acosta was killed in a gunfight with U.S. federal authorities in a village in Mexico south of Big Bend National Park. After Acosta's death, Mimi claimed his body at a Mexican morgue. In legend, Acosta was a benevolent, Robin Hood–like *narcotraficante* whose riches fed the poor and freed the oppressed. The truth, like that of many celebrated American gangsters, is not nearly as glamorous.

Four years after Acosta's death, one of his American associates, Robert Chambers, was arrested for drug trafficking on his father's ranch in Candelaria, about forty miles north of Presidio on the border. As part of the bust, Rick Thompson, then-sheriff of Presidio County, was also convicted. Sheriff Thompson had also been smuggling since the days of Pablo Acosta. Robert Chambers, who had also dated Mimi Webb-Miller, was sentenced to twenty years in federal prison. Sheriff Thompson was sentenced to life.

For years, Mimi was in the federal witness protection program. Eventually, as power coalesced around different cartel leaders, she stopped worrying about being targeted as part of the turf wars. She moved to Los Angeles and became a casting director for prime-time commercials. She still owns the ranch in Paso Lajitas, as well as a lodge in Terlingua. Her current list of lovers, if any, is not publicly known.

———————⟫•◦•⟪———————

On January 23, 2006, deputies working for Sheriff Arvin West of Hudspeth County learned that a drug load would be entering the U.S. that afternoon at a place called Neely's Crossing. Hudspeth County's southeastern corner is about thirty-five miles northwest of

Candelaria, where Robert Chambers and Sheriff Thompson had smuggled drugs for years. Neely's Crossing is another forty miles northwest. It is closer to El Paso than Presidio.

The officers set up a sting on the I-10 corridor, twelve miles from the Northern Rio Grande. Three Suburbans appeared; the deputies gave chase. One blew a tire. The other two SUVs exited the highway and turned south toward Mexico. The deputies followed the smugglers down the dirt road that ran back to Neely's Crossing.

When the deputies arrived at the border, they were met by a squad of men wearing Mexican Army uniforms and armed with AK-47 rifles. The soldiers were dispersed along the river. A military humvee with Mexican Army markings escorted the drug smugglers back across. The deputies could do nothing. Weeks later, aerial surveillance reported seeing bulldozers driving across from Mexico, plowing new off-road access routes through the desert to U.S. highways for the cartels. These incidents were reported, accurately, as armed incursions by persons representing the Mexican Army into the United States.

Two weeks after the Neely's Crossing event, Sheriff West testified before the U.S. House of Representatives that without significant increases in manpower, law enforcement was powerless against the cartels. We're outgunned, he said.

Ironically, it's likely that many of the guns pointed at Sheriff West's deputies at Neely's Crossing had been purchased legally in the U.S. by fixers like Robert Chambers, Sheriff Rick Thompson, or Mimi Webb-Miller. Since assault weapons are banned in Mexico, drug cartels often barter their wares for weapons, not cash. I wondered what would happen if drugs were decriminalized in the U.S. and gun ownership was legalized in Mexico.

I also wondered how far things could go before the U.S. government would order the Army or Marine Corps to fight the drug lords. This is, after all, our national border. Regardless of whether or not a drug cartel or corrupt general was responsible, an armed incursion would typically be considered valid cause for heavy reinforcements. In other nations in the world, either soldiers—not police officers—are used as border guards, or agreements are made with neighbors that dissolve the border and permit free travel. Since NAFTA, the

U.S. government has attempted to do both simultaneously. This has been a failure.

In 2006, President George W. Bush ordered 6,000 soldiers mobilized from the Texas, New Mexico, Arizona, and California National Guards to active duty on the U.S.-Mexico border. The program was called Operation Jump Start. The official purpose of the mobilization was to support the Border Patrol while they trained new agents and expanded the size of their force.

President Bush's decision created two separate outcries. On the one hand, the president—a former governor of Texas—was accused by allies of "militarizing" the border. Mexico reacted angrily. But when reports trickled in that soldiers would only be used in background roles—in command posts, auto repair warehouses, and, very rarely, for observation on the lines—the president was vilified for not doing enough. The Mexican Army is invading, critics said. Machine guns! Automatic rifles! IEDs! Why aren't we cracking down? Why aren't we getting tough? Why are we letting the terrorists win?

There is a reason we haven't been cracking down or getting tough. Experiments with the military on the border have been attempted in recent years, but in 1997, they were terminated after a calamity here in west Texas. Few communities on the Texas border are as vociferously antimilitary as those of Presidio County. When National Guard soldiers with Operation Jump Start were invited to a ceremony at a high school football game, the editor for the Marfa-based *Big Bend Sentinel* protested. An Army National Guard soldier told me that he had to drive to El Paso just to get a haircut.

To explain what happened in 1997, to whom, and why, I'm going to stop here and take a break from the journey. I also need to back up a few miles and return to the Rio Grande—the original river, not the northern one—just east of Presidio. A detailed discussion about what happened in Redford is critical to understanding this part of the border. It was clear to me—and to the Army National Guard—that the residents of this region will never forget this event.

# 6

Redford, a border village in west Texas, is bucolic in a quiet, scorching way—a poor man's Amish country in the midst of the Chihuahuan Desert. One hundred and thirty-two devout Catholics live in adobe, concrete, and cinder block houses. The town has a cheese cooperative and a handful of goat herds. There isn't much more. Redford is southeast of La Junta, the confluence of the Rio Grande and Río Conchos. The locals say that illegal drugs have never been seized in the village; most narcotics traffickers cross north of La Junta, where the Northern Rio Grande is shallow. Their poverty lends credence to that assertion.

From Redford, the closest legal crossing into Mexico is in Presidio, which is sixteen miles away but a thirty minute drive through mountain passes and switchbacks. But the closest stores and shopping centers are across the river in hamlets south of Ojinaga, Chihuahua. Until late 2001, the Border Patrol treated the arroyo at Redford called Polvo Crossing as a Class B port of entry.

What's a Class B port of entry? Sometimes at remote areas, the Border Patrol—Marfa Sector, in this case—waives the documentation requirements and allows local residents to cross back and forth between countries unofficially. Instead of driving to the port of entry at Presidio, villagers enter and exit Mexico informally at Polvo Crossing and then follow a dry stream bed south of town called Arroyo el Nogal (the respective names mean Dusty Crossing and Walnut Stream). The volume of traffic at a Class B port is never high, but no authority is present to check for any paperwork.

The Border Patrol's official position is to say that all Class B ports of entry on the U.S.-Mexico border were closed during the 1990s.

This was true on paper, but not in practice. Disregarding orders from bureaucrats, agents on the ground felt—not unreasonably—that small towns like Redford were actually made more secure by leaving the Class B ports open. Because they were quietly used by a handful of locals, new and therefore untrustworthy arrivals into town would stand out and be reported. The Border Patrol did not enforce the closure of Class B ports on the Rio Grande until after 9/11; at that point, Washington's demands could no longer be ignored.*

In 1997, the dusty arroyo that ran from Polvo Crossing to the two-lane asphalt highway that bisected Redford was not entirely empty. The ruins of a Spanish mission and an abandoned U.S. Army fort stood near the bluff that crested at the dirt lane. In the distance was a humble homestead where Esequiel Hernandez, his wife Maria, and his eight children lived a simple life. They cared for horses, worked their small ranch, and raised goats.

The primary custodian of the goats was Hernandez's seventeen-year-old son, Esequiel Junior. The sixth of eight children, "Junior" was a tall, thin, happy-go-lucky boy who enjoyed horses, dancing, and friendship. The late-blooming sophomore smiled easily and was popular at Presidio High School. He was entrepreneurial; he had expanded the family's herd of goats in an Isaac Guerra–like capitalistic endeavor to make money by selling milk, meat, and cheese. His buddies called him Zeke.

Beyond the unpretentious pleasures of his plain life, Zeke quietly nursed a private, personal ambition. There was something he contemplated beyond Redford. Perhaps it was an opportunity to give back to his village and beloved family. Or a team he wanted to be a part of that was known for excellence. Zeke hung a poster on his wall to sustain his dream.

Every day after school, Zeke took the family's forty-three goats down a dusty draw beyond Polvo Crossing, watching over the herd while they drank from the Rio Grande. Save for the backdrop of crops—alfalfa, melons, pumpkins—Zeke enjoyed a vista of gorgeous nothingness. Because wild dogs and coyotes occasionally went after a

* As of January 2003, twenty-three Class B ports remained open on the U.S.-Canada border. They were in six states (Maine, New York, Michigan, Minnesota, Montana, and Washington).

goat, Zeke carried a rifle. It was an antique single-shot .22-caliber rifle, a gift from his late grandfather that predated World War I. It was mechanically unreliable, but it shot straight enough. He hung the family heirloom above his bed, next to his poster, a portrait of the Virgin Mary, and two American flags.

In February 1997, Border Patrol agents James DeMatteo and Johnny Urias were working the 3:00–11:00 P.M. shift. Agent DeMatteo was a veteran at the station; Agent Urias was a new arrival and trainee. At sunset, the agents drove to Polvo Crossing. They exited their truck and went walking in the bush, cutting for sign. Nobody was visible. Goats grazed near the river.

Suddenly, the agents heard three popping sounds. One came right after the other. They sounded like firecrackers. The agents were not sure what was making the noise or where it had come from. They thought it might be gunfire. They looked around and drove away.

As they were leaving the riverbank and driving toward the village, Agent DeMatteo noticed two vehicles following behind them, flashing their headlights. The agents stopped, as did a weathered white pickup and another vehicle. Zeke Hernandez got out of the beat-up truck.

"I'm sorry that I was shooting," Zeke said to the agents. "I thought someone was doing something to my goats. I didn't know you were back there."

Agents DeMatteo and Urias looked Zeke over. He was just a nice kid; a fresh-faced, buoyant boy who had intended no harm. He didn't even know he was firing at them. Not only that, but he had even flagged the patrolmen down to apologize. It was logical that the agents could have been mistaken for wildlife. When you spend your days secretly scouring the backcountry, those risks come with the job.

Agent DeMatteo told Zeke Hernandez to use more discretion when shooting his weapon, especially at night. Having determined that no further action was necessary, Agents DeMatteo and Urias drove on and finished the remainder of their shift. The rest of the evening was uneventful. The agents made no formal report of the incident.

From the mid-nineteenth to the early twentieth century, the U.S. Army maintained a robust presence on the border with Mexico. Before and during the pre–World War I Mexican Revolution, shootouts between Mexican *federales* and U.S. soldiers were relatively common occurrences. During Prohibition, rum-runners and Texas Rangers fought with frequency. Forts were shuttered after the ban on alcohol was removed—thus far, I had encountered scores of abandoned outposts—but the Border Patrol still called on the cavalry during international firefights in the 1930s. Several bases reopened temporarily during World War II mobilization, but in 1945, the Pentagon became absorbed with defending against the Soviet Union. After the Cold War began, guarding the borders evolved into a matter that was supposedly left to civilians.

Things changed on November 13, 1989. With the media euphoric over the fall of the Berlin Wall, President George H. W. Bush's Secretary of Defense, Richard Cheney, and the Chairman of the Joint Chiefs, Gen. Colin Powell, announced the establishment of Joint Task Force (JTF) 6. "I believe that our military forces have the capability to make a substantial contribution towards drug interdiction," then-Secretary Cheney said in a written order. "I am instructing them to carry out that responsibility."

The Pentagon ordered JTF-6 to establish a headquarters in El Paso. The mission: support local, state, and federal law enforcement. The official area of operations: California, Arizona, New Mexico, and Texas. The press coverage: none. Compared with the end of the Cold War, a few soldiers on the border didn't seem particularly important.

A month later, JTF-6 seemed even less important to everyone, including the Secretary of Defense. In December 1989, 24,000 U.S. troops invaded Panama during Operation Just Cause, ousting the autocratic general and drug lord Manuel Noriega. In August 1990, Saddam Hussein's Iraqi Army invaded Kuwait. For a year, American ground forces were occupied in Saudi Arabia, Kuwait, and Iraq with Operations Desert Shield and Desert Storm. Several months after the end of the war, the U.S. military provided famine relief in Somalia. During this same period, the JTF-6 completed only 144 operational missions. Although the headquarters was established at El Paso, there were few available troops.

Things changed by the fall of 1992, and the Pentagon asked Army and Marine Corps units to volunteer for the counterdrug/border security missions. They were classified as "military operations other than war" and advertised as an opportunity to provide "real world experience" for soldiers and Marines. One of the units that volunteered for the missions was 1st Marine Division. This unit, based in Camp Pendleton, bills itself as the oldest, largest, and most decorated organization in the Marine Corps. At the time, the 1st Marine Division had about 15,000 Marines. The major subordinate commands were three infantry regiments, one artillery regiment, six battalions, and a headquarters battalion.

Between October 1992 and February 1997, the 1st Marine Division completed 119 of the approximately 3,300 counterdrug missions that JTF-6 executed during that time. In those four and a half years, eight shooting incidents happened to units stationed with the task force. Of those eight episodes, four involved the 1st Marine Division. In all four shooting incidents, the Marines chose not to return fire. Even in one case when a Marine was wounded, the Marines de-escalated the situation without retaliating.

In other incidents, however, U.S. forces did return fire. In March 1993, drug smugglers were firing on law enforcement officers with machine guns, and a unit from the 2nd Marine Division provided cover with .50-caliber weapons. In January 1997, a five-man Special Forces team was approached by three men who were told to halt. Instead the men charged the Special Forces team. One of them fired. A soldier shot back, wounding the assailant and dropping him to the ground. All three were arrested. The man who had shot at the soldiers was later found to be an illegal immigrant.

It's easy to forget that large military units—particularly in peacetime—operate in many ways like businesses or corporations. During fiscal years 1995–97, the 1st Marine Division performed seventy-six counterdrug missions. As compensation, the division received $2 million in 1995 from the Pentagon. The next year, the figure increased to $4 million. These funds were supposed to cover the costs for preparation, training, and deployment of the JTF-6 missions.

But the counterdrug money also functioned as a cushion for the penny-pinching Marine units, who were notoriously stingy with their

operational budgets. In his 1998 budget estimate, the division commanding general said this about the importance of JTF-6 counterdrug funds: "Unequivocally, my commanders depend on this annual
infusion. Withdrawal from counterdrug missions will impact small
unit training." The implication was that units could not afford to
train for combat unless the division saddled up for border duty.

Since the JTF missions did not involve full-scale war, Marine
authorities at all levels characterized them as "training deployments."
This meant they were not of serious importance to the division staff.
On the one hand, participation was "strictly voluntary" and "not
intended to take priority over division training." But somebody had
to do the mission, or else the money wouldn't roll in. So the division
handled this "strictly voluntary" event the way that military organizations generally do: all missions were divvied out evenly, and each of
ten subordinate commands took their turns "volunteering."

The problem: these were not training missions. Regardless of
what the staff officers said, the counterdrug deployments were actual
operations. Every counterdrug mission was formally briefed at the
Pentagon and approved by the Secretary of Defense's office prior to
execution. Granted, they were not major things, like fierce combat
or disaster relief. They were considered static, routine events. Nothing exciting. Because of this, many field-grade officers in the division
didn't think of JTF-6 operations as significant. It was good training
paid for by someone else.

From 1995–97, the 11th Marine Regiment handled seven JTF-6
missions for the 1st Marine Division. Assignments were rotated
evenly through the artillery battalions as training opportunities. In
May 1996, after Lt. Col. Douglas Montgomery took command of the
5th Battalion, 11th Marines, he said that the unit should complete a
JTF-6 mission within a year. Specifically, Montgomery wanted "the
headquarters Marines to do a real world mission." In other words,
the JTF-6 mission, in Lieutenant Colonel Montgomery's view, would
be good training for noncombat Marines while the battalion's other
warriors were busy with their primary task: honing skills related to
launching explosives.

Inside the brotherhood, it's not fashionable to classify a Marine as
"noncombat." The Marine Corps proclaims that every Marine is a

rifleman, and whenever Marines who lack special training are required to improvise, adapt, and overcome a challenge, this adage is recited. But Marines—even those who aren't in the infantry—are still expected to train, prepare, and rehearse when called upon for a mission. Planning for contingencies enables Marines to handle the ad hoc nature of combat's chaos. In the peacetime Marine Corps of 1997, however, most Marines who ran supply warehouses, worked on trucks, or fixed radios did not train routinely on how to react under fire.

Because of these deficiencies, the battalion commander believed that Headquarters Battery—the supply clerks, truck drivers, and radio technicians—were best suited for counterdrug duty. It will be a great training opportunity, they said. Staff officers identified April and May 1997 as the ideal time for the headquarters Marines to do their training. In the summer of 1996, they contacted the JTF-6 in El Paso and sent in their request.

A few months later, it was approved. During the month of May, Headquarters Battery, 5th Battalion, 11th Marines would deploy to conduct Mission JT414-97A: counterdrug operations in Redford, Texas. They would be attached to the Border Patrol in Marfa. They were told that Redford was chock full of bad guys. Headquarters had a real world mission.

⋘══════⟫⊶⊙⊷⟪══════⋙

Mission JT414-97A called for Marines to occupy four camouflaged observation posts from May 15–29, 1997, in order to detect, monitor, and report illegal drug activity. The positions, which the Marines called holes, had been dug into the ground and were well concealed. Two teams of four Marines were assigned to each hole. The teams would work the lines for three days straight, then switch out with another team.

The mission commander would be Capt. Lance McDaniel, an artillery officer who commanded Headquarters Battery. A blue-eyed, square-jawed 1988 graduate of Texas A&M University who grew up in Waco, McDaniel seemed a natural fit for the assignment given his regional background. According to written accounts, Captain

McDaniel's decisions during the planning process were clear, competent, and professional. After being assigned the mission, McDaniel met with senior staff officers, phoned the liaison officers at JTF-6, and arranged to meet in El Paso with military, law enforcement, and Border Patrol representatives.

This meeting happened in February 1997. It was the captain's first opportunity to learn about what his Marines would actually be ordered to do. From the 156 Marines in his battery, Captain McDaniel would need to select eight teams of four to accomplish Mission JT414-97A. Another twenty-four would be required for support duties off the line. He expected the JTF to prepare him with information—intelligence updates, mission orders, task lists. Like any good officer, he wanted to set his Marines up for success.

During the February meeting, Captain McDaniel was underwhelmed by the JTF-6 staff. On the one hand, the hazards appeared deadly serious. McDaniel was given a letter stating that "there are several areas of special concern when conducting counterdrug military operations." The most significant threat, the letter said, was from drug smugglers, who were characterized as "an organized, sophisticated, and dangerous enemy." They were warned about gangs that were "extremely dangerous" and prepared to kill. Operations were "dangerous" for the unprepared. In a single paragraph, the word dangerous emerged three times.

But the JTF-6 staff offered McDaniel no advice on how to deal with this organized, sophisticated, and dangerous enemy. They told the captain where he was going, when he should show up, and what gear he would need. They gave McDaniel a formal packet titled: "Operational Considerations for Counterdrug Missions." It contained a checklist with titles of things he was supposed to know—Border Control Measures, Immediate Action Drills, Communications Procedures, Posse Comitatus Rules. There was no explanation of what these things actually were. The packet was a generic document that applied to the entire border. In terms of preparing for Mission JT414-97A, the information was functionally useless.

Nevertheless, Captain McDaniel followed up on the letter and the packet. Would his Marines receive any training? Would they have classes? What kind of intelligence would they receive for this dangerous mission? Who would respond if the Marines came under fire? He got the runaround from JTF-6.

The Border Patrol seemed helpful, saying they would respond to any calls from the Marines in fifteen minutes or less. They didn't have a choice; the Marines would be coming to the border whether they liked it or not. As far as the Border Patrol was concerned, the job of the Marines (or soldiers, or whoever the JTF sent down to the border) was to crawl into their holes, be quiet, and stay put.

To the Border Patrol agents, the Marines sent on the line to support them were hardly essential. Having the steely-eyed young men around was helpful, but they were also an intrusive annoyance. At best, they provided agents with another set of eyes for a few days. At worst, they compromised the Border Patrol's comfortable routine with their incessant demands for information, responsiveness, and action.

———————⟫⟩·◉·⟨⟪———————

Headquarters Battery encompasses the smattering of Marines who are needed to run an artillery battalion, but whose jobs don't fit neatly into a box. Administrative clerks, truck drivers, Humvee mechanics, computer repairmen, radio operators, and "mess management specialists"—cooks—all have a home in headquarters. From among these 156 men of varied talents (female Marines are not stationed with artillery units), Captain McDaniel needed to select the eight best as team leaders. Several Marines—McDaniel included—had been seasoned under fire in the Gulf War or Somalia. All but one were ranked sergeant or higher.

The exception was Cpl. Clemente Banuelos. Although he was only twenty-two years old, Banuelos had impressed the senior enlisted men and officers of Headquarters Battery. A whip-thin Hispanic with brown eyes, bushy eyebrows, a dimpled chin, and a crooked smile, Banuelos, from a San Francisco suburb, had been in the Corps for three years and married to his high school sweetheart, Luz, for one. His awards included a Navy Achievement Medal—not an extraordinary accolade, but also not a ribbon tossed out like a candy wrapper, particularly for a Marine in headquarters—and he sought a long-term career in the Corps. At any rate, Captain McDaniel didn't have eight qualified sergeants to lead the teams, and Corporal Banuelos had stood out for his bearing and maturity.

What Corporal Banuelos did not have was training in any specialty beyond his official job as an artillery scout. The corporal performed well as a headquarters liaison to infantry units, but he had never been in combat or led Marines on any tactical missions. Banuelos knew how to observe and relay reports. He knew how to remain undetected. He knew how to lead four Marines in a flanking maneuver to surprise an enemy. And he was an expert shot.

Despite a plan from Captain McDaniel that included several training exercises, the Marines assigned to Mission JT414-97A only conducted about six hours of classes from February to May. They didn't train as units or teams, but on an ad hoc basis. The men studied camouflage, cover and concealment, movement techniques, and hide sites. More instruction had been planned for headquarters—in particular, a detailed practical application class with scenarios involving the use of deadly force. That class was supposed to come from veterans of counterdrug missions. Various conflicts arose, and the class kept getting bumped back.

In the meantime, a military lawyer taught Headquarters Battery about rules of engagement. After the instruction, wallet-sized plastic cards were handed out to Marines, detailing the legal dos and don'ts. The explanations seemed byzantine, and the Marines had a lot of questions. On the one hand, the cards said they could shoot to kill if they faced "imminent danger of death or grievous bodily injury." But it stipulated that they could only fire if "lesser degrees of self-defense had been exhausted." What constituted lesser degrees on the U.S.-Mexico border—against a reportedly dangerous enemy—was unclear.

One person who spoke up with concerns was Staff Sgt. R. R. Macias. A veteran of Desert Storm and Somalia, Macias, who had just been promoted, was one of the most experienced men in the battalion. To him, there was an important distinction between hostile forces and U.S. citizens that wasn't being carefully addressed. Macias had taken some night classes at a sheriff's academy, and he felt the Marines should be briefed by a civilian law enforcement officer prior to the deployment. Macias told his boss, a gunny, that he was both-ered by the lack of focus for Mission JT414-97A. The gunny agreed, but said the unit had a busy schedule and they just had to deal with it. Improvise, adapt, and overcome. Ooh-rah.

During the first week of May, the scenario training was cancelled yet again: a surprise inspection team had arrived from Marine Head-quarters in Washington. These "readiness drills"—part competition, part audit—happened to Marine units at random every two years. Paperwork was reviewed. Gear was checked. And Marines were tested on basic things all Marines were supposed to know—including a comprehensive dress uniform inspection. Headquarters Battery was tasked with the dress inspection. Captain McDaniel protested, but his higher-ups told him the uniform inspection took priority. The scenario training with the counterdrug veterans never happened.

On May 12, 1997, Captain McDaniel and fifty-five other Marines arrived in Marfa, Texas. They linked up with the Border Patrol and established two headquarters near Presidio. The teams went out with Captain McDaniel and the Border Patrol agents to look around at the areas near their holes. The holes were placed along a shallow ridgeline facing the Rio Grande. The most challenging assignment was Hole Three, overlooking Polvo Crossing. Captain McDaniel gave that hole to the teams led by Staff Sergeant Macias and Corporal Banuelos. Two days later, on May 14, Mission JT414-97A was opera-tional.

The day the mission began, Staff Sergeant Macias sat inside Hole Three with his team. The Marines wore ghillie suits—utility blouses and trousers covered with stitched strips of camouflaged fabric. Their faces were painted brown and black. They looked like shrub-bery, not people. They were told to remain concealed and not reveal their presence to anyone.

Unlike Arizona, where a substantial portion of the border is pub-lic land, most of the border in Texas is privately owned. This included Hole Three. The JTF staff had asked for and received per-mission from the landowner, Mr. Carmen Orozco, to use Hole Three at any time. Other than the Border Patrol agents, the JTF staff, and a handful of law enforcement officers, Carmen Orozco was the only person in Texas who could have known the Marines were there.

Orozco lived 221 miles north of Redford and rarely visited his border property.

As Staff Sergeant Macias and his three charges settled in for their first clandestine night on the border, another event was happening in a small pueblo a few hundred yards from Hole 3. Music and laughter echoed from the thin windows and spilled onto the dusty porch. The Hernandez family and their friends were having a celebration. It was Junior's eighteenth birthday.

———————————— ◆◦◆ ————————————

More than 85 percent of all illegal drugs—including nearly all of the heroin, cocaine, and methamphetamines—enter the United States through official ports of entry. These are the "plazas" drug lords fight over. The exception is marijuana. Only half of the marijuana entering the U.S. comes through the ports; the rest is physically transported by human mules. Because over half of the marijuana consumed in the U.S. is domestically grown, the demand—and subsequent profit margin—is much lower for narcotics smugglers. Heroin and coke are big business. Marijuana is, comparatively, a mom-and-pop operation.

Marijuana is an interesting illegal drug. Unlike alcohol, which kills if you drink too much at one time, there is no known quantity of marijuana that can threaten your life. Driving stoned is bad, but so is driving after taking sleeping pills. In 1972, President Richard Nixon's National Commission on Drug Abuse recommended that consumption of marijuana be decriminalized under state and federal law.

In 2002, when asked if he had ever smoked pot, New York Mayor Michael Bloomberg replied: "You bet I did. And I enjoyed it." According to the National Institute on Drug Abuse, almost 98 million Americans over age twelve have admitted to smoking marijuana at least once. Over half of Baby Boomers and Generation-Xers say they've inhaled (and enjoyed it).

But what is tacitly acceptable in society is a deadly sin in the Corps. Weed makes a person sleepy, relaxed, and lethargic, and those are not qualities the Pentagon wants from its warriors. Drug testing happens early and often in the U.S. military; failure results in dishonor, discharge, and jail time. For this reason, service members are inclined to replace bud with Bud (or Corona) during their years of social experimentation.

At any rate, having ceded their individual freedoms on behalf of their band of brothers, the Marines sitting inside Hole 3 were sworn to forsake the leaf. Regardless of what you did in your former life, drugs were viewed within the traditional Marine culture as a menace to society. And drug smugglers were the greatest threat of all.

This mindset toward contraband, combined with intelligence briefs from the JTF that had been gleaned like the children's game of telephone, caused the Marines in Hole 3 to paint an inaccurate portrait of their surroundings. They believed that Redford was a "high risk" area, not a friendly town. (False.) They thought 75 percent of Redford was involved in narcotics and that the drug traffickers were connected with all the locals. (False.) And they were supposed to be watching out for drug gangs who used armed scouts to conduct reconnaissance. (True, but none had been caught doing so at Polvo Crossing.)

The day before the mission started, Staff Sergeant Macias and Corporal Banuelos discovered an empty box of .22-caliber bullets. They were inspecting the base of the hill behind Hole 3. Did the bullets belong to hunters? Recreational shooters? Or were they the property of Redford's drug smugglers who preyed upon the good people of America?

For three days, Staff Sergeant Macias and his Marines broiled in sweltering heat. Insects bit them. The afternoon temperature approached 130 degrees. They dined on MREs and forced scalding water down their throats to slake their thirst. They prayed for nights.

On May 18, the teams changed over. Corporal Banuelos appeared with his three charges: a junior corporal, Ray Torres, and a pair of lance corporals, Ronald Wieler and James Blood. Corporal Torres and Lance Corporal Blood were in the same motor transport platoon. They drove trucks. Corporal Banuelos and Lance Corporal Wieler, a radio operator, had worked together in a training exercise the year before. But the first time Lance Corporals Blood and Wieler met was when they arrived in Texas. Prior to May 12, the teams for Mission JT414-97A did not train together at all.

The day of the changeover, traffic at Polvo Crossing increased. Because the life-giving waters of the Río Conchos were not flowing, the Rio Grande was shallow. Trucks piled high with tires, concrete, and furniture drove back and forth. Men on horseback rode into Redford from ranches in Mexico. A Ford Bronco carried six people. There was no urgency to the movement; the men weren't rushing to get across the line in fear of *La Migra*. This was how they lived. It was their home. The same thing happened again the next day.

Dutifully, the Marines called in report after report. Eventually, they stopped counting the number of illegal transits. On May 18, the Border Patrol responded twice. On May 19, the Border Patrol finally told the Marines that Polvo Crossing was a Class B port of entry. After that, they only reported for a single call. Each time, it took the Border Patrol fifteen minutes to show up. And when agents finally arrived, the people who had crossed were long gone.

This confused the Marines, especially Corporal Torrez and Lance Corporal Blood. They were supposed to be on guard against Redford's dangerous criminals. They were told to report every illegal passage of this depleted river into the country. And now the Border Patrol tells them—on a blistering afternoon, right in the middle of their mission—that all this activity is actually okay? "If they don't care," Blood said to Torrez, "why do we need to be out here?"

⟫·◊·⟪

On the afternoon of May 20, less than half a mile from Hole 3's position, Zeke Hernandez arrived home from Presidio High School. Zeke went into his room and studied his driver's education handbook for about an hour. Then he helped his father unload some hay from the truck. It was time to water the goats.

Sometime after 5:00, Zeke grabbed this .22 rifle and went to the makeshift pens where the Hernandez family kept their animals. He led his herd past the abandoned Spanish mission and the old fort down a stony bluff to the river. It appeared to be an ordinary afternoon. Hole 3 was on the other side of the slope.

As Zeke Hernandez watched his goats, he noticed something in the brush. Movement. Two hundred yards away. Not long ago, a wild dog had taken one of his goats. He wasn't about to let that happen again. That was why he carried the .22: to defend his herd.

---

While Zeke was walking his forty-three goats down to the river, the Marines were not occupying Hole 3. During the day, they kept an eye on Polvo Crossing from a hidden spot on the high side of the bluff. There was some shade. They were still concealed. And they could sleep, clean their weapons, and eat.

Ordinarily, the Marines traveled from their rest area to Hole 3 either after sunset (8:30 P.M.) or before sunrise (5:30 A.M.). The darkness masked their movements. But because they were changing out the next morning with Staff Sergeant Macias's team, they left the bluff early, about 6:00 P.M. They had a bunch of gear—radios, food, ammunition—to carry down to the observation post, and they wanted plenty of time to settle in. They were wearing their ghillie suits and walking in a low crouch. They blended in with the yucca, ocotillo, and creosote, just as they had been taught.

At 6:05, Corporal Banuelos put his Marines into a halt. He had noticed something too. He grabbed his handheld radio and called back to the operations center in Marfa. "We have an armed individual, about 200 meters from us," Banuelos said. "He's heading toward us. He's armed with a rifle, appears to be, in, uh, herding goats or something."

This was odd. On the previous afternoons, goats had grazed right next to the Marines. But this was the first time the Marines had seen a man accompany them. They all stopped. Corporal Torrez thought the shadowy figure with a rifle had a visual on them.

---

Zeke was certain. There was some kind of animal. He couldn't make it out at the distance, but it was definitely a scavenger. Wild dog? Coyote? Maybe even a bobcat. Whatever it was, he had to protect his goats from the threat.

At 6:07, Zeke raised his .22-caliber rifle, pointed toward the silhouette, and fired two shots at the predator hiding in the brush. That silhouette he shot at wasn't an animal.

≈≫·◇·≪≈

Captain McDaniel was working out in the gym at Marfa Sector's Border Patrol headquarters when someone ran in and told him the Marines were taking fire. Immediately, he ran to the Mission JT414-97A operations center, which was about forty yards away. Before McDaniel arrived in the command center, the watch officer was a second lieutenant who had arrived at the unit a month ago. An experienced noncom, Sergeant Dewbre, was also in the operations center. Lance Cpl. James Steen manned the radio.

The shot had cracked past Lance Corporal Blood's shoulder. The men froze. A drug smuggler had discovered their position and attacked them, they thought. Corporal Torrez and Lance Corporal Wieler believed he fired a second shot, but Banuelos and Blood didn't hear it. "Lock and load," Banuelos said, motioning his Marines face down on the ground. "If he raises that rifle again, shoot him." The Marines hit the deck, got behind creosote bushes, inserted magazines into their rifles, and pulled back, then released, the charging handle. Their M-16s were ready.

Banuelos was on the lower edge of the ravine. He could not see the man with the rifle, but Torrez and Blood could. The man had lowered the rifle and was standing on his toes. He appeared to be looking for something in the distance, Torrez later recalled, "Like when you . . . try to move your head around to see."

After the Marines radioed that they were taking fire, the Marfa dispatcher for the Border Patrol began organizing backup response. Agents Rudy Martinez and Johnny Urias were the closest agents on duty. They were sixteen miles away, had just detained four illegal aliens, and were missing their body armor. They would not arrive for another thirty-eight minutes.

Meanwhile, back at headquarters Captain McDaniel was trying to figure out what was happening. Everyone was discussing the rules of engagement. Lance Corporal Steen asked Banuelos if he was still taking fire. Banuelos didn't reply. Then he came on the radio and told Steen that he was going to pull back and come around from the right flank. "Right now he's stationary," Banuelos said, "but he kind of knows the general vicinity where two of my men are."

This was a critical decision. Authorities later determined that, under the rules of engagement, Banuelos had five legal options. He could have remained in the ravine and assumed a defensive position; maneuvered the team onto the bluff and stayed there; retreated through the low ground; identified himself and offered a verbal warning to cease fire; or moved along the ridgeline parallel to Zeke Hernandez, ensuring visual contact and preventing his team from being flanked.

If Banuelos thought that someone with a rifle was trying to flank them, staying put in the open ravine or on the ridge made no tactical sense. And four Marines wouldn't consider retreating from "the enemy." The only other logical choice besides the one Banuelos made would have been to identify themselves as U.S. Marines and call for him to drop his weapon and cease fire. Unfortunately, he followed the attacker.

Banuelos later said he made the call because he thought Zeke Hernandez was a drug smuggler who had initiated an unprovoked attack. And he hadn't been taught to consider the possibility of making an arrest, especially from a distance of two football fields. If the young Marine had been trained like a police officer or a Border Patrol agent, he would have acted accordingly. But he was a Marine who was told to watch out for dangerous criminals. If he moved, then so would they.

At 6:11, Banuelos radioed the command center: "As soon as he readies that rifle back down range, we are taking him."

"Roger, fire back," Lance Corporal Steen said.

The officers and senior enlisted men went ballistic. Steen had blindly authorized the discharge of a weapon he couldn't see based on a report that he couldn't verify. Captain McDaniel pulled Steen off the radio watch, replacing him with Sergeant Dewbre. But in the commotion, "fire back" was not corrected or rescinded.

It didn't matter, at least not immediately. The radio went silent. At 6:14, Sergeant Dewbre asked Corporal Banuelos for an update. "I have a visual on the suspect, in front of the church," Banuelos said. "He knows we're out here. He's looking for us."

Dewbre acknowledged the transmission. "You're to follow the ROE," he said. Banuelos did not reply, which concerned the command center. Five minutes passed.

Around 6:20, Agent Johnny Urias called. The Border Patrol was on their way. So was the county sheriff. Agent Urias asked Banuelos where Hole 3 was, and to describe what they saw. Was the man armed? "He's armed with a rifle, a .22," said Banuelos. Apparently, Agent Urias did not remember his personal involvement in a similar incident that had happened three months ago at Polvo Crossing. If he did, he didn't mention it over the radio.

Zeke started moving again. Banuelos didn't want to take any chances. He saw a second point of high ground that would provide a better angle of observation. To get there, Banuelos would need to go down the hill, across a draw, and then back up another slope. He motioned for Blood and Wieler to follow him. Then he passed off the handheld radio to Corporal Torrez, giving up his only link to higher headquarters.

The three Marines moved into the gully, dispersed by ten to thirty yards. Banuelos was in the middle; Blood on his left, Wieler on his right. For six minutes, they took turns sprinting and kneeling behind scrub brush. They arrived at the base of the hill. Banuelos ascended, took a knee, and motioned for Blood and Wieler to spread out along the high ground. As they dispersed, Banuelos watched Zeke, who was now about seventy-five yards from his position.

Corporal Torrez, who had the radio, also had Zeke Hernandez in his line of sight, but he was unable to see the other three Marines. Blood and Wieler were moving laterally amid the desert brush and watching their footing. (Wieler had slipped and fallen several times while descending into the draw.)

At 6:27, Torrez heard a burst of static on the handheld radio. The Marfa dispatcher was directing the backup team to the wrong location. Torrez looked away from Zeke and down at the radio. He was about to call to correct the Border Patrol.

Suddenly, a shot rang out.

"We have a man down," Torrez said.

The 5.56mm bullet that Cpl. Clemente Banuelos fired from his M-16A2 rifle entered Esequiel Hernandez Jr.'s body below his right arm. The instant the round pierced Zeke's skin, it fragmented, as the bullet is designed to do. It sliced two trails through his chest, shredding flesh, tissue, and organs along the way. Zeke fell backward into an old stone well that was shaped like a square and filled with sand.

When the Marines ran up, Zeke Hernandez was unconscious. His body weight rested upon his grotesquely twisted neck. His legs protruded in midair. Because they didn't see any blood, Banuelos and Torrez initially thought Zeke was faking his injury. Then they saw his body. In basic first aid, they had been taught that it was better to leave someone immobilized with neck injuries. They seized Zeke's rifle, but didn't touch him at all.

Twenty minutes later, backup finally arrived. The Marines had secured the perimeter, as they were trained, and challenged the deputies, officers, and agents when they ran toward them. They were allowed to pass after identifying themselves as law enforcement. A local deputy pronounced Zeke Hernandez dead. Even if the Marines had rendered first aid, the autopsy revealed that they could not have saved his life. The bullet had done its job.

Thus ended Mission JT414-97A, the last of 3,300 U.S. military counterdrug missions on the border. The promising career of a young Marine also died that day. Banuelos was investigated for over a year by the Texas Rangers, the Justice Department, Joint Task Force-6, and the Marine Corps. Three grand juries—one federal, two from Presidio County—concluded he had committed no crime. All four investigations determined the same result.

Clemente Banuelos left the Marines honorably, as did Ray Torrez, Ronald Wieler, and James Blood. For ten years, Banuelos has refused all requests for contact. He lives in San Diego and has no public comment on the incident, beyond those in his official statements from the many investigations.

The U.S. government paid the Hernandez family $1.9 million to settle a wrongful death claim for their role in the loss of their son. But that didn't bring Zeke back. Nor did it cause anyone in Presidio County to forget that Esequiel Hernandez Jr. was the first civilian killed by the U.S. military on American soil since four students at

Kent State University in 1970. His memory lives not only in Redford, but throughout west Texas. And because of his death, the active duty soldiers from the Texas National Guard sent to support border security in 2006 were not welcome in their hometowns. They can't be supported or trusted. Ever. Not after what they did to Zeke.

When his son was killed, Esequiel Hernandez Sr. had been chopping wood. He saw a crowd gathering on the hill across from his home, and drove the old pickup over to see what was happening. Lance Corporal Blood, still wearing his ghillie suit, ordered him to stay back. Hernandez obeyed. Then a sheriff's deputy, who did not know who he was, called Hernandez over to the cistern and asked if he could identify the boy who had just been killed.

Weeping and screaming, the Hernandez family was kept away from their beloved for the rest of the evening as the sheriffs tried to assemble the pieces. That night, Esequiel Senior took Zeke's ten-year-old brother, Noel, down to the river so they could round up the goats and put them back in their pens. When they finished, Noel went into his dead brother's bedroom, ripped the image hanging next to the Virgin Mary from the wall, and shredded the placard with unbridled fury.

It was a U.S. Marine Corps recruiting poster.

# 7

**M**ost nomads moving west are sapped when they arrive in El Paso. The clock has advanced an hour—El Paso runs on Mountain Standard Time—and the lights visible from the southern edge of the pass call to weary travelers like a mild, rustic oasis. The rays of the early sunset whisper with a sultry, relaxing silence, descending into the 3,700-foot basin the Northern Rio Grande carved—over 200 miles northwest from its juncture with the Río Conchos—between the Franklin, Hueco, and Juárez Mountains.

El Paso is the fulcrum of the border. Other than Las Cruces, the New Mexico suburb that sits thirty-five miles northwest, El Paso and its Mexican mirror, Juárez, are the largest cities within a 250-mile radius in either country. Somewhere between three and five million people live in the *barrios, colonias*, suburbs, neighborhoods, tribal jurisdictions, and gated communities that form this southwestern metropolis. Except for San Diego/Tijuana, more humanity is concentrated on this line than anywhere else along *la frontera*.

The gated communities for the wealthy are on the north side, tucked safely between downtown El Paso and Las Cruces. Bright red adobe roofs, painted stucco walls, rock desert gardens, and savory cuisine are the hallmarks of the sunny suburbs. From there, the conurbation trickles southeast along the river though Ysleta, Socorro, and San Elizario. Twenty miles of rusty metal, chipped concrete, and stained asphalt sprawl along a border corridor of barbed wire and chain link. Only when the urban jungle terminates into pecan and alfalfa farms near Fabens and Fort Hancock does the jagged prairie appear to regain sanity.

The U.S. military drives El Paso's economic engine. Each year, 23,000 soldiers and their families stationed at Fort Bliss pump an estimated $3.2 billion into the city. The Army base is the only force preventing El Paso from being swallowed entirely by Juárez. South of the border, Juárez—locally, "Ciudad" does not precede the name— thrives on the 400 *maquiladoras* that line the city's slums. Four of the 23 bridges spanning Texas and Mexico are in the El Paso/Juárez vicinity. Only Laredo ranks higher in Mexican imports entering through Texas.

The afternoon I drove into El Paso, gray clouds had darkened the sky and the stiff wind smelled like creosote. A thunderstorm was coming. I saw a sign ahead for McDonalds and decided it was time to pull over. I was hungry and had to use the bathroom; Mickey D's seemed like a good, quick pit stop.

It was 2:45 P.M. on a weekday, but tractor-trailers were stacked on the access road like it was rush hour the day before Thanksgiving. I studiously ignored the bearded man holding the "homeless veteran" sign who was begging near the overpass. The veterans I know would cut off their right arm before asking for a handout from strangers. Crawling through diesel exhaust, I analyzed the vagabond and rejected his claim as a hollow plea. I inched along the highway for eighteen minutes before reaching the restaurant.

In the McDonald's restroom, I noticed a curious sign: "Please Dispose of the Used Tissue Paper Into the Commode." It was also printed in Spanish. It was not the sort of guidance you would expect to receive, or need. I looked down next to the porcelain throne. Sure enough, three or four wads had been tossed into a plastic trash can.

I realized something interesting. If I ever wanted to know if a border region had a high population of immigrants, all I needed to do was check the bathrooms. In countries as diverse as Ethiopia, Vietnam, and Kuwait, toilet facilities aren't built to handle paper inside the plumbing. Water closets are equipped with wastebaskets; after wiping, you fold up your tissue and put it in the plastic bin. Much of the world—including rural Mexico and Central America— uses the same system. Of the 12 to 20 million legal and illegal immigrants in the United States, 750,000 are unable to read and write in any language (and the proprietors of this McDonalds had probably learned this from multiple unsanitary experiences).

I finished, flushed, washed my hands, and grabbed a burger. When I entered the diner, I had noticed a dark-skinned man sleeping near the door. He wore a red cap, dirty white t-shirt, jeans, and work boots. On my way out, he woke up and called to me.

"Hey," said the man, "you know where I can get a lift to Houston?" His eyes were cloudy and bloodshot. He looked filthy and smelled high.

"Sorry, pal," I said. "I'm headed west."

"Oh, okay. I'm just looking for work. Say, you wouldn't have any spare change? I'd like to get a burrito."

I didn't have any change. But I did have five dollars, which was more than he had expected. I enjoyed the look on his face when I told him to go buy something to eat and keep the rest. He laughed, thanked me, and went inside.

I felt different about this stoned *caballero* than the "homeless vet" I had seen minutes before on the overpass. Maybe it was because he addressed me, politely, man-to-man, with a self-respect that I appreciated. Inebriated or not, I could tell that if I had asked him to join my painting team or hang some drywall to work off the meal, he would have done it. He was a tough man who lived on handouts, but he seemed to do so with vigor. Not happiness—that would be a stretch—but a certain level of enthusiasm that suggested he saw his cup as half full, even when it was mostly empty. I hoped he found a decent work crew.

But there was another realization I had to acknowledge. I turned my face away from the homeless veteran because I was angered by the thought that his sign could be a lie, but also shamed in the event that he was telling the truth. I didn't want to accept that war had scarred him to the point that he could not stand on his own, although I knew full well it was possible. There, but for the grace of God and supportive comrades, goes any troubled warrior.

I discovered another distressed warrior of sorts on a foreign land near Ysleta, twenty miles north of Fabens and less than five miles from the border. The Tigua Indian Reservation of Ysleta is the only federally-recognized tribal nation in Texas located inside a major city. The tribe, whose sovereign nation is formally called the Ysleta Del Sur Pueblo, claims much of the land in El Paso, Hudspeth, and Culberson counties. They are fortunate to have any at all.

In November 1864, the United States Congress issued land patents to the seventeen Pueblo Indian tribes in New Mexico territory. As formal recognition of their sovereignty, President Abraham Lincoln presented the *caciques*, or Pueblo chiefs, with black ebony canes. The scepters were between three and four feet long and tipped with a white tassel, leather string, and a polished silver crown. They were replicas of canes that had denoted authority under the Spanish Crown. Even today, *caciques* pass these canes from one chieftain to the next as a symbol of power and responsibility.

In 1864, however, America was engaged in a great Civil War and the state of Texas was governed by the Confederacy. Consequently, the Tigua Indians of Texas became the only Pueblo tribe in the United States not covered by the Act. After the war, the Texans were hardly eager to relinquish any terrain. Although the Treaty of Guadalupe Hidalgo had granted the Ysleta Del Sur Pueblo over seventy-two square miles of land, in 1871, the Texas legislature voted to incorporate the Yselta Pueblo into El Paso County. The Tigua protested, but it meant nothing. Their land was gone.

This knavery was only the latest in a long line of degradations the Tigua endured under European hands. For millennia, Pueblo tribes farmed and fished this river valley. In 1541, during Francisco Vázquez de Coronado's quest to find the mythical seven cities of gold, they had their first encounter with another civilization. The Spanish confiscated Pueblo food, destroyed houses, and raped women. After the Tigua resisted, Coronado slaughtered several hundred.

Forty years later, under orders from King Philip II, Don Juan de Oñate moved to colonize the northern lands for Spain. Flanked by knights and friars during an ornate ceremony in 1598, Oñate claimed possession of the fertile land of the Rio del Norte—"and all its native

Indians"—for God and King on April 30 of that year. Through bribery, coercion, and war, the Spanish subdued the natives.

This pattern of oppression continued for over a century, and was briefly interrupted in 1680 by a regional Pueblo uprising. Upon learning that the slaves had revolted and chased their masters south, Spanish reinforcements marched from Mexico City the following year and extinguished the rebellion in a brutal series of campaigns. Following the seventeenth century insurgency, which marked the last violent challenge to European rule, the Tiguas of Texas joined in Pueblo negotiations. For the next two hundred years, the Pueblos were recognized as peaceful allies by both Mexicans and Americans against the Apache and Comanche.

Natives and colonists buried the hatchet, but the Pueblos have not entirely forgotten their past. In April 2007, an eighteen-ton, thirty-four-foot statue of a triumphant Oñate on a horse was unveiled at the El Paso International Airport. The $2 million statue took ten years to complete, and is the largest bronze equestrian statue in the world. Indian tribes protested the use of taxpayer funds for the project.

Since the Tigua were overlooked during President Lincoln's 1864 land grant, the *caciques* of New Mexico's Pueblo tribes believed their southern cousins no longer existed. At a series of ceremonies and tribal councils during the twentieth century, Tigua leaders offered proof of their lineage. In 1968, the U.S. government restored a portion of the claim, returning sovereignty over the Ysleta Pueblo to the Tigua.

Today, in addition to their homes, the Tigua own and operate the Ysleta Del Sur Mission, Speaking Rock Casino, Tigua Indian Cultural Center, and a 70,000-acre ranch. In May 2007, the Ysleta Pueblo's *cacique* received formal recognition from the King of Spain acknowledging the Tigua Nation. Along with a letter, the Spanish king sent a cane.

I know this because I took a wrong turn on my way to the Ysleta Del Sur Mission. While looking for the correct street, I saw a posted sign informing me that I had just entered a different country. Unaware that any other nations existed on the Texas-Mexico border, I stopped at an unassuming adobe compound. A twenty-foot statue of a sinewy, dancing Indian resplendently clad in ceremonial regalia peered out, arms opened towards the sky. I had arrived at the Tigua Indian Cultural Center.

Sammy Gutierrez, thirty-one, is one of the center's curators. When I met him, Gutierrez wore jeans and an untucked collared shirt. His long black hair was braided into a ponytail that stopped at his waist. He has light brown skin, a soft serene face, thick black eyebrows, and a scraggly mustache. He and his wife, Angie, have two daughters, ages ten and four.

The Tigua Indian Cultural Center is an adobe pueblo. It has three or four display rooms, a snack bar, restrooms, and a gift shop. A traditional garden grows in the middle. In April 2007, there were 1,558 Tigua enrolled on the tribal roster. This cultural center is, for the Tigua, a national museum.

Gutierrez escorted me from one exhibit to another, detailing the Tigua's story as we walked from room to room. He spoke without anger of the Spanish, American, and Texan occupations. I have known Native Americans who retain immense resentment towards the white man because of their forefather's sins. Gutierrez recounted the past studiously, but he did not seem consumed with any grudges. He said that he liked to live in the present.

The Ysleta Pueblo divides their leadership into two councils: tribal and traditional. The tribal council includes the governors, jurors, administrators, and police. The traditional council is the war council. The four *capitanes* who sit on the traditional council are elected from among the Tigua people, and they report to a senior war captain who sits on both councils. The *capitanes*, who are marked by the red headbands they wear in council, are charged with defending the tribe against all foreign threats. If the Tigua Nation declared war, these four men would theoretically lead their tribe into battle. Sammy Gutierrez was one of the *capitanes*.

I was not expecting much when I asked Gutierrez about his views on the Border Patrol. I figured he would include *La Migra* among the forces of oppression. I was wrong.

"I definitely want more Border Patrol agents," Gutierrez told me. "It's in my Nation's interest for the United States to have a strong border." He had grown quiet and sober; his seriousness communicated a deep feeling. He measured his words thoughtfully, as if he was seated at the council fire of his people. "We keep getting overrun by outsiders," Gutierrez said. "If we don't protect ourselves, it will happen again."

To explain his perspective, Gutierrez told me a story. A year earlier, his four German shepherds had interrupted his spring cleaning at 4 P.M. with a furious round of barking. He walked behind his property and discovered a dozen illegal aliens hiding in an irrigation ditch. One had two cell phones; he was a *coyote* calling for a pickup. The aliens eyed Gutierrez and ran to another part of the ditch. They remained on Tigua land.

Gutierrez drove off, calling the tribal police on his cell as he shadowed the smuggler and his human cargo. He then phoned the Border Patrol and worked with agents to corral the illegal aliens. Two escaped; the others were apprehended on tribal property.

In part, Gutierrez was motivated by his position as a Tigua *capitane*. Ceremonial or not, Gutierrez saw his responsibility as protector of his people against foreign invasion. To him, the smugglers fit the bill. "Most people don't know what these guys are capable of doing," he said. "These smugglers are a danger to my community."

Throughout the American southwest, Indian reservations have cultivated a reputation as being safe zones for drug use. I asked Gutierrez if his views on smuggling included narcotics, or if he was aware of a drug problem in the Ysleta Pueblo. He acknowledged that marijuana was easy to find, but said that the tribe was adamantly against all heroin and cocaine. He also did not believe that anyone with the Tigua police was accommodating smugglers.

Mostly though, Gutierrez was concerned about his children's safety and the tribe's future. "It's not only my people I care about," he said, "but the American people as well." I asked him if he hesitated to assist the Border Patrol. Not at all, he said. If it didn't harm his tribe, he was happy to help in any way he could.

By now, I had monopolized two hours of Sammy Gutierrez's day. Five other visitors had come and gone, but the *capitane* was gracious and answered each of my peppering questions in careful detail.

Finally, he needed to return to his cultural duties—there was a traditional dance in a few weeks and more guests had arrived—but not before sending me on my way with a remembrance. He walked behind a counter at the gift store and presented me with a small, sage-filled leather pouch made by his wife. The sage was for good luck, Gutierrez said. It would keep me safe on my journey.

I wondered why it was a point of pride for Gutierrez to support the Border Patrol. A few miles back, Sheriff Ronny Dodson had emphasized that the local police refused to grant the federal government any authority in their jurisdiction. It seemed that Gutierrez felt an alliance with the Border Patrol was necessary to strengthen his defenses and safeguard his tribe. Sheriff Dodson, on the other hand, believed that since the agents were unable to secure the border, their illusory presence did more harm than good.

I slipped the leather pouch into my front pocket, more appreciative of Gutierrez's gift than words could say. It was his way of honoring my quest and my journey. Not only that, but if I was ever going to make sense of the border, I needed all the luck I could get.

⟫⟩·◦·⟨⟪

Leaving Ysleta and driving north through traffic, I learned that McDonald's commodes are not the only public places in El Paso where the normal American routine has been altered by the undocumented. On Interstate 10, the speed limit is a comfortable (and mildly patrolled) 80 mph. It appears copacetic.

But the instant you enter the city limits, the traffic crawls at exactly 55 mph. And there is no fast lane—that's the speed that you're stuck driving, period. It doesn't matter how many cars are on the road. It's as if the population of El Paso has collectively decided that traffic laws need to be obeyed, if only because of the threat of deportation. Enough people fear the punishment of one set of laws so much that they reduce the citizen's ability to violate other rules.

In south Texas, a welcoming, affable, gracious border had invited me to reap the fruits of bi-nationalism and benefit from its economic bounty. In west Texas, an empty border wanted me to visit occasionally, leave only footprints, and stay the hell away after I finished examining their environs. Here, on the edge of El Paso, I first glimpsed the angry border—the seething racial tensions, the class animosities, the nationalist furors. For another six hundred miles, this clash became typical.

Since the border is both a physical and cultural estuary, the transition from American to Mexican is rarely as simple as crossing the line. Generally, the break occurs somewhere from the north to the south. In Texas, San Antonio and Austin—geographically closer to Mexico—are less divided by border issues than Dallas and Houston. Along the Northern Rio Grande corridor, the split between racial majorities happens somewhere south of Las Cruces. This means that if you are white in downtown El Paso and you stay for awhile, you will be reminded at some point that this is not your turf.

Instead of taking the interstate all the way into downtown—it was late on Friday afternoon, and the roads were clogged with truckers, commuters, and weekend vagabonds—I exited the freeway on Airway Boulevard, a busy four-lane road that ran at an angle to the highway. It wasn't the quickest route to my destination, but I wanted to explore the area. I found a collection of auto mechanics, dentist offices, and Starbucks kiosks: the new norm in American office park exurbia.

As I was driving on Airway Blvd, two Hispanic men pulled alongside me in a black Jeep. One pointed and laughed. They revved their engine, sped ahead, and swerved into my lane, braking abruptly before the traffic light turned red. Then, they drove off. As they sped away, I saw a sticker on their rear window of Calvin, the cartoon character, urinating on the word *Migra*.

I arrived downtown and checked into the Camino Real hotel, which was surprisingly affordable given its crystal chandeliers and Tiffany glass dome above the bar. The Hampton Inn in Laredo had cost twenty dollars more—and that was on weeknights, when rates are normally lower. It seemed like the demand for hotel rooms was higher in Laredo because more business transactions were happening on the American side. In El Paso and Juárez, the *maquiladora* industry is robust, but also routine. It wasn't primed for the post-NAFTA explosion the way that Laredo and the Rio Grande Valley appear to have been. El Paso and Juárez will probably look the same ten years from now, give or take a few dozen *maquilas*.

Having donned my last change of clothes that morning, I asked the Camino Real clerk about the available laundry facilities. The hotel didn't have any do-it-yourself machines, so I walked outside towards the plaza in search of a laundromat. I was wearing a grubby t-shirt, faded khakis, white socks, and running shoes, carrying three plastic bags stuffed with dirty garments, and sporting wraparound sunglasses. I looked like a hobo with UV-protection.

After hoofing eight blocks north on Mesa Street, I still couldn't find anything. Finally, I saw a dry cleaning store. I walked inside and found a Latina teenage clerk pounding her thumbs on her cell phone. She glanced at me for a second, and then looked back down at her phone.

"Excuse me," I said, "are washers or dryers available here?"

"No," she said, staring at her phone.

"Sorry. Uh, I just drove in. Do you know where I could find a laundromat?"

"Nope." Still no eye contact. Another five seconds passed while I waited for the clerk to acknowledge my presence beyond a monosyllable.

Maybe she was just a sullen teenager, but I doubted this, especially after I left the dry cleaners and found a laundromat half a block away. It was pretty clear to me what she was trying to communicate: *Chingate, gringo.* And, yes, that means what you think it does.

Welcome to the *barrio*.

El Paso has a history of division and conflict. After the 1848 Treaty of Guadalupe Hidalgo defined the waterway as the international boundary, the shifting course of the Northern Rio Grande caused land to exchange ownership between nations and states intermittently for over a hundred years. Land barons from Texas and New Mexico fought over the river's western alterations, and homeowners would begin one summer as Mexicans, but end the season as Americans. Although the treaty defined the border as the mid-point of "the deepest channel" in the river, nature inconveniently took its own course, depending on the weather. Most seasons, the river ran further south and west, granting fertile soil to the United States, and, specifically, to the farmers, ranchers, and businessmen of Texas. Prior to 1964, the shifting flow of the river made this the most controversial section of the U.S.-Mexico border.

In 1895, Mexico lodged a formal complaint to get its land back. The dispute was not resolved until 1963, when President John Kennedy negotiated the Chamizal Treaty with Mexican President López Mateos. After five thousand El Pasoans were evicted from their homes and businesses, 437 acres were returned to Mexico. American and Mexican engineers cemented over four miles of the riverbed, permanently draining the river's course into a concrete trench.

At this man-made hinge, the river flowing south from New Mexico is no longer wide and friendly. It becomes a shallow creek and even, in places, a concrete drainage ditch. It also ceases to define the space between nations. Thanks to the Gadsden Purchase in 1853, the Northern Rio Grande—we are now well beyond the life-giving source of the Río Conchos—becomes the western boundary between Texas and New Mexico for twelve miles. The border abruptly, sharply, and incongruously changes here, transforming from water to land as you travel west.

The difference is unsettling. Back in Eagle Pass, where Yee-hah met Olé, the border had appeared stable; there was separation, but also a natural rhythm and harmony. Likewise, in Laredo, the city water from the river quenched throats and cleansed bodies in both new and old municipalities. The day I kayaked north of McAllen, I watched Mexican and American children frolicking across from one another in swimming areas roped off for picnicking families. In Brownsville and Matamoros alike, the river nourished crops and harbored fish for food.

Unlike a river, a line in the sand invites tension and dispute. It forces you to pick a side. The border normally seen on CNN's Lou Dobbs Tonight begins in El Paso, and it only gets more intense from here to the west. In El Paso, Yee-hah doesn't embrace Olé. Either one avoids the other entirely, or Yee-hah waves from across the street because Olé has three times as many *hombres* and he has no choice. If Yee-hah doesn't smile, Olé will kick his *pendejo* ass.

The cultural discord around El Paso is like quicksand. On the surface, you cannot see it. White and brown families intermarry, mingle, and professionally merge. Colleagues and friends relate with mutual courtesy and respect. Caucasian teenagers jokingly call their Latino pals *mojado*, or wetback. One minute, you're walking on stable ground. Then, a step later, you've stumbled into a morass and plunged in to your waist. At that point, there is no escape.

The divide is not always racial, but it often overlaps into national or class distinctions that polarize sympathies. Each type of border clash—rich vs. poor; government vs. individual; military vs. civilian; federal vs. local—is invariably cast through the lens of a white civilization that has cemented a boundary against a brown nation. Tempers flare easily on both sides.

In addition to this, El Paso is also a headquarters for the various organizations and committees that the U.S. government has chartered to supervise the frontier. The El Paso Intelligence Center, or EPIC ("eh-pick"), is an informational clearinghouse based at Fort Bliss. The DEA, FBI, ICE, Homeland Security, Border Patrol, and half a dozen other alphabet soup organizations from the federal government staff the building. Joint Task Force 6—now called JTF North— is also headquartered at EPIC. For border guardians, EPIC is the equivalent of the Pentagon.

The overall significance of El Paso for the border's federal agencies is one reason the story of Border Patrol agents Ignacio "Nacho" Ramos and Jose Compean evolved into a furor that resulted in one of the most bizarre court cases in recent history. On February 17, 2005, Agents Ramos and Compean fired fifteen bullets at Osvaldo Aldrete-Davila, a drug smuggler who was spotted south of El Paso fleeing from a van that contained 743 pounds of marijuana. One of those bullets hit Aldrete-Davila on his left buttocks, which the agents gathered at the scene may or may not have known. The agents did not formally report the shooting. If it hadn't been for a phone call between Osvaldo Aldrete-Davila's mother, Macaria, and her close friend, Gergoria Toquinto, the facts of the shooting would never have come to light. Ms. Toquinto's son-in-law was Rene Sanchez, a Border Patrol agent stationed in Willcox, Arizona. Acting on his mother-in-law's behalf, Agent Sanchez reported the shooting to his supervisor at Willcox. This began a chain reaction within the Border Patrol/Customs and Border Protection/Department of Homeland Security bureaucracy, which led to an internal investigation. A month later, a full-on sting operation was initiated by two dozen SWAT agents while Ramos and Compean were at home with their families on a Friday night.

According to U.S. District Attorney Johnny Sutton's team of prosecutors and investigators, this is what happened. Three agents—Ramos, Compean, and Oscar Juarez—pursued Aldrete-Davila's blue van at about 1 P.M., corralling him at a sewage canal that drains into the Northern Rio Grande near Fabens, thirty miles south of El Paso. Shit Ditch, as agents call it, is about fifteen feet deep and thirteen feet wide, with three feet of muck at the bottom.

As Aldrete-Davila sprinted for Mexico, Compean pointed a shotgun and, according to the smuggler, yelled: "*Párate, mexicano de mierda!*" which means "Stop, you Mexican shit!" Aldrete-Davila-a poor man who testified that he had been smuggling to make money so he could care for his infirmed mother-lifted his empty hands. Then, according to Compean, either Ramos or Juarez yelled: "Hit him!"

"Take it easy, man," Aldrete-Davila claims to have said. "*No me pueges.*" (Don't hit me.) Ignoring his pleas, Compean swung the butt of the shotgun, but Aldrete-Davila dodged it, causing Compean to slip and fall face-first into Shit Ditch. Aldrete-Davila took off for Mexico.

Compean says he climbed out of the ditch and tackled Aldrete-Davila, but the smuggler wrestled free and headed again towards Mexico. Compean may or may not have seen something shiny pointed at him. Regardless, he pulled his pistol and fired ten rounds towards the fleeing smuggler. All missed. He reloaded and shot four more times. Those shots were also off the mark.

After Compean started shooting, Ramos sprinted from his vehicle across the ditch to back up his fellow agent. This took about forty seconds. Ramos passed Compean, who was still on the ground, pulled his pistol, and drew a bead. Aldrete-Davila turned back around and appeared to be pointing something at Ramos, who then fired a single shot. The round struck Aldrete-Davila, severed his urethra, and knocked him to the ground on the U. S. side of the river. Whether or not Ramos knew he hit Aldrete-Davila is uncertain. Ramos says that Aldrete-Davila was forty yards away and disappeared after the shot was fired.

After he was hit, Aldrete-Davila hid inside a thicket of carrizo. He waited to be arrested, but nothing happened. Sutton's prosecutors said the agents holstered weapons and walked back to their vehicles without searching. The defense disputed this, saying Ramos watched the brush but went back to the ditch to check on Compean. Once he realized that the Border Patrol was no longer in pursuit, Aldrete-Davila hobbled back into Mexico. Minutes later, he got into a vehicle and drove into a Juárez *colonia*. From that time on, Aldrete-Davila had to urinate with a catheter because of his wound.

This account was presented in court by Ramos and Compean, by other agents who were present, and by Aldrete-Davila, who had been granted immunity in exchange for his testimony. While the agents conceded that portions of Aldrete-Davila's testimony was true, both Ramos and Compean say that the drug smuggler falsified the unsavory anecdotes of their behavior, such as swearing at an illegal alien or wielding a shotgun.

Ramos and Compean also argued that their boss, Field Operations Supervisor Jon Richards, lied on the stand. They say Richards arrived on the scene and was livid to learn the smuggler had escaped. Ramos said he told Richards the smuggler had assaulted Compean. Richards, who never walked across the canal or checked on Compean, ordered his agents to load the marijuana onto their vehicles and report to the station.

Compean, who had cuts on his face and hand, said that Richards asked him if he was okay soon after the agents returned to Fabens.

Seven agents and two supervisors had responded to the incident. According to Ramos and Compean, all nine men present knew that they had fired their weapons. One agent, Oscar Juarez, was standing right behind Compean when he shot. Another man, Vasquez, helped Compean pick up his shell casings.

Prosecutors said that Compean's removal of the brass from the shooting area was evidence of intent to cover up the shooting. But Supervisor Robert Arnold testified that the agents had done firearms qualifications the day before. In his book *On Combat*, U.S. Army psychology professor Lt. Col. Dave Grossman tells of a police officer who was shot to death during a firefight after thoughtlessly pausing to pick up his shell casings. Likewise, in hundreds of post-shooting investigations, police have reported that they involuntarily picked up their shell casings, since they usually do so as part of cleanup on the firing range.

Ramos and Compean both knew they were supposed to fill out firearms discharge reports if they shot their weapons. They were also supposed to verbally notify their supervisor within one hour of the shooting. Days before, Agent Juarez had shot at a snake while on patrol. Juarez was supposed to fill out a firearms discharge report, and he did not. By the book, the penalty for failing to do so ranged from a written reprimand to a five-day suspension without pay. But nothing happened to Agent Juarez.

In contrast to the quiet village of Redford where Zeke Hernandez was killed, Fabens was known as a narcotics trafficking hotspot. According to Border Patrol agents, rock throwings, verbal taunts and drug busts-at one point, over three a week-were common occurrences in and around the station. For this reason, Ramos later said that he never pressed the issue with Richards on the shooting because he didn't want to put his supervisor in a bad position.

Compean said that Richards discouraged him from notifying the FBI, as Border Patrol agents are required to do if assaulted. "If we call the FBI, we are going to be here all night doing paperwork," Richards said after the shooting, according to Compean. "We will never know who the person was that assaulted you." Richards congratulated him on getting the van and the marijuana. Then they went back to work.

The truth appears messy on all sides. It turns out that Ramos was twice arrested in connection with domestic violence. However, Ramos was subsequently diagnosed with Tourette's syndrome after the arrests, a physical condition that can cause spontaneous verbal outbursts and lower inhibitions. Ramos was slated to attend a government-sponsored anger management program; after he asked for counseling, his wife and father-in-law had rescinded all accusations. He was never charged or convicted.

A year after he was shot, Aldrete-Davila was arrested and held without bond for smuggling another load of marijuana. At the time, he was on a humanitarian visa that permitted him free passage to and from Mexico. The U.S. attorney issued this passport. The prosecutors, zealous for a conviction, refused to grant jurors access to this information, which helped turned the drug smuggler into a sympathetic figure. Even the jurors were dissatisfied; three signed affidavits when the trial concluded saying they were pressured to concur with the verdict so the trial could end. Nobody comes out clean, including Field Operations Supervisor Jon Richards.

According to the court records, Nacho Ramos and Jon Richards have an interesting personal history. At a station of fifty, they were the only two members of a sector-wide Special Response Team, which meant the pair had likely attended special training together. Additionally, prior to Ramos's March 2005 arrest, Richards had intended to nominate him for Border Patrol Agent of the Year. In court testimony, Richards claimed that he first learned about the shooting from Homeland Security investigators on March 22 of that year. That was a Tuesday. But the Border Patrol agents were arrested by a Homeland Security SWAT unit on the previous Friday, March 18. It seems unlikely that Supervisor Richards would not have known the reason why two of his men were arrested for five full days. When interrogated by Ramos and Compean's attorneys, Richards often responded with: "I don't remember"; "I couldn't tell"; and "I don't recall." Candid, he was not.

On October 19, 2006, all Border Patrol agents below supervisory rank assigned to the Fabens station that were not on duty asked for a day of leave to attend the sentencing of Agents Ramos and Compean. These two men were going to prison for at least a decade, and their comrades wanted to show their support. Supervisors denied all requests.

In an interesting show of solidarity, *Immigrantes Sin Fronteras*, an Arizona-based immigrant rights group, spoke out against the sentencing. "Ramos and Compean are just two more victims of the broken immigration system that burdens our nation," said Mr. Elias Bermudez. "Injustice is happening at all levels when it comes to immigration: against the undocumented immigrant looking for a better life, the legal immigrant already in this country, and uniformed officials doing their best to interpret and apply these byzantine laws."

U.S. District Attorney Johnny Sutton has made the official transcripts of the *United States vs. Ignacio "Nacho" Ramos and Jose Alonzo Compean* trial available on his official Web site. Nacho's father-in-law, Joe Loya, has published his version of events, including a letter to his congressman on another Internet site advocating his son's release from prison. In response to Loya's piece-as well as a series of inflammatory broadcasts by CNN's Lou Dobbs Tonight, FOX News's Sean Hannity, and numerous conservative talk shows—Sutton issued a "Myths vs. Reality" statement regarding the court's ruling. This only fueled the fire, and the National Border Patrol Council penned a "Facts vs. 'Myths vs. Reality'" counterargument.

Reality boils down to this: the United States government sent two Border Patrol agents to prison for over a decade because they shot a drug smuggler and failed to file any paperwork. Prosecutors also may have coached Supervisor Jon Richards in the betrayal of his own men. In January 2007, Ramos and Compean were jailed in separate federal penitentiaries. In March, Latino inmates associated with narcotics cartels punched and kicked Ramos for a full minute during a prison riot. For their future safety, prison officials ordered both agents into solitary confinement. Supervisor Richards was promoted.

Soon after I encountered the mute clerk at the dry cleaners, I discovered a peculiar building in downtown El Paso two hundred yards from the border. The single structure looked like a village with an interior plaza. Murals of *campesinos,* or farm workers, cover the tan exterior. On the outer wall, in spray-paint, a black fist jutted out from a red background. The symbol of defiance was bracketed by two phrases: *Segundo Barrio*—the downtown neighborhood surrounding the building—and *Resizte,* or Resist. The slogans, colors, and symbols of the graffiti urged the workers of the world to unite.

I had arrived at the headquarters for *Sin Fronteras,* or Without Borders, the largest migrant welfare center physically located on the U.S. side of the border.* Since 1993, *Sin Fronteras* has "fought against the injustices and inequalities faced by the farmworker community of West Texas and New Mexico." Federal tax dollars via the Department of Housing and Urban Development, disbursed by the City of El Paso, built this structure.

Inside *Sin Fronteras,* I met Javier Pérez, a twenty-six-year-old El Pasoan who had been on staff at the center for three years. Pérez first learned about *Sin Fronteras* at age sixteen, when he heard a speaker from MEChA, or Chicano Student Movement of Aztlán, give a talk at his high school. MEChA was started in 1969 because: "The Hispanic is a person who lacks respect for his/her cultural heritage." In contrast, the Chicano rejects these terms of cultural oppressions, asserting their true identity as Spanish descendents of the Aztec people. Indigenous community, class consciousness, and social justice are popular phrases among militant Chicanos.

MEChA exercises little power beyond college campuses, but what they lack in strength is compensated for with inflammatory rhetoric. "MEChA must bring to mind that the liberation of her/his people from prejudice and oppression is . . . greater than personal achievement and more meaningful than degrees." In other words, devout Chicanos believe that the leaders of the National Council of La Raza, an organization promoting civil rights for Hispanic-American, are sellouts. By being Hispanic-American, they've ceased to support the *Resizte.*

---

* *Sin Fronteras* of El Paso and *Immigrantes Sin Fronteras,* the Arizona-based group that called for the release of Agents Ramos and Compean, are not affiliated.

Such is the intellectual background of Javier Pérez, a pudgy, quiet man with brown skin, short hair, and a smooth, clean-shaven face. Pérez chose his profession from an admirable sense of cultural compassion, but he also brimmed with naiveté and youthful idealism. "We emphasize openness in our culture, and you lose that in this country," Pérez said, also emphasizing his disdain for the American way. "Here on the south side, we still have that community feeling."

South side El Paso, also known as "*Chihuahuita*," is a *barrio*; more like a *colonia* in Juárez than a suburb in the United States. Open-air markets sell tacos, cheap clothing, and secondhand electronics. Radio stations like "Super Estrella" feature bilingual pop sounds that blossom like flowers on a prickly pear cactus. I heard the aggressive hip-hop of Calle Trece as I strolled Segundo Barrio, as well as Shakira, Ricky Martin, and a Spanish version of the Bryan Adams song "(Everything I Do) I Do It for You." Laborers drifted in and out of safe houses, seeking one of the dozens of contractors who represented businesses throughout the region. A migrant slept on the sidewalk in the shade of a van.

In addition to being a kitchen, shelter, and halfway house, *Sin Fronteras* functions as a place for migrants to connect with smugglers, purchase fake documents, and skirt the American legal system. The chain fence facing south towards Mexico, near the railroad tracks that run adjacent to the barbed wire and the Northern Rio Grande, has been flattened by a plywood plank. The detritus of migration— shoes, bottles, sweatshirts, backpacks—littered the cracked sidewalk and parched earth.

Before I met with Pérez, I had noticed two men talking to a *Sin Fronteras* attendant at the front desk. They were obviously from Immigration; only rookie U.S. government agents travel in pairs, wear ironed jeans, and tuck in shirts when visiting civilians in a professional capacity. They had asked the attendant a few questions and left. I asked Pérez if he worried about Immigration agents clearing out the premises. He said no. "We won't allow them in without a court order."

Pérez also told me that anyone without documentation was not allowed to stay at *Sin Fronteras*. Instead, they were referred to Annunciation House, a Catholic sanctuary that had opened its doors in

1978 for those lacking papers. Pérez said there was an agreement between Annunciation and *La Migra*. Thus, migrants who did not have identification were in a safer situation.

While this may have been true, I sensed that Pérez was hiding something. On the street, I had noticed a handbill asking $150 for anyone who wanted to buy immigration documents registered for "Jose Velazquez Mata." It was written in Spanish. Interested parties were told to go to *Sin Fronteras*.

In McAllen and Laredo, I had seen vibrant communities. I attended multiple *pachangas*—not only Don Medina's picnic at the Cine El Rey, but backyard barbecues in Laredo where city council-men assembled informally with the mayor and county judge. At those gatherings, local leaders were not urging their children to *Resizte*. They wanted them to go to college, learn impeccable English, and seize the American dream. I didn't hear nonsense about strug-gling against capitalist oppression in south Texas; officials discussed responsible change, sustainable development, and regional eco-nomic growth. Save for the Spanish and Tex-Mex cuisine, men and women accustomed to New England town meetings would have felt at home.

The distinction between the communities of south Texas and the *barrios* of El Paso and beyond is best explained by the varying attitudes on the border towards NAFTA. While locals from the Rio Grande Valley recognize that many American workers have derided the trade agreement for pushing thousands of jobs south of the bor-der, they argue that NAFTA has brought greater prosperity to north-eastern Mexico. By improving Mexico's economy, government, and social structure, America has become safer, more stable, and less vul-nerable. NAFTA advocates in south Texas said that without the trade agreement, the efforts to fight poverty and create a Mexican middle class would fail.

Javier Pérez begs to differ. "NAFTA is the main enemy," he said. "Free trade has created poverty and suffering for the indigenous Mexican farmers." I asked Pérez if he believed that free trade could be restructured fairly. "I don't believe in fair trade." His comments continued in this vein (businesses are greedy and evil, etc.) as he launched further into his anti-globalization rant. After a few minutes, I tuned him out.

Beyond high school and his volunteer work for *Sin Fronteras,* Pérez was a professional student. He had attended the University of Texas at El Paso, and had at least a year before he would earn a political science degree. Pérez spoke of heroic *campesinos* forced by malevolent global agricultural conglomerates to sell farms they had tilled for centuries. NAFTA is increasing unemployment and killing the *campesinos,* and we will defeat it. His undergraduate Marxist vitriol might play well in the *barrio,* but I thought it was of little practical value beyond.

Unfortunately, Pérez—despite his myopic worldview bequeathed to him by utopian academicians—is right: NAFTA has not been the panacea that was promised. The agreement has created as many problems as it has solved. Mexico, Canada, and the United States pretended to level the playing field and lay the conditions for Mexico's economy to improve. But while NAFTA has worked for some Mexicans in the upper and middle classes, the treaty has further alienated the laboring class from upward mobility.

Ironically, this has not dampened public enthusiasm for free trade. In a July 2004 survey by CIDE, a Mexico City–based economic think tank, 64 percent of the Mexican public said they approved of NAFTA. In an October 2006 survey by the Chicago Council on Foreign Relations, 60 percent of responders said that the "increasing connections of our economy with others" created by globalization was "mostly good" for the United States. At the same time, 67 percent said that trade agreements like NAFTA were dangerous for the job security of American workers. And 93 percent said that minimum standards for working conditions should be enforced as part of any eradication of trade barriers. This data suggests that Americans and Mexicans want to be connected, but not in a way that is unfair to either country. Given the economic, political, and cultural disparity between the two nations, that is an awfully tall order.

For hundreds of thousands in the Latino working class, downtown Juárez is a cross between Ellis Island and Detroit. Mexico's tired and poor, joined by women and children from Central and

South America, stream north in search of employment at $1.25 an hour. If they are fortunate, they find work in one of the 400 *maquiladoras* that churn out auto parts, plastics, textiles, compact discs, stereos, and other related merchandise that fuels the American engine. Those who ascend to the height of the Juárez social ladder live near the Pronaf District, where El Paso's elite go to enjoy entertainment and nightlife. In contrast, the plywood-and-tin *colonias* where the poor live on the city's expansive southwestern outskirts make the hardscrabble west Texas estates appear palatial by comparison.

If the *maquilas* cannot give them what they need, the women ply the world's oldest profession in one of the city's 6,000 bars and cantinas. This is dangerous work in Juárez, and not only because of sexually transmitted disease. Since 1993, over 360 women—some as young as twelve—have been violated and murdered in and around Juárez (an unknown number were kidnapped or missing). No one knows who started the murdering or why the bloodshed happened. Drug cartels, serial killers, and abusive lovers have been blamed. Although there have been several arrests, the violence has continued.

In December 2007, the Mexican government exhumed over 4,000 bodies in unmarked graves to take DNA samples. They hope the database will eventually provide answers to the mystery, perhaps by tying the identity of an unknown body to a known victim. In the meantime, the Juárez murders are the largest string of unsolved crimes on the entire border.

———————————— ❧❀❧ ————————————

North of Segundo Barrio and a hundred yards from the Northern Rio Grande, a white concrete obelisk called Monument One stands on a platform. This granite pillar is the first of 276 markers dispersed from this river to the Pacific Ocean. Officials from the International Boundary and Water Commission place these markers a few miles apart to delineate the line between U.S. and Mexico. Spanish graffiti covers many of the markers associated with the border near Juárez, including the base of this concrete pillar.

There is no fence at Monument One, but this space north of Juárez is a poor smuggling spot. To the east is an old smelting plant, along with the trickle of the Northern Rio Grande. Mounted inside Suburbans, astride horses and atop all-terrain vehicles, Border Patrol agents peer menacingly from perches hidden amidst the hills.

At Monument One I observed some similarities to the scene at Boca Chica on the Texas coast, except the families on the Mexican side were no longer fishing. Children squealed while weathered men and women gazed listlessly at their progeny chasing one another in the dust. Before the border became an iron curtain, Mexican worshippers would walk miles from the surrounding *colonias* of Juárez and ascend a nearby American mountain each Easter, holding sunrise services on the summit they called Mount Cristo Rey. The sunrise service had been sponsored by Catholic churches in both nations, and was meant to symbolize the communal oneness of humanity despite the national divide. Today, the cross remains, but the relaxed attitude towards sojourners is gone. And so are the pilgrims.

# 8

I unearthed a lot of nothing in New Mexico and southern Arizona, but it was a different type of nothing than the emptiness I had discovered in west Texas. Between the Pecos, the Rio Grande, and the Northern Rio Grande, the water bounding the vast *tierra despoblada* had provided a reference point. Driving west on New Mexico's Highway 9 through the Potrillo Mountains, I had no idea where the U.S. ended and Mexico began. I looked out my car window and saw waves of unmarked rock and sand crest and fall. Three miles to the south, somewhere amid the *montañas*, small gray obelisks marked the line between nations. Because they were a substantial distance from any major city, these monuments were free of graffiti.

It takes an hour to drive Highway 9 from El Paso to Columbus, New Mexico. Other than pickups operated by ranchers and Border Patrol agents, the only things I saw in motion were antelope jackrabbits and tumbleweeds stuck in saguaro cacti that swayed slightly in the stiff wind. Staked out at two or three locations were tan-colored observation towers that ascended fifteen or twenty feet into the air like skyboxes mounted to staircases. Soldiers from the New Mexico National Guard manned the observation posts.

Columbus is home to Pancho Villa State Park, a bank, a handful of restaurants, a bed and breakfast, and about 1,000 people. Near the state park sits an adobe plaza called the Hacienda de Villa Hotel (it's more like the Hacienda de Econo Lodge). Martha Rodriguez, a weathered, kind, woman in her fifties, has managed the Hacienda de Villa since 2005. Her husband lives in Phoenix and runs another business. Martha grew up in Palomas, the Mexican city of 8,000 across from Columbus, and has lived throughout New Mexico and Arizona. It was not clear exactly how she became a legal U.S. resident.

What was clear—at least in her comments to me—was that Martha Rodriguez supported the law and opposed smuggling. "Palomas was beautiful before the drugs arrived," she said, expressing strong ire for two specific substances. "Crystal meth and crack ruined the town." The previous owners of the Hacienda de Villa allowed _coyotes_ to pack up to thirty illegal aliens into a room each night while they waited for a pickup. Martha will not rent a bungalow to anyone unless she sees some ID. It wasn't about the "illegals"—it's possible that Martha may have been one herself—but the malevolent forces that manipulated them for their ends.

The first year she was in Columbus, Martha said she had "a lot of problems" with smugglers. "It was bad." She didn't want to elaborate on the details. But according to Martha, human smuggling decreased in Columbus after soldiers from the National Guard arrived in 2006. Although a drug war flared up in the spring of 2007—presumably the same type of _plaza_-related rivalry that had engulfed Nuevo Laredo two years before—Martha says life is better. She thinks drugs still come across the border, but she feels much safer, now that the soldiers are here.

Ninety years ago, Columbus residents had other reasons to appreciate a U.S. military presence. In 1916, a Mexican rebel named Pancho Villa was angry. Three years earlier, when he was a general in the army of Venustiano Carranza, Villa had represented the revolutionary faction during negotiations with the United States at Fort Bliss. At the 1913 meeting, Villa posed for a friendly picture with another Carranza loyalist, Álvaro Obregón, and U.S. Army general John J. Pershing. Among the crowd who gathered for the photo, only General Pershing's aide, Lt. George S. Patton, failed to sport a wide grin.

Patton might have sensed that Villa's days in popular favor were numbered. Villa was a small, swarthy man with rough dark skin, a thick mustache, and a reputation of being crude, cunning, and cruel. As the _caudillo_ of Chihuahua—the governor-general of Mexico's enormous north-central state—Villa had switched allegiances between several factions which had been fighting for control of Mexico since 1910, when the dictatorship of Porfirio Díaz ended and the nation plunged into violence and intrigue. A year later, after Carranza occupied Mexico City, Villa rebelled against him.

In April 1915, as Villa prepared to battle his old comrade, Obregón, at Celaya (120 miles northeast of Mexico City), he sent a messenger north to purchase weapons from the United States. Although President Woodrow Wilson had previously communicated to Villa that the U.S. would support his insurrection, the Americans denied Villa's request for arms. As a result, the *Villistas* lost the Celaya fight. The crowning insult for Villa came six months later, when the U.S. government formally recognized Carranza as the Mexican leader. In three years, Villa had fallen from favored neighbor to international outlaw.

Villa vowed to avenge what he saw as treachery. Just before dawn on the morning of March 9, 1916, about 500 of Villa's men slipped north of the border, surrounded Columbus, and called out *"Viva Villa!"* and *"Muerte a los gringos!"* (Long live Villa, and death to the gringos.) Businesses were robbed, buildings were torched, and men, women, and children were shot both in their sleep and fleeing in terror.

But because the U.S. Army's 13th Cavalry had garrisoned Columbus, 330 American soldiers quickly organized for a counterattack. By 7:30 A.M., the Americans chased Villa's men back into the south. Eighteen Americans died, including ten soldiers. The Mexican bandit captured most of the 13th Cavalry's arsenal of rifles, ammunition, and machine guns, as well as a stable of 100 horses and mules, while losing ninety men.

Beyond the fury of American betrayal, the practical need to steal more supplies may have contributed to Villa's selection of raid sites. Whatever his motivation, Villa's attack sparked a public outcry and prompted a loud call for reprisal. President Wilson asked for, and received, Carranza's blessing to pursue Villa into the Chihuahuan heartland. Ten days after the Columbus raid, General Pershing led 10,000 U.S. soldiers south on a mission to bring Villa to justice.

For eleven months, Pershing's forces foraged through Mexico, skirmishing with Villa's generals, the regular Mexican army, and a rogue's gallery of bandits whose allegiance was unknown. Mexican civilians resented the trespassing gringos; many aided Villa or others in resisting the American presence. By February 1917, all U.S. forces returned north of the border.

Although General Pershing declared the expedition a tactical failure, the incursion—combined with the mobilization of 112,000 National Guard soldiers—produced several interesting strategic consequences. The Columbus raid was only one of dozens that occurred from July 1915 to June 1916; in all, Villa attacked U.S. citizens on American soil thirty-eight times, killing twenty-seven people. But three months after the U.S. Army pushed south and the National Guard fortified the line, the border was secure. Meanwhile, with Villa occupied, Carranza consolidated executive authority, stabilized the government, and drafted a constitution.

In 1923, an assassin killed Pancho Villa in Mexico City. In this way, Villa rose and fell like so many Mexican strongmen who sought power through revolution: although he could elude the Americans, Villa could not escape the tyranny of his own country's political chaos. Carranza was also assassinated in 1920, but the Mexican constitution lived on, shining forth as an ember of hope that a stable, democratic order might survive in the troubled nation.

---

Forty-five miles west of Columbus and nine from *la frontera*, I found signs of the smuggling that Martha Rodriguez had mentioned. In Hachita, another mining camp–turned–ghost town, the village's abandoned church, St. Catherine of the Siena, reeked of stale urine. Dozens of empty backpacks, stacks of half-eaten food plates, and piles of dirty clothes were strewn across the dust-covered wooden floor.

"The wets come quite a lot," said Elizabeth Larkins, seventy-five, a sturdy, thin widow who lived next door to the church. Her use of the ethnic slur, spoken in the accent of her native Alabama, was more colloquial than derogatory. "Last time they came was a week ago. They're usually young men in groups of five or six. I feed them sometimes. They always want to use the phone."

Many think that the term "wetbacks"—still commonly used by older Anglos in the West like Mrs. Larkins—refers to the sweat formed on the leathered frames of farmers, or to the drenching caused by swimming the Rio Grande. Wet/dry references to alcohol, however, are common throughout literature and popular culture in the decades leading up to Prohibition. This was the same time that large-scale smuggling operations began in Mexico. Perspiration and river crossings may have sustained the term, but the combination of prejudice and Prohibition likely started it.

Mrs. Larkins wasn't taking sides. To her, aiding the needy was a practical matter of kindness that had nothing to do with politics. Mrs. Larkins held the Border Patrol agents in esteem; after all, they were the face of local security. "They drive around here day and night," she said, smiling. "They're good boys."

Larkins said she only felt threatened once by "the wets" in the thirty-seven years she lived in Hachita. Twenty years ago, when her husband was still alive, a migrant worker snuck into their bedroom while they slept. She sensed his presence, awoke, and screamed. The man fled, and that was that.

Despite that memory, she harbored no grudge, or fear, toward migrants. And she saw nothing wrong with offering food and water to the hungry, tired Latin American men who trickled onto her doorstep a dozen at a time as subjects of the agent's endless hunt. Why? She smiled again, fixing me with a grandmotherly stare. "Because they are human beings."

If only it were that simple.

The duality in Hachita was an omen of sorts, a harbinger of the clash between reason and emotion that fueled passions to white-hot, scalding levels on the western side of the aptly-named Continental Divide. This irregular dotted line that runs south through the Canadian Rockies and the Sierra Madres separates the two major watersheds of North America. Water that falls on the eastern side of the divide flows into the Gulf of Mexico; the west drains into the Pacific Ocean.

A few miles from Hachita on Highway 9 amid the Peloncillo Mountains, a stoic sign pays homage to the naturally appointed north-south line where east becomes west. Continental Divide: Elevation 4,520 feet. It is a peculiar touchstone, and feels like a type of altar to the divisions that humanity has wrought over centuries upon itself and this terrain. These kinds of monuments dotted the border in strange places: an abandoned corral, a statue of Geronimo, an obelisk placed in memory of a sixteenth-century Spanish explorer. Each in its own way honors the timeless external and internal conflicts between nature, man, and mankind.

I stood at the foot of the Continental Divide sign, gazed south into Mexico, and pondered the magnitude of it all. In the back of the car, untouched since I kayaked with Eric Ellman in McAllen, was a cooler with a six-pack of Tecate. I fetched a can, approached the divide, and stood at the base of the sign. With a solemn, reverential air, I cracked open the brew and poured it on the ground, sweeping my arm across the east-west line as the savory ferment emptied from its aluminum container. It seemed the least I could do to mark the moment.

I hadn't set out expecting to feel moved by the border, but I did. Looking back on it, the Continental Divide marker still resonates— pointing, perhaps, to my ongoing, futile attempts to fully comprehend *la frontera*. The land demands reverence, and this seemed as good a place as any to nominate as its temple. There are other places in the U.S. where you can observe nature's Continental Divide, but this marker is situated adjacent to the man-made partition that rends asunder two distinct ways of life. Stand next to the sign and stare into the ruggedness after listening to so many people with passionate opinions, and you'll know exactly what I mean.

After pondering the great divide for several minutes, I drove into a magnificent, blinding sunset, edged out of the Peloncillos, and, clattering through the Coronado National Forest along rutty federal roads, crossed into Arizona.

⊸⊷⊷•0•⊶⊶⊷

When the U.S. Army hunted Geronimo and Cochise in the latter years of the nineteenth century, the Apache warriors took refuge in the Chiricahua Mountains. The volcanic peaks rise to almost 10,000 feet in southeastern Arizona, where mule deer, antelope, and cattle graze on the fibrous portions of spruce, fir, and cottonwood. Yuccas and tumbleweeds conceal rattlers and roadrunners. Cacti of all types dot the lava landscape. Wrens chirp. Coyotes howl.

In 1881, while the Army was chasing Apaches, a Pennsylvania mining company sent a man named James Douglas to Arizona on a quest for buried treasure. Soon after Douglas arrived, Geronimo was captured, and the frontier supposedly brought under control. Douglas succeeded in a southern ridgeline of the Chiricahuas, where he found deposits of copper and founded the Phelps-Dodge Mining Company to procure the ore. The vein that ran through the craggy basin of Bisbee, south of Tombstone, would make him one of the richest men in the newly-established Cochise County. Twenty five miles from Bisbee, north of the Mexican border town of Agua Prieta, Douglas built a smelting plant and bestowed his name on the resulting American town.

The Wild West was a place where fortunes were made and lost; where lawmen and outlaws roamed (and were often one and the same); where towns took brawny names like Tombstone because they were "too tough to die" (and instead of dying, evolved into tacky tourist attractions). Southeast Arizona remains unaltered; it is a region engaged in ideological, psychological, physical, and legal dispute over its law, its residents, its policies, and its international southern neighbors. In Arizona, Yee-hah and Olé are hurling insults and flipping fingers faster than bullets cycling through a tommy gun.

The 1987 closure of the copper smelting plant in Douglas should have been the kiss of death for the border village. With no economy beyond a state prison and community college, any typical border city of 15,000 would eventually become desperately poor. But enterprising officials, propelled by the seedy cocktail of drugs, money, and greed, had other plans. Leading the charge was a dastardly, conniving politician with an unparalleled track record for graft. "Judge Joe Borane has no scruples whatsoever," said Alberto Rodriguez, a retired Army colonel who has known Borane since childhood, to a reporter. "He's the greediest man I ever met."

Culture wars frequently mask real ones, and few understand this as well as Lee Morgan, a retired U.S. Customs agent who worked in and around Douglas for twenty-five years. In his colorful and candid 2006 memoir *The Reaper's Line*, Morgan details the sordid web woven by Judge Ronald "Cocaine Joe" Borane. His revelations, along with testimony involving the misdeeds of numerous local, state, and federal officials, earned Morgan the title "Serpico of the Desert." He wasn't the first to pinpoint the issue; in 1998, the late John F. Kennedy Jr. identified Douglas as the third-most corrupt city in America in *George* magazine. Two years later, *The New York Times* published a story that did little to dispel this perception.

Avarice was the Borane family business. Cocaine Joe—the corrupt Douglas judge, real estate baron, and well-connected drug kingpin—pulled the levers of power from his perch as a chief justice. In the meantime, his brother, Ray, covered his tracks as the city mayor. Although Morgan and others say that Ray Borane isn't the type to be directly involved in crime—he was a school superintendent before becoming a public official—he made little effort to restrain his brother's excess.

In 1990, Morgan led agents from the FBI, Border Patrol, and other federal organizations into a tunnel used to smuggle cocaine and heroin from Agua Prieta into Douglas. Traffickers enslaved and exported about forty poor Mexican Indians from either Oaxaca or Chiapas to build the tunnel—and then killed the laborers when they were finished. On the U.S. side, the tunnel terminated in a warehouse once owned by Judge Joe Borane. Borane walked away clean on legal technicalities, offering the spurious claim that he had no idea the new homeowners—who paid cash for the house—were drug dealers.

In 2000, after a two-year federal investigation culminating in Borane being videotaped—twice—in sham drug deals, he was indicted on four felony counts that carried a maximum sentence of fifty years. Unfortunately, the undercover FBI agent bungled the investigation by sleeping with both the sister and the niece of another trafficker. Cocaine Joe cut a deal with the Arizona Supreme Court, resigned, and agreed never to seek office again. Borane never spent a day in prison.

This might sound clever or even charming—no more disturbing than the juvenile, ruffian antics of Judge Roy Bean. But Judge Borane's Mexican partners in corruption exhibited a chilling, bestial streak of brutality that went far beyond any of Bean's comical misbehavior. Consider Lee Morgan's 1989 discovery of twelve men and women at the bottom of a well near Agua Prieta whom the drug lords had found expendable:

The bodies resembled anything but humans. The slimy skins and raw flesh of the corpses were covered with flies and maggots crawling up and down their oozing nostrils and leaking skulls. The horrendous stench of death hung in the air above the beaten faces that now resembled those of a blowfish instead of human beings. Their rotting cheeks were grotesquely swollen out of proportion to the rest of their faces. . . . Some of the females' fingers had been cut off and tossed on the ground for the coyotes and dogs to feed on.

It was almost like they were trying to hold their breath, like they had taken their last, desperate gasp of air before being dumped into the well to suffocate under the weight of the torsos to follow. Their open eyes, some protruding out of their sockets, were testimony to a slow, agonizing end of life. Some of their mouths were gaping in a now silenced terror, reminding me of the dying screams I had heard as a youngster in Vietnam.

Little has changed in Douglas and Agua Prieta since the days of Cocaine Joe Borane. Though out of office, the old judge remains a formidable figure in the border underworld. When asked, the Borane brothers will, of course, deny all knowledge of any illicit relationship with drug lords. These protestations sound acutely like the denials of athletes accused of taking steroids, or of politicians whose private liasons are brought before the public eye.

The current justice of the peace, Alma Vildosola, was Borane's secretary when he wielded power. She is a naturalized U.S. citizen from Mexico and holds a degree in tax law, which she obtained at a university in Guadalajara. Beyond her title in Douglas, Judge Vildosola has never practiced law in the United States.

In a phone conversation, I asked Lee Morgan if he had received any lawsuits for libel or defamation of character from the current or former leaders of Douglas after the publication of his 2006 book. He had not. "They know everything I wrote is true," Morgan said, adding a cryptic post script. "They also know I've got more ammo that I held back." I'm not prepared to argue this case, but Douglas residents of many ethnicities told me that the last honorable community leader to set foot in Cochise County was Geronimo, the renegade Apache warrior tamed a century ago by the U.S. Army. The sad commentary on the bankrupt leadership in Douglas reminded me of Agent Walter King's "homeland security" poster I had seen in Brownsville heralding the native fight against terrorism since 1492.

⟫⟩─○─⟨⟪

Arizona's Tucson Sector is a war zone. Here, the Border Patrol agents are ragged soldiers, not Maytag repairmen. They call it the "Smuggler's Ground Zero," and for good reason. Every year since 2000, more than half of all illegal aliens caught sneaking into the United States were apprehended in Arizona. Since 1998, the Tucson Sector, which covers the entire state of Arizona minus three western counties, has annually recorded almost 400,000 arrests.

In contrast to the Texas border—which, between the cities, is predominantly private farms and ranches—Arizona's borderlands are primarily federal, consisting of wildlife preserves, Native American reservations, and military training grounds. The Coronado National Forest, Tohono O'Odham Nation, Organ Pipe Cactus National Monument, Cabeza Prieta National Wildlife Refuge, and Barry M. Goldwater Training Range all lie inside the Tucson Sector. The National Park Service, Departments of Defense and Interior, and Bureau of Land Management share ownership of this rugged terrain. The parks, reservations, and bases comprise 68 percent of the Arizona border.

Although agents monitor these areas, the Border Patrol cannot place permanent stations on the federally owned land. Instead, park rangers scatter impotent signs throughout southern Arizona, warning that: "Smugglers and Illegal Immigration May Be Encountered in this Area." Such is the helplessness, confusion, and incongruity of border security—although the federal government owns two-thirds of the land, its stewards cannot make it safe for visitors. The rangers can only inform like hurricane forecasters who anticipate a storm's arrival.

Agent William Fimbres, the Douglas station's official spokesman, told me the noticeable spike in smuggling activity began in 1997. Two years later, Douglas saw its highest migrant traffic in history, when agents detained over 1,500 per day—per day!—in Cochise County, the Douglas station's 1,600 square mile area of responsibility. Twelve miles of fencing, more cameras, and additional agents brought the station's tally down to only 150 per day. "Things have gotten a lot better," said Agent Fimbres. "The quality of life has improved." Unfortunately, 150 is the same number of aliens caught daily in the entire 100,000 square miles of Laredo Sector, which is the size of Colorado.

For tactically sensible reasons, the agents in Tucson Sector embrace barriers and fencing even as those in the Rio Grande Valley, Laredo, and Del Rio Sectors remain ambivalent about it. The twelve miles of fencing in Douglas were fashioned from portable steel airstrips that were scrap leftovers from the Vietnam War. After the migrant tidal wave hit Douglas in the late 1990s, agents built the fence themselves. Metal patchwork covers the steel where repair crews fix the holes that *coyotes* have cut with welding torches.

Conventional wisdom attributes the dramatic increase in human smuggling through Arizona's Sonoran Desert to the illegal immigration crackdowns in San Diego and El Paso from 1993–95 that "pushed" the migration into the hinterlands. Though these actions certainly played a major role, there was another element to the shift that border analysts usually neglect to mention. According to the Redford shooting investigation, most of the 3,300 JTF-6 counterdrug missions completed prior to May 1997 happened on federal property. (The exact statistics remain classified.) According to Timothy Dunn, author of a book about border militarization, those missions were also "directly as well as indirectly focused on undocumented immigration."

After Zeke Hernandez was killed on May 22, 1997, the Pentagon publicly ended all counterdrug missions involving the U.S. military. This action drastically lowered the number of Americans patrolling the Arizona-Mexico border, which gave *coyotes* a new opportunity. They exploited it, and haven't looked back since.

———————=>-0-<=———————

During the copper boom a century ago, Bisbee was the crown jewel of the southwest—the largest city between St. Louis and San Francisco. Ten thousand people crammed into this rocky basin eleven miles north of the border town of Naco, chipping, picking, and dynamiting their way through the picturesque terrain until they finally extracted their burnt orange prize. Demand for copper slowed after World War II, which caused yields from Bisbee's largest mine, the Lavender Pit, to plummet. The Phelps-Dodge Company finally ended mining in 1974.

Instead of dying out and becoming a tourist attraction (Tombstone) or turning to smuggling (Douglas), Bisbee followed the Marfa pattern and became an artist colony. Painters, poets, hippies, hairstylists, natives, and New Agers commune in the breezy alcove. Today, coffee, crystals, and cannabis are as cool in Bisbee as peace signs.

If it was not for the charm of Arizona's weather and their pride in ownership of the Copper Queen Hotel, Bisbee would not be Dan and Connie Finck's kind of town. Built in 1902, the Copper Queen is Arizona's oldest continually running lodge. It has four stories, forty-eight rooms, and, according to local legend, three ghosts. Although the Fincks do not drink alcohol, they sell an aromatic homemade microbrew in a saloon that retains the period's architecture and décor. On the wall of the bar, a full-size mural of Lillie Langtry pays silent tribute to Judge Roy Bean and her other late admirers.

Dan has short gray hair, a salt-and-pepper goatee, and the height, bearing, and girth of an offensive lineman. He wore a short-sleeve collared shirt, baggy jean shorts, and running shoes. Connie has sandy brown hair, blue eyes, and a pleasant, warm smile. She wore a light blue cotton skirt, a white t-shirt, a blue jean vest, and sandals. They are conservative Mormons who have been married to each other since they were both twenty-one. They own the largest hotel in Bisbee.

I met the Fincks thanks in part to my own countercultural behavior. While seated at Winchester's, the hotel restaurant, I wore a black short-sleeve t-shirt emblazoned: Iraq and Afghanistan Veterans of America. Most cars in crunchy Bisbee featured bumper stickers with "Visualize World Peace" slogans. As I sat alone, Connie approached, thanked me for my service, and mentioned that her husband was in the Army during Vietnam.

The Fincks' first foray into the restaurant business was in 1981. They were living in Fairfax County, the upscale Northern Virginia suburb of Washington, D.C., and had been married for ten years. In two decades, the Fincks bought and sold several eateries in Fairfax. Longing for the southwestern beauty, mild weather, and wide space, Dan and Connie purchased the Copper Queen in 2006. With their children gone, the empty nesters could work a few more years while looking forward to retirement. They also felt a spiritual compulsion, a calling of sorts. "I just felt like we should be here," Dan said.

Bisbee turned out to be a little different than they had expected. The Fincks weren't prepared for the town's lackadaisical attitude toward immigration. Since Bisbee is only twelve miles from the border, it's a popular linkup point for migrants who evade the authorities from Naco, but need a pickup to travel further north. The previous owners of the Copper Queen had allowed migrants to lounge in the hotel lobby late at night as they were passing through.

Dan and Connie told their clerks to end the practice, which left many on the Copper Queen staff in a huff. ("The new owners aren't very popular," one employee admitted, anonymously.) Dan knew his decision wouldn't win friends, but he didn't want to be responsible for aiding and abetting. "People who have lived here forever don't let this bother them," Dan said, amazed. "They just haul away tons of garbage and go on."

One day, Dan and Connie were riding horses in the mountains near Carr Canyon, about twenty miles northwest of Bisbee and the same distance north of the border town Naco. Rounding a bend near a campground—Carr Canyon is government-owned property– the Fincks suddenly realized that they were approaching a man armed with a rifle. "Turn around," the gunman said. They had little choice, and departed the area.

"If you call the Naco Border Patrol, nothing happens," Dan said. Placards plastered throughout southeast Arizona advertise a toll free number citizens can use to report on smugglers or illegal aliens. "They say 'Thank you.' And then they do nothing."

"Every homeowner in Bisbee has dogs," Connie chimed in. After thirty-six years of marriage, Dan and Connie seemed comfortable finishing each other's sentences. "I don't know a single family that doesn't own at least one. They're the best deterrent." Connie said her friends leave gallons of water outside at night. "If they don't, the illegals just take it from the hose."

The Fincks felt conflicted. After all, immigrants had washed their dishes at restaurants in Fairfax County. "They would show me documents," Dan said, "but I knew they weren't legal. There were always two or three named Johnny Muñoz." He would discover the same Social Security numbers, circulated time and again. I chose not to ask about the Copper Queen's employees, but I suspected some of the maids were in a similar situation.

Dan said he hired the migrants for the same reason every employer does: nobody else wanted the work. "I tried to get kids to work," he said, "but it was Fairfax County. What suburban parent wants their high school teenager washing dishes in a restaurant?" The immigrants—Hispanic and Lebanese—would work construction during the day, wash dishes for Dan at night, and send whatever money they made back to their homes. Some lived in squalid apartments and shared rooms with as many as twenty.

"We sponsored half a dozen people for permanent residency," Dan said. For an immigrant, a permanent residency sponsor is the ultimate benefactor—the one individual or organization that puts a man or woman on the glorious path to citizenship. "The only thing they asked for was Sunday off so they could go to church, be with their families, and play soccer."

Dan and Connie Finck knew that they—like many Americans—used differing standards when dealing with immigration. On the one hand, they did not want to flaunt the law. They sought to be upstanding citizens, and could not bring themselves to openly support those who were illegally entering the land. But as employers seeking to run a business—and as Believers in extending the Church's compassion—the Fincks were unwilling to condemn the men who labored honorably; whose work brought hope, dignity, and survival to the impoverished.

"I can remember the day he got his citizenship," Dan said with a smile, referring to a Lebanese man whom he had sponsored. After he became an American citizen, two of his brothers came to the United States and followed suit through a separate employer. One became a police officer; the other joined the Air Force.

According to Dan, all three Lebanese brothers went to the FBI after 9/11 and volunteered their efforts as translators. Although once illegal, the men still wanted to give something back to their adopted homeland. The FBI took their names and said they would call. They never did.

⟞⟩━◦━⟨⟝

The U.S military plays an odd supporting role in this cast of border characters. Although the Department of Defense does not have any overt security task, their institutions, bases, and activities sustain the lives of many local residents. In a way this is unsurprising; if the Defense Department were a nation, its 2008 gross domestic product would be an estimated $811 billion. Ironically, that ties the Pentagon with Mexico as the fourteenth-largest economy in the world. Without the influx of military dollars, southern Arizona—like El Paso—would not survive for long.

Fort Huachuca, the U.S. Army's National Intelligence Center and southern Arizona's largest employer, sprawls alongside cattle ranches and retirement communities an hour west of Bisbee. In total jobs, Fort Huachuca is slightly ahead of Raytheon Missile Systems and Davis-Monthan Air Force Base. Taken together, these three organizations—all of which the Department of Defense owns or directly supports—account for over 32,000 jobs, or 34 percent of southern Arizona's work force.

West of Fort Huachuca, the mountains descend into the expansive, creosote covered San Rafael Valley. Among the ranches near Lochiel—where a single strand of barbed wire marks the boundary between the U.S. and Mexico—an unobtrusive grotto honors the exploration of Father Marcos De Niza. On April 12, 1539, De Niza, who commanded Spanish delegation from Mexico, became the first European to set foot west of the Rocky Mountains.

Like the Continental Divide marker, the grotto was a stunningly simple place. It seemed worthy of Smithsonian-like attention, but judging from the food wrappers, dirty socks, and soda cans, the only regular visitors to the monument were migrants. Many of the Latino outlaws who stopped by this unusual memorial had begun their journey twenty miles west of the grotto in the largest city on the Arizona-Mexico border.

Although it has the same name on both sides of the border, the Mexican-American town of Nogales owes more allegiance to Mexico than the United States. The population of Nogales, Arizona, is about 30,000. The sprawling Nogales, Sonora, has at least ten times as many residents—since so many come and go because of the smugglers, the exact count is uncertain.

There are a handful of legal businesses in Nogales; the usual mixture of discount goods sold to retirees and tourists at border towns. But from the nighttime activity of the Border Patrol, it's evident that the largest overall industry is smuggling. Douglas unfolds on relatively flat terrain, but the 4,000-foot hills of Nogales dip and spike into rocky ruts and dusty crags. On both sides of the line, sagebrush, Joshua trees, and cacti dot the terrain. The fourteen-foot-tall corrugated metal fence that divides Nogales for several miles has only slowed migrant traffic, not stopped it. Most of its panels are scarred with rusted pieces of replacement metal to cover holes sliced with a welding torch. The fraying strands of barbed wire at the top have been cut many times over.

More than 570 agents are assigned to Nogales, more agents than any other station in the States. (Douglas, which has the nation's largest facility, claims to be second; they would not disclose personnel statistics.) Recently, Nogales has also been the busiest; in 2007, on average, 1,000 aliens were processed each day at their detention facility. They were interrogated, fingerprinted, herded onto buses, and dropped off at the downtown gate to walk back into Sonora. Almost all were Mexican migrants—at least they claimed to be (in Arizona, smugglers teach Central Americans to say they are from Mexico to avoid deportation)—and almost all would cross again.

To better understand this cyclical phenomenon, I went on another ride-along with the Border Patrol. Although my sunset event with Agent Walter King in Brownsville had been benign and relatively quiet, the Tucson Sector was a different place. At Nogales, I met Zulma Gomez, twenty-seven, who grew up in El Paso, Texas, and had been with the Border Patrol for five years. Like Agent King, she wore a weathered green uniform and hat, and carried a pistol, handcuffs, flashlight, and handheld radio on her equipment belt.

Gomez was amiable, friendly, and considerate; I could see why she had been assigned to public affairs. She originally joined the Border Patrol because her best friend's father didn't think she could pass the initial screening and dared her into making an attempt. After proving him wrong on the test, Gomez became intrigued with the intense rigors of federal law enforcement. She quit her job in retail customer service and accepted admission to the Border Patrol Academy in Artesia, New Mexico. Five months later, she was an agent.

For liability reasons, the Border Patrol prefers to keep reporters away from apprehensions. Consequently, ride-alongs are typically interesting and educational, but they usually feel scripted. Not here in Nogales. The evening I visited, the station was overwhelmed, even with almost 200 agents on duty. All of them were busy, and the authorities needed every vehicle and person to pitch in. Including Agent Gomez.

"Did you say a group of four or six?" Gomez held the push-button radio linked to headquarters while I sat in the passenger seat.

"Six," responded the dispatcher. "We already found four in the brush, and there's another group."

"Ten-four," said Gomez. "What do you want me to do?"

"Go to the fire tower. You should be able to cut them off there." The fire tower was roughly two miles north of the border.

"Attention all agents," said the dispatcher. "Three more groups just came across."

We sped off in the Suburban toward the fire tower, scanning the undulating horizon for movement. Was this a typical night in Nogales? "Oh, absolutely," she said.

In 2003, after the Department of Homeland Security was reorganized, the Border Patrol officially said agents were the first line of defense in the nation's strategy against terrorism. But along the border, I didn't see any would-be terrorists being arrested. What I saw were agents going about the necessary, often tedious work of their jobs: querying drivers of suspicious vehicles, studying footprints in the sand, and examining clothing, garbage, and bottles of baby formula left in an illegal wake. Agents spend most of their time seizing drugs and illegal aliens. This made finding a potential terrorist threat seem like a search for a needle in the haystack.

A handful of threats have been discovered. Agents have caught individuals from more than seventy countries other than Mexico since 9/11. Although most were from Central and South America, the Border Patrol has apprehended people from places as diverse as Poland, Palestine, and Iraq. Some appeared to be political or economic refugees, but others—including a Farsi-speaking group found less than a year ago near Sasabe—may have posed tremendous danger.

For migrants, the challenge is not jumping the fence. (Although Arizona-based agents support the barrier's existence far more than those stationed in Eagle Pass, McAllen, and Brownsville.) The real obstacle is crossing the stretch of mountainous, parching desert north of Nogales. Although nature has provided trees and ravines for cover from *La Migra*, it offers little to sate hunger, slake thirst, or protect against thorns, coyotes, or rattlesnakes. For fifty miles, the voyagers seeking the Promised Land must avoid the trucks, airplanes, and helicopters of the Border Patrol, who scan for them like eagles for prey as they march toward their destination: the urban oasis of Tucson.

It was dark by the time we finally arrived at the fire tower. Grabbing a flashlight and radio, Gomez jumped out of the vehicle to reconnoiter with another agent. Together, they headed down a foot path. Gomez told me to wait in the vehicle.

Annoyed with my inability to observe the action, I listened to the dispatches. Another group had crossed, but this one was larger. About fifteen to twenty. There were not enough agents to respond. The migrants might be caught later at an interior checkpoint, I thought.

Or perhaps not. I discovered later that Tucson Sector was the only region in the entire Border Patrol without permanent interior checkpoints established on roads leaving the border. Although agents were allowed to set up temporary roadblocks, funding (and permission) to build the checkpoints was blocked for years in the U.S. House of Representatives by former Tucson Congressman Jim Kolbe. A population of retirees and artisans in the city of Tubac that straddles Interstate 19 (the highway running from the border to Tucson), had long opposed a checkpoint because of the possibility of waiting in traffic lines while traveling to and from home.

Agents from several sectors had told me that fixed interior checkpoints created a blocking position, enabling them to predict the alternate routes where aliens are more likely to flee for escape and evasion. In the Laredo Sector, which has six permanent checkpoints, more than 25 percent of the marijuana and 89 percent of the cocaine that agents confiscated in 2007 was found at the fixed instillations. Absent those interior checkpoints, the Border Patrol seemed like a football defense that didn't have linebackers or safeties.

Twenty minutes later, Gomez and her weary partner returned, shaking me from my reverie. At the same time, another Border Patrol vehicle approached. A third agent, who had caught one migrant, drove up, said something, and raced off. Gomez walked back.

"They got away," she told me. "We were too late to stop them." Chalk up another addition to the get-away ratio. Gomez's face looked like that of a beaten athlete who wanted to move on to the next play. Or like an exhausted soldier wishing for reinforcements.

━━━━━⟫⋅○⋅⟪━━━━━

Despite their failures, the Border Patrol still catches one-third of the economic refugees fleeing north soon after they cross the line. Hundreds of these unlucky men, women, and children are dumped back into the city each night. The mélange *La Migra* captures forlornly departs from buses and trudges through a revolving, grated steel door back into Nogales, Sonora, Mexico like inmates reentering their cellblocks. Wackenhut, a Blackwater-like private security contractor hired by the Department of Homeland Security, operates the shuttle service. The would-be migrants are easy to spot; they return to Mexico without shoelaces. Before returning them through the Nogales gate, drivers and security guards remove the laces to deter future crossing attempts.

Hundreds more would-be migrants pour north into Nogales, Sonora from western Mexico's largest city, Guadalajara, and smaller states like Oaxaca, Querétaro, and Michoacán. They feed north into the Sonoran cities of Hermosillo and Altar, where entire blocks of open-air *mercados* sell backpacks, shoes, water, food, and clothing required for the journey north. Networks of competing *coyotes* funnel their migrants, whom they nickname *pollos*, or chickens, into Nogales. They jam the *pollos* into motels and shelters until they have enough for a full load.

The *coyotes* are not always men. A woman known as Gaviota told a reporter from the Los Angeles–based Spanish newspaper *La Opinión* that she made $50,000 a month in human trafficking. Female *coyotes* depend on a network of relatives, usually single mothers, to arrange food and lodging, line up customers, and launder money on both sides of the border. They pay *jefes*—affiliates of a major cartel—up to $15,000 each month for the right to operate in a *plaza*. Gaviota said that she, like other female *coyotes*, prefers to run *pollos* through the port of entry *plazas* rather than march them across the desert.

Another *coyote*, Cristal Ontiveros, said she ran her first *pollos* when she was nine. Like Veronica Reyes of B&V Logistics in Laredo, Cristal worked with her mother in transport. Rosa Emma Carvajal Ontiveros was the infamous *La Güera Polvos*, or Blonde Powder Woman. She controlled the drug trade into Columbus, New Mexico—Pancho Villa's old stomping grounds—until she was killed by rivals on October 6, 2007. "My mother taught us the business," said Cristal, who also spent three years in prison for drug smuggling, where she picked up a tattoo featuring a sun and moon face. "She made us tough."

There was no shortage of toughness in Nogales, Sonora. At night, the Mexican town pulses with the rhythm of both benign and malevolent crime. Tattooed, rail-thin Latino men stand in sleeveless wife-beaters, smoking cigarettes, wearing caps sideways, and eye-balling pedestrians. Pairs of overweight hookers sashay on sidewalks, seeking their nightly score. Souped-up Chevys, Camaros, and Ponti-acs with rims, stickers, and tinted windows thump bass as they speed down narrow, potholed streets.

I walked into Nogales at about 10:00 P.M. one night. A dozen people were waiting to talk to me. Some were more fascinating than others.

"You want taxi?" a potbellied man called out. "You want tittie bar? Sixty-nine?"

I wanted none of the above. Just like in Matamoros, I was inter-ested in finding a fixer; hopefully someone more connected and dependable than José. Even though I had traveled almost 1,500 miles, I still had not talked in detail with any actual migrants. My lack of Spanish fluency was only compounded by my gringo appearance and a few remnants from military training. One person told me that when I walked, I looked like I was going to head butt something. This may have had the unfortunate side effect of frightening interviewees.

Fortunately in Nogales, mean-looking and curious works as an acceptable substitute for *Español*. In no time at all, I was introduced to Pedro Portugal, thirty-six, who looked like a stronger, fatter, and more responsible version of José. He had four kids—ages six to eighteen—and his wife worked at a *maquila* fabricating mother boards for computer systems installed on Ford cars. Pedro had lived in Oakland for fifteen years before being deported to Nogales in 2000. Initially, he told me that he was discovered after receiving a DUI, but later I heard a different story.

"Can you find me a *coyote*?" I asked.

"Sure," Pedro said. "When do you need to talk to him?"

"Tomorrow night."

"No problem. You want to go tonight?"

"I've got another idea," I said, satisfied that Pedro was the real thing. "What about Grupo Beta or some other migrant shelter?"

"Yeah, we can go by Grupo Beta." The government-sponsored shelter was twelve blocks west. "You want to take a taxi?"

"No," I said. "Let's walk."

Pedro was reluctant to go on foot; he said we'd be passing through an area—including a cemetery—that wasn't his turf. But sometimes you miss the sights and sounds of a place from the back of a taxi. My feeling was that Pedro was trying to hook up one of his *compas* by making me pay for the ride. After a couple of minutes, Pedro agreed that hoofing it for a few blocks wouldn't be excessively dangerous.

The limits of Pedro's safe zone—the part of town owned by whatever syndicate, cartel, or gang he worked for—intrigued me. If Pedro didn't have protection twelve blocks from downtown, it meant there were a lot of rival organizations competing for the smuggling market. Nogales wasn't as big as Juárez, but the growth in smuggling in the 1990s—combined with deported arrivals like Pedro—had tripled the city's population.

Walking toward Grupo Beta on a street adjacent to the border, we saw two men sitting inside a gray pickup. As we passed the truck, the driver received a call on his cell phone. The truck drove ahead two blocks. We stopped to watch.

"They're waiting to send over a load," Pedro said. "In a few seconds, we'll hear a quail call." He was correct. The truck stopped and the men fetched several parcels from inside the cab. They slid them under a gap in the fence.

"They were waiting for the Border Patrol to pass," Pedro said. "Someone was probably running back and forth to distract whoever is watching the cameras."

We walked on. Pedro pointed to a wide culvert near the cemetery that led into Arizona. "You know about the tunnel, right?" He was glancing around and had quickened his pace.

"Of course," I said. I knew nothing about this particular tunnel, but Pedro wasn't going to say anything else. By now we were way out of his turf, and the short, swarthy streetwalker had grown a little tense.

We arrived at the Grupo Beta building without incident, and found a man sitting at a desk watching Univision. Through Pedro, the attendant said there were no migrants at Grupo Beta. The building was closed for the evening and he was the only one on duty. He invited me to return the following day and speak with his boss.

I had been under the impression that Grupo Beta was where deported migrants went for help. The man at the desk said, no, they usually stay at one of several churches in Nogales, and then come to Grupo Beta for paperwork or assistance. In other words, Grupo Beta, according to this representative, had outsourced its job to the Catholic Church. The inefficiencies, contradictions, and hypocrisies of federal bureaucracies were apparently without borders.

The church/shelter was back across town, at least twenty blocks away. Pedro was happy, though—it was back in his turf. We took a cab. On the way over, Pedro told me his life story.

He was born in Guadalajara and came to Oakland through Tijuana as a teenager under illegal circumstances. For a decade and

Border graffiti:
Juarez, Chihuahua/
El Paso, Texas
PHOTO BY THE AUTHOR

Border graffiti:
Juarez, Chihuahua/
El Paxo, Texas
PHOTO BY THE AUTHOR

SE GRATIFICARA
CON $150 DLS A
LA PERSONA QUE
ENTREGUE
DOCUMENTOS A
NOMBRE DE
JOSE VELAZQUEZ
MATA
EN
SIN FRONTERAS
201 9TH AVE
532-0921

Sign outside of
*Sin Fronteras*:
El Paso, Texas
PHOTO BY THE AUTHOR

Javier Perez of Sin Frontreras:
El Paso, Texas
PHOTO BY THE AUTHOR

Statue: Ysleta Del Sur Pueblo
PHOTO BY THE AUTHOR

Sammy Gutierrez:
Tigua Indian Cultural Center
PHOTO BY THE AUTHOR

Elizabeth Larkins:
Hachita, New Mexico
PHOTO BY THE AUTHOR

Highway 9:
east of Columbus,
New Mexico.
PHOTO BY THE AUTHOR

CONTINENTAL DIVIDE
ELEVATION 4,520 FT.

Highway 9: east of
Antelope, New Mexico
PHOTO BY THE AUTHOR

**Vehicle barriers: Douglas, Arizona** PHOTO BY THE AUTHOR

**Hay bales informally mark the international line: west of Douglas, Arizona**
PHOTO BY ROBIN BHATTY

Memorial for migrants who died crossing the desert: west of Douglas,
Arizona PHOTO BY ROBIN BHATTY

The Border: east of Douglas, Arizona PHOTO BY ROBIN BHATTY

Douglas Fence:
Tucson Sector, Arizona
PHOTO BY ROBIN BHATTY

Nogales Fence:
Tucson Sector, Arizona
PHOTO BY ROBIN BHATTY

Douglas Station:
Tucson Sector, Arizona
PHOTO BY ROBIN BHATTY

Fence construction:
Tucson Sector, Arizona
PHOTO BY ROBIN BHATTY

Coronado National
Forest, Arizona
PHOTO BY ROBIN BHATTY

**TRAVEL CAUTION**
SMUGGLING AND ILLEGAL
IMMIGRATION MAY BE
ENCOUNTERED IN THIS AREA

Dan & Connie Finck:
Bisbee, Arizona
PHOTO BY ROBIN BHATTY

Retirement homes:
north of Nogales,
Arizona
PHOTO BY THE AUTHOR

Grupo Beta
official vehicle:
Nogales, Sonora
PHOTO BY THE AUTHOR

West of Naco, Arizona
PHOTO BY THE AUTHOR

Baboquivari Peak: Tohono O'Odham Nation, Arizona PHOTO BY ROBIN BHATTY

Abandoned building/safe house: Tohono O'Odham Nation, Arizona PHOTO BY THE AUTHOR

*Los Samaritanos* volunteers: Tohono O'Odham Nation, Arizona

PHOTO BY THE AUTHOR

Migrant's
discarded shirt:
Tohono O'Odham
Nation, Arizona

PHOTO BY THE AUTHOR

Gringo Pass:
Lukeville, Arizona
PHOTO BY THE AUTHOR

Brother David Buer,
Order of Friars Minor
(Franciscans): San
Xavier del Bac, Arizona
PHOTO BY ROBIN BHATTY

Rescue station:
Sonora Desert,
Arizona
PHOTO BY THE AUTHOR

**Organ Pipe Cactus National Monument, Arizona** PHOTO BY THE AUTHOR

**All-American Canal: east of Calexico, California** PHOTO BY ROBIN BHATTY

New River:
Calexico, California
PHOTO BY ROBIN BHATTY

Pedestrian crossing:
Calexico, California/
Mexicali, Baja
California
PHOTO BY ROBIN BHATTY

Recent international
marker: Imperial
County, California
PHOTO BY ROBIN BHATTY

Original international marker: Imperial County, California
PHOTO BY ROBIN BHATTY

All Terrain Vehicle team: El Centro Sector, California PHOTO BY ROBIN BHATTY

Rick van Schoik: San Diego State University, California
PHOTO BY THE AUTHOR

**The Fence: San Diego Sector, California.** PHOTO BY ROBIN BHATTY

**Efficiency housing: Tijuana, Baja California** PHOTO BY ROBIN BHATTY

**Watching Tijuana: Border Field State Park, California** PHOTO BY ROBIN BHATTY

**Pacific Ocean: Border Field State Park, California** PHOTO BY ROBIN BHATTY

a half, he fit pipes, poured concrete, and hung dry wall. But Pedro wanted more cash for his wife and children, and, in 1997, he was offered several thousand dollars—along with the necessary fake documents—to drive marijuana. Customs agents arrested him five months later at the San Ysidro port of entry, south of San Diego.

"I got greedy," Pedro said. "I did something illegal, I got caught, and I got busted." He didn't think his migration north was wrong, but he believed that God had punished him because he tried to get too much. Before that, he had only done hard work. When not escorting inquisitive gringos, Pedro sold bootleg DVDs. I sensed that his wife—who was not deported, but followed him back home after his misfortune—was paying their $120 monthly rent.

When we arrived at the church, two men were loitering in the parking lot. One man, who was sitting on an asphalt landing, wore a light blue t-shirt and faded jeans. He looked tired and spaced out, like he had spent twelve hours filling potholes in the Mexican sun. The other, who was standing and holding a clipboard, wore a collared, button-down shirt, khakis, and brown shoes. He looked fresh and scrubbed, like he had stepped out of a J. Crew catalog.

A minute later, three young men and a heavyset woman walked out of the church into the crisp night air. The youths, who had been deported just an hour earlier, were wearing baggy denim, long-sleeved shirts, and hats. They claimed to be in their early twenties, but looked younger. The woman excused herself to cook dinner for the deportees; Pedro and I declined her offer for food, but accepted two Cokes.

As we sipped soda, the woebegone trio told their rueful tale. They had crossed near Sasabe, a border town west of Nogales, and marched through the desert for a day and a half. As planned, they met up with a *coyote* on Highway 86 southwest of Tucson. Three hours later, they were in Phoenix. It was their first attempt and they made it. They were thrilled.

The friends were so fired up that they went to a raucous house *fiesta* to celebrate. They were in *El Norte*! Music blasted and booze flowed. The scent of pot floated through the air. Inevitably, though, all wild parties end the same way: the neighbors call the cops. When the police showed up, *los tres amigos* were happily inhaling. They tossed their roaches and tried to run away, but their attempted escape wasn't even close.

So fortune had kicked the Three Amigos back down into Mexico. They said the local cops were decent, but the Border Patrol had kept them in flexi-cuffs for hours. "They were assholes," said one of the *hombres*, prompting a torrent of Spanish swear words. They told their story with enthusiasm and color, but none wanted his picture taken or name printed. At one moment they were sullen convicts; at another, silly teenagers.

The Three Amigos stopped talking as soon as the woman working the church kitchen brought out their platters of beans, rice, wilted lettuce, and tortilla chips. While they ate, I turned my attention to Luis Martinez, the preppy professional. For Martinez, the shelter was a job fair of sorts. He was a project manager for Collectron International Management, a Nogales-based company that goes above and beyond international logistics service. Collectron not only performs customs services; they also find *maquila* sites and laborers for specific production requirements of American companies. Xerox, Alcoa, and General Electric are among the largest of more than 150 U.S. manufacturers who use Collectron's services.

Martinez grew up in Ciudad Obregón, about 200 miles south of Hermosillo, the capital of Sonora. Three years ago, he graduated from Obregón Technical Institute with an engineering degree. Eventually, that landed him a position with Collectron and required him to move to Nogales with his wife and children. Martinez was at the shelter because he needed to find three men skilled in soldering and/or welding for an aerospace engineering project. Ever the company man, Martinez exuded ambition, upward mobility, and naïveté. It was his first week on the job.

As Martinez knew, the Three Amigos were neither criminal illegals nor militant Chicanos. They were merely roughnecks who wanted to pound nails, pick crops, or turn wrenches. With so much work available in *El Norte*, an attempted crossing into the U.S. was like applying to Harvard. Going back to the farm near Guadalajara was like staying with mom and dad while attending community college. Martinez was pitching a third option: *maquila* work at a Nogales plant two miles away. The Three Amigos weren't interested.

Unfortunately, the Three Amigos were Martinez's best recruiting opportunity. The remaining man, José Bracamontes, had lived in Los Angeles for nineteen years before being deported. He earnestly believed he was a psychic hired by the National Security Agency, San Fernando Valley City Council, and President George W. Bush to spy on terrorists. "I used the crystal with my third eye," he said. "I got into the machine in China." He also mentioned the Masons.

This machine, according to Bracamontes, was a sinister device that "the secret people" used to control our thoughts. These secret people, he said, were the ones who hired him. Now, in some strange twist, they were also trying to kill him. In fact, they were using his ex-wife against him, who had taken custody of their three daughters. He thought they might need his help again after all, but he wasn't holding out much hope. "If they don't come and pick me up from here," Bracamontes vowed, "I'm not gonna help them anymore." I wondered whether it was mushrooms or meth that had conjured this powerful a hallucination.

It was an interesting evening at the shelter. Pedro, who knew he would make more money from this excursion than a trip to a strip club, seemed content. The Three Amigos—who had emerged victorious over the desert and then lost everything in Phoenix—were depressed and weighing their options. (It sounded like they were returning to Guadalajara.) Martinez was leaving his business card with the kitchen worker and then heading on to another shelter. And Bracamontes—who had decided that, as a writer, I must "know things" too—was asking me to put in a good word for him to the machine masters in China.

Just as Pedro and I were preparing to leave, one of the Three Amigos turned to me. "Why do Americans hate Mexicans?" he asked.

I paused. He wasn't asking the question with petulance. It was innocent, almost childlike. As far as he knew, Americans hated Mexicans and that was that. At least, that had been his experience in Phoenix.

"Most Americans don't feel that way at all," I said.

"Then why do they pay us so much to work for them and then kick us out?" he asked. "Why do they bribe us with riches, and then throw us away like whores?"

I'm sure there are thousands of immigration activists on both sides of the issue who would have had a snappy comeback. One faction would have blamed him for being illegal and said he should be staying home and fixing his broken country. The other would have showered him with artificial compassion and drafted him into an empty, banal *Resizte* against his white colonial oppressors.

But all the men in that parking lot—probably even Bracamontes—knew that any fancy explanation was no real answer to their imminently fair question. I ignored the query, thanked them, and wished them all luck. I felt my irrational anger returning, but kept it to myself.

**M**any people refer to the U.S.-Mexican border as though it were the same thing as the U.S.-Mexico border. The latter is the boundary of sand, water, and steel. The former is the filter somewhere north of the line; the place where you no longer smell fajitas grilling at a stand, see signs for discounts at an open-air *mercado*, or hear the sounds of the *mariachis* at midday. The U.S.-Mexican border blends amiably in San Antonio, but crackles divisively in Houston. In Arizona, Tucson beats Phoenix in the percentage of radio stations that broadcast exclusively *en Español*. Geography defines one limit; culture delineates the other.

Here in Arizona, the only U.S. interstate that uses metric—Mexican—signage is Interstate 19, the Nogales-Tucson highway. I'm not sure exactly why the exits are marked with kilometers, although I doubt the highway engineers who built the metric highway were in overt collusion with MECha or other members of the *Resizte*. But given the contrast between Nogales and *El Norte*, the irony does not seem accidental.

From Nogales to Yuma, where the Colorado River partitions Arizona and California, the U.S-Mexico border points diagonally northwest. It forms the hypotenuse of a triangle, with I-19, the Nogales-Tucson highway, as the short, flat base and the combined highways of I-10 and I-8 that stretch from Tucson to Yuma. Inside the triangle is a vast nothingness. The U.S. government has partitioned this particular *despoblada* into four enormous regions: the Tohono O'Odham Nation, Organ Pipe Cactus National Monument, Cabeza Prieta National Wildlife Refuge, and Barry M. Goldwater Air Force Training Range.

Who meanders through the Sonoran *despoblada*? It's hard to say. An enormous chunk of the land belongs to Native Americans, who police their own through tribal law enforcement. As many as 7,000 of the O'Odham Nation's population of 20,000 live in Mexico while maintaining tribal identification cards issued by the U.S. Department of Interior. Since the border inconveniently cuts the Papago tribal lands in half, natives often sneak in and out of the country through unofficial Class B ports of entry south of the O'Odham capital of Sells. Smugglers traverse both sides of Baboquivari Mountain and Kitt Peak Observatory, funneling their cargo north through Three Points and Ajo.

West of O'Odham Nation, ranchers graze their cattle on open ranges along the fringes of the national parks and preservations west. Hikers and naturalists take in the trails. In Arizona's southwest corner, Marine Corps aircraft use tank carcasses for target practice on the bombing range. Throughout the area, helicopters ferry the Border Patrol Search, Trauma and Rescue—BORSTAR—who keep watch for men, women and children dying of hunger and thirst.

Two groups of citizens are among those who patrol these places. Both are on the lookout for migrants, claim humanitarian intentions, and attempt to gain the moral high ground through compassionate ideological narratives. Indeed, both seem stricken with the conviction of the True Believer; their actions—even to the point of civil disobedience—are necessary. With the zeal of William Wilberforce's opposition to slavery, they roam this dusty purgatory in an effort to stop an evil that will destroy society if left unchecked. Believing they have been betrayed by the ignorance of their leaders, both groups feel they have a duty to confront the malevolence in their midst.

Chris Simcox, forty-seven, is white, clean-shaven and has short brown hair. In 2002, he was hiking in Organ Pipe when he encountered an armed caravan of drug smugglers. Coming on the heels of 9/11, Simcox saw the smugglers as evidence that the U.S. was being invaded. Soon thereafter, he discovered an area in the desert where migrants changed clothes and dumped trash before walking north. These discoveries were, for Simcox, a type of conversion experience. Chris Simcox is the president of the Minutemen Civil Defense Corps.

On selected weekends during the year, Simcox and the Minutemen go into the desert, look for migrants, and report them to the Border Patrol. If the migrants are thirsty, they give them water. When we spoke over coffee, Simcox told me that Minutemen have assisted with apprehending more than 10,000 illegal aliens, rescued more than 300 migrants in distress, and recovered 36 dead bodies over the past four years. In 2007, Simcox was retained by the John Birch Society speaker's bureau, which charges $1,000 fees for his appearance.

Brother David Buer, fifty-three, is also white, but he wears a long gray beard and has a ponytail. In 1975, he hitchhiked to California and began a lifetime career as an advocate for the homeless. After his own conversion to Catholicism, Buer's faith journey led him to become a Franciscan friar. For years he worked in Las Vegas, where he angered city officials with his determination to force an increase in the city budget for the poor. (In 2004, Las Vegas spent 0.02 percent of its annual budget on the homeless.) In 2006, Buer moved to the San Xavier del Bac Mission, a small Franciscan order near the Tohono O'Odham land. He is the leader of *Los Samaritanos*—The Samaritans—a humanitarian group that offers first aid to stricken, poor migrants.

About three times a week, Buer and his *Samaritanos* volunteers go into the desert, look for migrants, and ask them what they need. If exhausted migrants have given up and want to turn themselves in, the *Samaritanos* call the Border Patrol. Otherwise they give them water, food, and medical attention and let them go where they wish. If they do not meet anyone, the Samaritans carry cheap backpacks filled with gear which they place along trails. As a Franciscan friar, Brother Buer has taken a lifetime vow of poverty. If Brother Buer has a rare speaking appearance beyond the pulpit, he receives nothing.

Both Chris Simcox and David Buer think the current U.S. immigration policy is immoral, unjust, and unethical, even though they've reached opposite conclusions on how it should be fixed. The Minutemen Civil Defense Corps believes we should station large numbers of U.S. troops on the border to prevent illegal entry. Simcox feels that both sets of borders—the physical and the cultural—should be sealed and closed to protect Americans from threats to their way of life. Unintentionally, the Minutemen's international model is Russia.

The Kremlin authorizes 200,000 Border Guards—an official branch of the Russian military—to use deadly force to prevent any unauthorized crossing. It is a position Simcox would support.

*Los Samaritanos* thinks that the border should be opened completely. Their international model is more like Europe; where the 1990 Schengen Agreement—a treaty between twenty-eight European nations—have removed all border controls, turning checkpoints from Estonia to Spain into political boundaries of no greater physical significance than the line separating Arizona from California. Brother Buer believed that personnel, technology, and infrastructure should not oppress the poor; that these synthetic, artificial boundaries do not change the intrinsic value—or extinguish the divine spark—inside every human soul, regardless of its nationality.

A clear majority of Americans agree that the U.S.-Mexico border—the line separating the legal systems, political jurisdictions, economic zones, and military realms of two distinct nations—should be stabilized and controlled. For a small, vocal minority, however, the summons to secure the border has to do with culture, not security.

The unspoken, and flawed, assumption is that by controlling the U.S.-Mexico line, the U.S.-Mexican border will also be regulated. Defeating smugglers and deterring terrorists is an important national security goal, but accomplishing it will not alter the demographic and cultural shifts already happening within the United States. In other words, even if the Department of Homeland Security can fortify the political border, it cannot do likewise with the cultural one.

⟨⟩⊙⟨⟩

Staring at footprints with Brother David Buer or hearing stories of rifle-brandishing invaders from Chris Simcox could only teach me so much. The *coyotes* obviously had an effective business model. The question that stuck with me, though, was tactical. Was an individual crossing in western Arizona actually as easy to complete as it had appeared to be in Nogales?

For the smugglers, the answer seemed straightforward. Using couriers throughout Mexico, they funnel their *pollos* north into

Altar, the Sonoran staging ground for *coyotes* smuggling cargo from western Mexico or Central America. Rows of backpacks, hats, shirts, water bottles, canned food, and other supplies are sold at Altar's markets—the Wal-Mart for a hopeful migrant.

From there, *coyotes* stash the migrants in the safe houses and hotels they own and operate along the Arizona border. Pedro showed me several of these in Nogales; all were adjacent to the border gate. According to Pedro, abuse and violence is at its worst at the hotels. Migrants waiting to cross are robbed and deported. Migrants unable to pay their *coyotes* are abused, assaulted, or tortured. Pedro was relieved that he had not been forced into collecting. It was a job he felt would have damned him to hell.

The night before migrants attempt a crossing, they go to churches, memorials, or makeshift grottos. They light candles and pray for God, *María*, Jesus, and everyone in between to grant them safe passage. They gossip, network, look for tips, and swap contacts with the recently deported.

At night, it is time to go for it. They jump in groups over the fence in places like Nogales, or tunnel through holes cut by *coyotes*. Like salmon fighting against the current, they sprint past the line of cameras and sensors. They are mice that the hawks of *Migra* are waiting to snatch. If they escape Agent Zulma Gomez and the other 200 agents scouring the countryside on the manhunt, they hike miles to the west and find a cut or pass where they can walk north.

After eluding their captors, the migrants find a rhythm. In the city, they look for a street with the safe house. In the desert, they settle in for the long march, watching out for headlights, helicopters, and rattlesnakes. On the road, they look for their pickup—a hollowed-out truck or Suburban where they cram in with others in their situation. If they approach a Border Patrol checkpoint, they are dropped off, so they can walk around and meet back up with their ride.

From there, it's off to Phoenix, which is to human smuggling in the United States as Laredo is to international trade and freight logistics. Some pay their *coyotes* at the hub, and strike out on their own from Phoenix. More likely, the smuggler escorts them to their final destination, whether it is Chicago, Nashville, Cincinnati, or New York.

By the time I was driving down I-8 toward Yuma, I thought I had a clear understanding of how illegal crossings for narcotics smugglers and *coyotes* worked in theory. As mentioned, more than 90 percent of the cocaine and heroin entering the U.S., as well as half the marijuana, is smuggled through the ports of entry. The remaining stashes are packed across by "mules," who work for their bosses using an arrangement that appears to be somewhere between sharecropping and slavery.

For human smuggling, the best bargain for poor migrants appears to be the $20 trip across the Rio Grande. It is also the least certain: the journey only buys you a crossing, and nothing more. The best overall value, however, is clearly the most expensive: fake visas, documents, and a new name that will guarantee employment credentials (such as Joel Garibay-Urbina from Pilgrim's Pride Chicken). Sonora-based *coyotes* persuade migrants into the third option of the desert trek, putting them on a credit card–like payment plan that forces them into years of indentured servitude if they survive the journey.

In a bizarre way, the *narcotraficantes* and *coyotes*—not the Border Patrol, FBI, or Department of Homeland Security—are the real first line of defense between the American people and a terrorist. Despite the cruelty and brutality of the *narcos* and *coyotes*, one U.S. federal agent told me that they do not believe the smugglers are running IEDs, explosive-laden artillery shells, or dirty bombs into the United States. "Competition is much too fierce," he said. "Any 9/11-style involvement in domestic terrorism would destroy their business model."

This, however, does not mean that terrorists lack ties with drug cartels. Back in Nogales, the Border Patrol rounded up a Palestinian man one night amid their nightly game of hide-and-seek. The man was on an FBI terror watch list. What were his intentions? Had he entered the country with a plan to attack innocent civilians? The federal agent did not know—the FBI had whisked the man away for interrogation. The agent suspected he was involved in trading drugs for weapons, which he planned to export overseas. It made me wonder if the terrorists—actual or hypothetical—who may or may not be crossing the border were doing so to plot against American civilians or simply as fundraising for their international criminal enterprises.

One of the many valuable habits I learned in the Marines was to "turn the map around." To understand a problem, think about how your adversary or opponent would approach it. If I were a terrorist, how would I cross the border? Is it as easy to do as people say? And if so, is it possible to separate the issue of national security—protecting the country against terrorists—from drugs and illegal immigration?

Before I started theorizing, I needed to test the hypothesis.

<hr/>

From the time I started my journey in Boca Chica, attempting an illegal crossing of the border had appealed to me for several reasons. One is that I am a sucker for challenge. In college and in the Marines, I was often quick to fall for the "nobody calls me chicken" routine to prove one thing or another. I thought it might be interesting to gain an unvarnished account of the experience, both for the story and for the adventure. Could I slog for days through the desert—like the men who picked the fruits I ate, or the women who cleaned the hotels where I stayed—and survive to talk about it?

A wilderness escapade, however, would not illustrate whether or not the border could be crossed easily by a single terrorist. No sane criminal would hoof for days on foot through searing heat—especially solo—if there were better ways to enter illegally. Gangs of bandits prey upon lone wolves; one reason that migrants use *coyotes* is because of the safety that larger numbers bring. I had hiked in hard desert, so I knew how much water to carry for survival, and the feeling of a parched, dehydrated throat. A desert trek might prove solidarity with migrant workers, but it would not tell me how easy it was for one man to get into America.

Other than swimming the Rio Grande, I had few options to simulate an illegal terrorist entry. I could sneak through the desert at night and then make my way out to a remote road for a pickup. Or, I could just sprint pell-mell in broad daylight like the migrants, daring the Border Patrol to come after me. Either choice would require me to drive to a border crossing, park on the U.S. side, walk into Mexico, and then jump over a barrier or fence. Perhaps I would be lucky and *La Migra* would just ignore me, or I would elude and outrun them in a fair scrape. Using the football analogy, it was a choice of selecting the screen pass or the run up the middle.

Although the recon attempt might yield interesting intelligence, the plan also carried several risks. Even though I had my passport, Border Patrol agents would have a field day if they snagged a journalist—a journalist!—attempting an illegal crossing. At best, I would lose face among the healthy network of contacts I had established within the feds. At worst, I could be charged with failure to enter the United States without submitting to an inspection—a misdemeanor offense.

Would the brainy approach of sneaking through the desert be superior to the brawny sprint? Probably not. In this case, the clever method posed more physical danger and less likelihood for success. Rattlers, wolves, and bandits come out at night. In addition to natural obstacles, there was also the issue of me being me. Crawling through bush in the dead of night, my long stride and heavy footprints would easily set me apart from a Mexican man. Even the greenest of Border Patrol trackers would find it out of place when cutting for sign, and curiosity would prompt them to sniff me out. I was leaning toward in-your-face smashmouth as opposed to guile and stealth.

Since the Yuma/San Luis crossing was in a high visibility area on the Colorado River—the twenty-four-mile corridor connecting Arizona/Calfornia with Sonora/Baja California—I decided to make my test run at the Lukeville/Sonoyta border crossing. Best known as the "Gringo Pass" that runs south to the tourist resorts on the Baja coast, the Lukeville border crossing is where retirees, students, and twentysomethings line up their RVs, SUVs, and hybrids on their way to beach towns like Puerto Peñasco, or Rocky Point. The town of Gringo Pass—the map says Lukeville, but a green welcome sign labels it otherwise—has a motel, grocery store, and diner. The motel, crossing, and Mexican city of Sonoyta were the only amenities that made Gringo Pass, Arizona, any larger than Langtry, Texas.

Back to my plan. If I were going to try smashmouth, I would also have to arrange for a pickup. Assuming I parked in Gringo Pass and walked over to Mexico, I would need a few hours to find a fixer and feel out the area. From there, I would stay the night, wait, and make the jump in town just before sunrise. The late shift of Border Patrol agents would still be groggy and the early birds would either not have arrived or still be settling in. After I made the jump, it would be an all-out sprint from one hiding place to another until I made it to my getaway car.

Driving south on Arizona Highway 85, I called up a friend I hadn't seen in years who lived in Colorado and asked if he would be available—sight unseen—to pick me up. (Surprisingly, he was.) Given that an international fugitive would probably require a similar arrangement, I figured that would enhance the realism of the test. If I made it to the car and drove off undetected, I would declare the mission complete.

It was just after 1 P.M. when I arrived at the Gringo Pass Diner. A dozen cars and trucks were in the parking lot. The diner was on the west side of Arizona Highway 85; to your right if you are facing south. The U.S. Customs building was to the east, on the other side of the road. It was sunny and 95 degrees—pleasant for southwestern Arizona, where the temperature can rival Baghdad for its ability to asphyxiate. Signs, barricades, and fences forced vehicle traffic from Mexico toward four lanes of traffic that were halted by traffic cones and spike strips underneath a canopy. Even though it was "only" 95, the relentless light was hot enough to drive all the American federal authorities either under the shade or inside. Only a sidewalk and arrows directed pedestrians walking from Mexico to enter the customs building.

After parking at the diner, I wanted to explore the Mexican town of Sonoyta to scout for good crossing locations. This time, my question about finding a *coyote* would not be a ruse. I didn't want the smugglers to actually take me over—it would not be worth risking in case we got caught—but I would need some good intel if I were going to pull this off solo. Plus, I figured that any skilled terrorist would do the same thing.

Entering into Mexico, I saw a three-foot-high chain-link fence and four uniformed Mexican officials standing underneath a pavilion. I noticed that the Mexican entrance was not guarded by Americans; the Border Patrol had a casual eye on the crossing from the U.S. into Mexico, but the passageway was not being carefully observed. The Mexican police were only interested in collecting the money from cars heading south to the coast. I filed this away.

On the outskirts of Sonoyta south of Gringo Pass, a small column of bars, pharmacies, and dental offices appeared alongside the two-lane Mexican highway. Fifty yards past the entrance into Mexico, the steel horses of America—Yukons, Durangos, Winnebagos—paid the customs fee required to travel into the Mexican interior and caravanned off to the resorts of Rocky Point. Tin-roofed huts were dispersed to the east and west. Five hundred yards ahead, dust devils vanished behind an empty, tumbleweed-laden road that led toward the city.

Ten minutes later, after I had walked to the end of the highway, I turned around and looked back at the international border. Then it dawned on me. It was obvious what a terrorist would do. They would choose the path that was hidden in plain sight.

In Nogales, I asked Pedro how he had crossed the border illegally several years ago. "I just walked through the Mariposa port of entry," he said, referring to a gate twelve miles west of downtown. Pedro had not gone with a group or a *coyote*—he had crossed alone. When he explained it to me, I had not understood the significance of the remote location. When I stood on the street and peered back at the Sonoyta gate, it finally made sense.

At checkpoints along the border like Gringo Pass, bustling parking lots with duty-free stores lie adjacent to the international line. The traffic is steady, but routine. In the heat of the day, while shoppers are coming and going, Border Patrol and Customs agents sit inside air conditioned buildings and vehicles.

Since it is not illegal in Mexico to cross into the U.S. from the south, the Mexican police have one main job at their northern border: collect customs fees from non-Mexican citizens traveling beyond the sixteen mile "border zone." That's it. A circular iron gate stopped travelers from using the pedestrian entrance at Gringo Pass, but there was nothing that could block someone from using the two-lane road to walk from Mexico into America.

This is the sort of thing a terrorist might know. If it were really this easy, an enemy of America could simply find a time at midday, have someone drop them off at a border crossing, and stroll into America using the road heading into Mexico. This would not work on the Rio Grande—the toll bridges are more secure—but at any land border crossing west of El Paso that was both remote and busy, it would be a viable option.

As I ambled toward the checkpoint, I stayed on the left side of the road instead of following the arrows toward the U.S. Customs station. I felt a brief sensation of nervous excitement. The first Mexican policeman I passed ignored me. The second one nodded without interest. I strolled quickly into the United States.

A Border Patrol vehicle patrolling the line approached from the left side, driving west to east. The freshly-built fence blocked their field of vision. I walked fifteen yards behind the vehicle, which then turned north onto the road. The fence, which also cut north to the Gringo Pass Diner, offered concealment. The agents had no idea I was there.

I walked over to the parking lot, jumped into my rented hatchback, and drove away from Gringo Pass at a normal speed. Eighteen miles north, a Border Patrol agent waved me through a checkpoint. I called my friend and told him not to worry about picking me up.

⟫-◦-⟪

When I told Border Patrol union president T. J. Bonner about my breezy illegal crossing at Lukeville, he chided me with sarcastic cynicism. "It's not like you deserve a gold medal or anything," he said dismissively. "Thousands of people jump the border every day."

Bonner's remark unsettled me, as did the entire experience of proving it really was that easy to illegally cross the border. Swimming the Rio Grande or trudging through the remote desert was one thing, but I had skirted the system right under the noses of the agents. I did not intend to take anything away from the individual agents, men, and women who perform brave, humane, and unheralded feats on America's southwestern frontier. But institutionally, it seemed that the Border Patrol had been set up for failure. Bonner agreed, although I was unable to get a full explanation of his earlier animus towards Chief Carlos Carrillo's remarks about focusing on preventing terrorism. To me, they both seemed to be saying the same thing: the Border Patrol can only do so much.

By now, I was convinced: no amount of personnel, technology, or infrastructure focused exclusively on barricading the line could stop determined souls from coming into the United States. Nothing good could come from spending the next thirty years watching 21,000 grown men and women play hide-and-go-seek with thousands of other adults along a 1,952 mile corridor.

I stopped in Yuma that night—a border city on the Colorado River home to a robust Marine Corps Air Station—and pondered the consequences of my success. Once again, my thoughts turned to the tactical: how do you actually stop people from coming across? More and more, I thought there might be some answers in the small classrooms on this base where thousands of Marines have trained for counterinsurgency operations in Iraq. It wasn't Yuma *per se* that offered the solution, but also Fort Leavenworth, Marine Corps Base Quantico, and, ultimately, the forging grounds in Iraq and Afghanistan where American soldiers and Marines have discovered what they can expect from twenty-first-century conflict.

Although I had learned many lessons on the border, two points kept coming back. First, excluding U.S. military forces from solutions to this international dilemma is terribly flawed—border security is ultimately a foreign relations problem and cannot be solved by an organization modeled only on domestic law enforcement. Second, and perhaps more importantly, border security can be achieved only through binational collaboration and not unilateral protectionism. Unless the citizens and government of Mexico are equally invested in the final outcome, any attempt to seal the border will fail.

Pondering the first point reminded me of an article in the U.S. Naval Institute's military journal *Proceedings*. Marine Gen. James Mattis and retired Marine Lt. Col. Frank Hoffman defined a theory of twenty-first-century combat called hybrid warfare. "Irregular methods—terrorism, insurgency, unrestricted warfare, guerrilla war, or coercion by narco-criminals—will challenge U.S. security interests," the pair wrote.

Mattis and Hoffman stressed that hybrid wars—a more refined type of counterinsurgency—would not be won by focusing on technology or other one-dimensional solutions. Victory, they said, would not come from conventional military solutions, but from unconventional strategies blending global statecraft with local security. The essential elements of this theory—which were codified with surprising simplicity in the U.S. Army's 2007 Counterinsurgency Field Manual—have contributed to the U.S. military's tactical success in cities such as Mosul, Tal Afar, and Ramadi during the Iraq War.

Whether we like it or not, a hybrid war is happening on the U.S.-Mexico border. Studying the border through the template of counterinsurgency helped me understand why anarchy had spread through Arizona and farther North, but had not infected south Texas. For soldiers and Marines in Iraq, the barometers of regional support are not only politicians or police chiefs, but also tribal leaders and sheikhs. Capt. Scott Cuomo, a Marine infantry captain with two tours in Iraq, summed it up best: "It's the people, stupid."

In the conduct of hybrid warfare, understanding the entities that wield power beyond the government is essential. North of the U.S.-Mexico border in south Texas, the strongest nongovernment forces are multinational corporations. In Brownsville, McAllen, and Laredo, companies like Motorola, Nokia, and General Motors drive the border agenda. South of the border, however, the *narcos* reign with impunity in many areas. In the case of the Nuevo Laredo shopkeeper, his belief in American power was such that only America—not his corrupted local government—could bring peace to his neighborhood.

In terms of hybrid war, the western portion of the land border has a different balance of power than the area surrounding the Rio Grande. Along the line in the sand, corruption has spread more corrosively to both sides of the border; in many regions, the drug lords hold more sway over local leaders than any other business interest or government official. Of the 226 reported incursions onto U.S. territory committed by the Mexican military from 1996–2005, 180 took place from El Paso west. They may have been fakirs contracted by drug cartels, or they may have been actual members of the military. Either way, 80 percent of all invasions by armed men wearing Mexican uniforms took place on the western borderline.

While there is little need for soldiers and Marines to patrol Brownsville, McAllen, or Eagle Pass, Border Patrol agents armed with pistols do not stand a chance in the federal land in Arizona against two squads of *narcos* packing AK-47s. Although Border Patrol agents possess certain paramilitary skill sets, their organization is structured for law enforcement, not combat. As I listened to the aircraft come and go at Yuma, I pondered whether or not the Department of Homeland Security could fight the hybrid war I had seen on the border without ample assistance from the Pentagon. Then, I wondered if Marines had really learned enough counterinsurgency to successfully conduct hybrid war on our own continent. I gnawed on these questions as I entered California.

———————⟫•◦•⟪———————

The way we use water tells us a lot about who we are. In Texas, most of the Rio Grande is privatized, independent, and left as a public resource. The water that feeds the farms in the Rio Grande Valley is dammed for flood control and irrigation along the Pecos, the Río Conchos, and the Northern Rio Grande. To maintain the flow of the water they need, south Texans must negotiate with New Mexico, Colorado, and, most of all, Mexico. Their survival depends on forging a fair compromise.

Without the Colorado River, which I crossed as I left Yuma and drove west into California, the All-American Canal would not exist, nor would the desert miracle of the Imperial Valley in southeastern California. Built during the Great Depression as one of several public works/infrastructure projects accomplished by the Bureau of Reclamation, the eighty-two-mile canal diverts more than 3 million acre-feet of water each year from the Colorado River and into Imperial County. Thanks to the canal, this stretch of the California desert has turned into an unexpected breadbasket. It's also a deceptively dangerous waterway where would-be immigrants are sucked into vortexes and pulled into hidden undertows. Rafts litter the fences along the canal where *coyotes* charge premiums for escorted crossings.

Ironically, the names of both features—"All-American" Canal and "Imperial" Valley—point to the attitudes Californians have displayed toward their resources, entitlements, and southern neighbors. Having haggled with municipal managers from four other states and twice as many cities, the "water buffaloes" of the U.S. Department of

Interior, Imperial Irrigation District, and San Diego County Water Authority have little interest in negotiating with another party. As several American writers have observed, "In the West, whiskey is for drinking, and water is for fighting."*

Some fights are easier to resolve than others, particularly when the water at stake is spoiled with chemicals and sewage. In 1983, the U.S. and Mexico signed a treaty to improve environmental cooperation and reduce pollution throughout the "border region," which was defined as 100 kilometers on either side of the U.S.-Mexico boundary. Of particular concern was the New River, an intermittent stream produced by industrial and human waste from both sides of the border that poured north from Mexicali, Baja California, into Calexico, California. The accord, which became known as the La Paz Agreement, has not entirely eliminated the cesspools, but the ongoing bilateral approach has halved the pollutant supply in the New River over the span of two decades.

Unfortunately, other international water disputes might undermine the progress. When the All-American Canal was completed in 1942, engineers who designed the 100-foot wide, 15-foot deep ditch did not seal the sides with plastic or concrete. As a result, almost 70,000 acre-feet of water seeps into the ground each year. For six decades, farmers in the Mexicali Valley have tapped this seepage as groundwater to feed wells, irrigate their own crops, and sustain the growth of Baja California's second-largest city.

Unlike Texas, California has no real incentive to negotiate water issues with Mexico. In the Rio Grande Valley, the waters of the Río Conchos that start in Chihuahua ultimately grow the fruits and vegetables in Brownsville. In the west, the positions are reversed. Once the Colorado River departs from its source in its namesake state, the stream is fiercely contested by Utah, Arizona, Nevada, and California. Decades ago, Mexico possessed a larger share of the twenty-four miles of the Colorado that separates Sonora from Baja California, but the explosive growth of the western sunshine paradise has trickled their share into oblivion.

---

* This quote has often been attributed to either Mark Twain or Will Rogers, because it seems like the sort of thing either one would have said. The actual etymology of this phrase—despite its veracity—is unknown.

Because 70,000 acre-feet a year would supply 134,000 families, and because Southern California's growth is expected to continue for decades, San Diego wants its water back. In 1988, the U.S. Department of Interior approved a plan to line the canal with concrete, which would seal the groundwater into the U.S. and eliminate the seepage. Throughout the 1990s and into this decade, Mexicali fought the plan, enlisting its sister city of Calexico and several California environmental groups to aid with a series of lawsuits. By early 2007, all legal challenges had failed.

For Mexico—which was not granted a seat at the negotiating table when the Colorado River distribution was negotiated among the five American states—the loss of the water was important enough to become an international issue. Mexicali's current and future needs were being discarded by the north. In March 2007, President Felipe Calderón made a personal appeal to President George Bush at a U.S.-Mexico summit to halt the canal lining. Calderón's pleas fell on deaf ears. Construction on the three-year project started in July 2007.

Driving north of Tecate, Baja California, on Highway 8—home of the working man's champagne that had earlier baptized the Continental Divide—I was forced to confront another unpleasant truth: I was not investigating with the same energy I had back in Boca Chica. Nineteen hundred miles had taken their toll, and the border's novelties were beginning to grow banal. At some level, it was interesting that Mexicali had the largest Asian-Mexican population in Mexico, and that the Mexican-Chinese still fought against virulent anti-Asian discrimination throughout Baja California. But just over the mountains was the Pacific Ocean. I could practically smell the salt, hear the waves and feel the breeze.

What I learned in the space between was that California's perspective on the border mirrored that of other Americans in ways I had not encountered in Arizona, New Mexico, or Texas. One example is the issue of birthright citizenship. David Green, the Chief Executive Officer and Administrator for the El Centro Regional

Medical Center, left a hospital north of San Diego for his current position. He says that he wanted a professional challenge: maintaining quality care at a border hospital without falling into bankruptcy. El Centro fit that description.

"The average charity burden for hospitals in the U.S. is 2 to 4 percent of all patients," says Green, referring to health care costs involving illegal immigrants. "El Centro's is 8 to 10 percent." In El Centro, most charity work can be triaged into three medical categories: dehydration aid to migrants lost in the desert, bone fractures sustained when climbing over the border fence, and—the largest charity category of all—newborn babies.

"El Centro delivers 1,600 babies per year," says Green. "Fifteen to twenty-five percent of all deliveries are charity." Since all children born on U.S. land are automatically granted American citizenship, expectant mothers often wait until late in their pregnancies to cross the border, find the hospital, give birth, and then return to Mexico. Green tells a story about a friendly greeting offered to one of his obstetrician/gynecologists. "Dr. Thomas, thank you so much," offered a Mexican mother. "You delivered my other three kids as well." A Border Patrol agent at the El Centro Sector told me that he knew of illegal immigrants who had gone into labor minutes after crossing. His fellow agents suddenly became midwives.

Citizen issues notwithstanding, charity work was not on the minds of most residents in the rugged Mountain Empire between El Centro and San Diego. In this sparsely populated retreat east of San Diego, I observed a hyperactive obsession with property values. The conditions of their communities, connections with drug cartels, or conformance to federal regulations had governed local attitudes in Texas, New Mexico, and Arizona. The closer I got to the Pacific Ocean, the more single-minded land barons became about their individual fixations with portfolios, assessors, and estates. Whether it was the Blackwater Training Facility being built in Potrero, the brush-clearing zone in Campo, or the zany hippie-style resort in Jacumba, the ultimate barometer to any local dilemma for residents was how it would affect the price tag of their land.

Finally, I found tremendous apathy among the U.S. populace about events taking place on the Mexican side of the border. Right or wrong, the Texas, New Mexico, and Arizona borderlands had tied their fortunes to the fate of their Mexican counterparts. California's security wall had transcended the public consciousness, feeding the ingrained cultural narcissism. Fitness, healthy eating, and alternative medicine, as well as traffic, air quality, and global warming, were the day-to-day concerns of Californians. The poor in Tijuana were not.

I had wanted California to teach me something about the border that I had not already learned. But beyond academics and activists, the Golden State seemed lethargic. In fact, California's lack of interest in Mexicali's water problems was all too revealing in the general attitude towards cross-border disputes.

While the usual suspects from both sides offered their talk radio rants, most Californians simply ignored Mexico. Even after decades of ranting, passing one proposition after another in an attempt to halt the state's evolution into "Mexifornia," the tide had not turned. Frustration, resignation, and a sense of inevitability combined with a not-in-my-backyard determination to enjoy their coastal bliss. With the exception of those who had families in Mexico, most Californians—even border residents—shrugged with indifference.

The clearest illustration of this indolent mindset came during the last week of October 2007, when the Santa Ana winds fanned a fiery assault on southern California. In Tecate and beyond, thousands of acres of Mexico were scorched by the Harris Fire. Dozens, perhaps hundreds, of homes and businesses had been destroyed. The general public was not informed, because San Diego only saw their nation's turf as newsworthy.

Remember the story of the tornado that hit Eagle Pass, Texas and Piedras Negras, Coahuila in April 2007? The largest local newspaper covering the event was the *San Antonio Express-News*. They reported the casualties and losses from both sides of the border; American and Mexican losses were treated as equally significant.

As the Harris Fire marched towards Chula Vista in southern California, the *San Diego Union-Tribune* appended a map graphic illustrating the western, web-like spread of the flames for their readers. The red zone spread through the border town of Tecate and moved west for nine miles. Amazingly and inexplicably, the fire-according to the graphic-halted at the U.S.-Mexico line. Apparently, the editors thought that San Diego's residents were not concerned about the effects of the disaster to the south.

The reference to Hurricane Katrina offered an interesting comparison. With his northern neighbor in distress, Mexican President Vicente Fox pledged 200 tons of food, bottled water, and medical supplies, $1 million in aid, and a team of doctors and nurses less than two days after the hurricane hit. In the shadow of the Alamo, 184 Mexican soldiers spent three weeks distributing meals and sorted food pallets at San Antonio relief centers.

A month after Hurricane Katrina struck, an earthquake hit the Pakistani province of Kashmir. After that disaster, the United States conducted a full-scale military relief operation and gave $156 million to the Pakistani government. Donation cans proliferated at Wal-Marts throughout America. According to the State Department, the aid helped 370,000 Pakistanis survive. The Pentagon said the aid was an important gesture to our partner nation in the war on terror. "We are not only together to fight, but we're also here to serve humanity," said a Pakistani general. "I think it won a lot of the hearts and minds."

Two days after the Tabasco floods, the Cuban government announced that it was sending a fifty-four-person medical relief team to Tabasco. The same day, Ambassador Tony Garza, who is the husband of Latin America's richest woman, announced the American aid package. The Bush Administration—which spends $14 billion annually in an attempt to secure the border—had pledged $300,000 for emergency assistance.

⸺⟫·◦·⟪⸺

If California is indeed a harbinger for the future of America, legislation will not reform immigration as we know it, stabalize the cartel violence, or prevent Spanish from becoming the common language of the working class. As California resident Victor Davis Hanson observed, when other states in the Union find themselves puzzled by dilemmas of border security and immigration, they will attempt to do all the things Californians have done for three decades. They will pass laws making English the state language; they will restrict welfare benefits and educational services; they will call for aggressive targeting of employers and identity verification programs. They will build walls.

Just north of the shadow of those walls, I spent an afternoon roaming San Diego State University, a gorgeous urban campus less than ten miles from the Tijuana border. At the college, I met with Rick van Schoik, a tanned, athletic man of average height in his mid-to-late fifties. He wears a bushy mustache and maintains the friendly, determined demeanor of a former Navy SEAL, which he is. After graduating from the U.S. Naval Academy in 1972 and finishing SEAL training in Coronado, California, van Schoik completed a year-long combat tour in Vietnam, a few missions in Latin America, and a classified operation on the Korean Peninsula that he still can't talk about. After leaving the Navy, van Schoik earned a graduate degree in biology from San Diego State University, became a Buddhist, and completed post-graduate programs in philanthropy at Harvard and sustainable development at Tufts. Since 1998, van Schoik has been the managing director of the Southwest Center for Environmental Research and Policy, a consortium of five U.S. and five Mexican universities that advises both governments on environmental issues relevant to the border.

Rick van Schoik thinks that the program he and his colleagues have developed over two decades to manage bi-national environmental concerns could be a model across the spectrum of border issues. "You can't fence out pollution," says van Schoik. But the officer-turned-environmental manager has seen few leaders interested in his systemic prototypes. "They are always looking at the horizon to the next election," he says, expressing disappointment at politicians who pander to an electorate whose views on border issues are shaped and stoked by polemic talk-show hosts. "The Daniel Patrick Moynihans of government have been replaced by actors," he said, obliquely comparing the lineage of a creative intellectual to former and current California governors Ronald Reagan and Arnold Schwarzenegger.

The former Navy SEAL's interest in border issues made him a minority on the San Diego State campus, where boys sauntered in tank tops and flip-flops and girls strutted in miniskirts and short-shorts. The varying degrees of exposed flesh suggested an afternoon on the beach, not an educational institution. Along the rest of the border, I had visited with women named Veronica, Rosa, and Isabel. Here, it was Devon, Brianna, or Krystal. No other border city is as white.

Caucasians are the numerical majority in San Diego, and they are a wealthy one. As such, the campus genuflects before multiculturalism's altar-learning about the border issues tepidly and diplomatically-while forsaking the plunge into the real thing. I asked a group of four sorority sisters wearing turquoise Kappa Delta shirts if they had any thoughts on the border. "I've never been over to Mexico," volunteered one nineteen-year-old. The others nodded. One had grown up in another part of California. Another candidly said she didn't care what was happening on the border. That was their side, not ours.

After surveying seventeen students passing to and from class, I finally encountered one who had actually been to Mexico. Nick, twenty-four, is a senior in his sixth year on campus. He scoots around the SDSU quad on a golf cart and picks up trash. He also surfs. Occasionally, Nick attends a class.

"The border is all about T.J.," says Nick, referring to Tijuana. "It's a place to drink, meet girls, and buy cheap stuff. It's the best black market around." I didn't ask Nick about drugs, and he didn't tell. Other than T.J., there wasn't much more he knew. "I've never been to the real Mexico," Nick says. "I wouldn't know anything about it." Nick didn't have anything else to say. I slipped my notebook into my pocket and headed for the ocean.

———————◆◇◆———————

Border Field State Park sits on three square miles of protected California real estate tucked south of a score of horse farms. Rusted steel spires slice through the final white obelisk that marks the line between nations and towers against a background of salty, endless blue. Waves crash along an empty beach; surfers and sunbathers are banned from this part of the coastline. A "Danger/*Peligro*" sign warns that those who—like me—walk down to the ocean should not dive in, lest we risk being infected by industrial waste. A Border Patrol agent sits inside a truck parked on a hilltop, scanning the sea for any migrants willing to take the plunge.

I gazed upon the vastness of the open sea, inhaled the wet, heavy fragrance of flora and fauna, and reflected on my quest to understand this complex 1,952-mile terrain. During the early 1990s, before the fence was installed, migrants used to sprint north from the flat floodplain stretching into Tijuana. Back then they would mass in groups and run on highways, dodging *La Migra* and traffic until reaching a pickup point. Today, the beach was quiet.

Rafael Peralta had been one of those illegals. He was twelve when he broke the law and ran across the border near this stretch of sand. For six years he lived illegally in San Diego. Somehow, he obtained a green card for one reason: he wanted to join the U.S. Marine Corps.

In November 2004, Sgt. Rafael Peralta, USMC—who had become a dual U.S.-Mexican citizen—was a platoon scout with an infantry company in Iraq assaulting the city of Fallujah. Prior to departing for the attack, Peralta wrote to his younger brother Ricardo, telling him not to worry. "Be proud of me, bro," he said, "and be proud of being an American."

On November 15, as the fighting spread from house to house, Sergeant Peralta stood at the front of several Marines and threw open a door to a room occupied by insurgents. As he entered the room, Peralta was shot several times in the torso and face. After Peralta's fellow Marines had flooded in, an insurgent threw a hand grenade. Bleeding and mortally wounded, Sergeant Peralta grabbed the grenade and cradled it, absorbing the blast with his body and saving the lives of four other Marines. Sgt. Rafael Peralta has been nominated for the Medal of Honor.

As I stood at the end of the border, less than ten miles south of Sergeant Peralta's final resting place at Fort Rosecrans National Cemetery, I wondered if anti-immigration activists would attempt to block his reception of America's highest honor for valor because of his former immigration status. And if they would not, I wondered why they would prevent millions of other Mexican men and women—who could grow up to be heroes like Sergeant Peralta—from being offered a pathway to do so. I knew what their answers would be, I did not find them satisfactory.

But despite my pessimism, I was unwilling to throw in the towel. To give up hope entirely on a rational solution to stabilizing the U.S.-

Mexico and U.S.-Mexican borders would dishonor Sergeant Peralta's memory. Someday, I thought, perhaps Americans and Mexicans will freely traverse this vast river and land. Perhaps citizens from both nations will have access to honorable work and fair trade, united against economic challengers across the Pacific. Perhaps the people will not fear their differences, because the police on both sides will be trustworthy. Perhaps the border will finally make sense.

I closed my eyes and let the ocean breeze embrace me. Accompanied only by Sgt. Rafael Peralta's memory, I welled with emotion as I tried to imagine the impossible: the day when both sides of *la frontera* would finally be at peace. That moment felt very far away.

# EPILOGUE

In 2008, the U.S.-Mexico border remained one of the most violent regions in North America. Within three months, 800 drug-related killings had occurred in Mexico, half of which had taken place in border cities. Campaigns of bribery, intimidation, and assassination prevented law enforcement officers in cities like Tijuana and Juárez from curbing the violence. The 210 murders in Juárez prompted President Felipe Calderón to deploy 2,500 Mexican soldiers throughout the state of Chihuahua at the end of March. Their presence created a temporary respite in Juárez, but left other parts of Mexico in greater turmoil.

I went to Juárez in March 2008 to see what the city looked like during a military deployment. I walked over the Stanton Street Bridge on a Friday night, crossing the Northern Rio Grande into the Santa Fe District opposite from downtown El Paso. Soldiers patrolled the street with weapons at the ready in teams of four, wearing Nomex masks on their faces to conceal their identities from enemy surveillance. Two policemen pulled me aside and politely frisked me, even asking me to count my money after they had emptied my pockets as evidence of their honor. They did everything but ask me to fill out a comment card. Someone had told them to be on their best behavior.

That first night, local residents had ignored the military presence. "It's just between them and the *narcos*," said a taxi driver. "All the killing has nothing to do with us." More than forty checkpoints were placed around the city, as soldiers took over for police in screening traffic and maintaining security. This left policemen emasculated, threatened, and intimidated. Some informed on the drug cartels; others ratted out the military. Fights broke out between the military and various factions of the cartels. The *policia* were stuck in the middle, and often played both sides. I had seen this same human dynamic at work in Baghdad, Fallujah, and Ramadi.

Students of both military history and Latin American studies often loathe the characterization of the U.S.-Mexico border violence as a war. Fortunately, President Calderón, who has sent over 25,000 Mexican troops into combat in the past two years against *narcotraficantes*, has not quibbled over that distinction. In perhaps the most underappreciated act of political courage in the last century south of the Rio Grande, Calderón has faced down critics and criminals by treating the *narco* threat to law and order as a military crisis, not a civil dilemma. The outcome of this twenty-first-century hybrid war-not conquering territory, but stabilizing society-will play a significant part in determining the future of North America.

It's a war that the U.S. has a vested long-term interest in resolving-perhaps even more so than the counterinsurgency in Iraq. For this reason, the common belief that an increase to the U.S. military presence on the border would inevitably result in chaos troubles me. Political advocates of a military deployment often see only the American side and fail to recognize the true nature of the border: it's a zone, and both sides of the line matter. Pacifists refuse to acknowledge that anarchy and injustice is already the norm in some areas of *la frontera*: there are places where "militarizing the border" will make things better, not worse.

The 2006 National Guard deployment of Operation Jumpstart was structured so troops assist the Border Patrol in static functions, but do not perform their own missions. In security terms, Operation Jumpstart offers valuable but minimal support. If current trends and violence levels continue, a broader U.S. military presence on the border may be necessary. The remote, federally owned lands in Arizona and California merit consideration for active duty operations, as do Mexican cities and states where Calderón's government might need assistance, such as Juárez or Tamaulipas.

To even have a chance of success, any American military operation on the border must be conducted in full partnership with the Mexican government. Regrettably, anti-immigration political activists view a forceful, one-sided deployment as the permanent cure for the border's ills. As this theory goes, a fierce aura of thousands of American warriors would end the scourge of illegal immigration by intimidating the labor-seeking Latinos from crossing the river or the line. But by using a unilateral approach instead of a bilateral model, they are encouraging a flawed, destructive application of U.S. forces. This would not help either side.

The sort of inane partisanship that Army Lt. Gen. Russell Honoré eloquently referred to as "getting stuck on stupid" during his command of Hurricane Katrina recovery operations is often on display during public discussions about the proposed border fence. Advocates of the fortification claim that the infrastructure creates the proper psychological deterrent—an indispensable severance between us and them. Good fences make good neighbors, they say. Perhaps some fences do mend relationships by delineating property lines, but a barrier imposed upon Brownsville, Laredo, or Eagle Pass accomplishes little. On this part of the border, the Rio Grande is a clear marker.

Instead of a fence, it seems that the inhabitants of the lower Rio Grande would be better served if the federal government widened the river, removed the carrizo cane, maintained the flow rate from the Río Conchos (by negotiating with the Mexican government), and equipped Border Patrol agents with shallow water boats to guard the waterway. The river is already a natural barrier and could be used as a road by boats, which would provide a more visible and mobile deterrent to illegal crossings. Chief Carlos Carrillo, who commands the Laredo Sector, is one of several agents who support this approach.

The Department of Homeland Security is listening to some border communities in an effort to create more productive solutions. In May 2008, Brownsville's Hidalgo County unveiled a cooperative agreement between the federal and local governments to shore up twenty-two miles of a worn Rio Grande levee. The flood wall is planned to double as a border fence, and will satisfy the requirements of the 2006 Secure Fence Act. Brownsville's college campus will be undisturbed.

The same cannot be said, however, for the Eagle Pass Golf Course. In January 2008, the Department of Homeland Security, via a lawsuit delivered to the Justice Department, commandeered 233 acres of land from the Eagle Pass City Council. The stated reason for the imminent domain seizure was to provide federal authorities with temporary access to survey the land. Mayor Chad Foster attacked the "sneaky, underhanded measures" of the Bush administration, but did not threaten a countersuit. Instead, Foster sought a meeting weeks later with Homeland Security Secretary Michael Chertoff. Negotiations were ongoing as this book went to print.

Fences are reasonable barriers west of El Paso, but it's doubtful that a Great Wall of America would end illegal migration into the United States. Divots from homemade rebar ladders dot the two fences in San Diego; the barrier slowed—but did not eliminate— criminal crossings after its 1994 installation. In 2007, the only sector on the border to show an increase in both apprehensions and violence against Border Patrol agents was the San Diego Sector, suggesting that the fence from Operation Gatekeeper has not provided an enduring fix. New obstacles may offer some deterrence, but they will have no long term effect.

I have to admit, the idea of sending the U.S. military to stabilize either side of the border bothers me. Young Americans brimming with duty, honor, and Red Bull are not always the ideal resolution to protracted peacekeeping enigmas. In the state of Chihuahua, the initial support for the military presence among civilians has given way to collective frustration. "These guys don't care about anything," said a Juárez resident in May 2008, referring to Mexican soldiers. "They came into my house without a warrant, searched through everything, and told me to sit on a couch."

As in Iraq, grunts who would carry out this theoretical mission would encounter one Catch-22 after another. They would patrol with Mexican soldiers they might not trust, deal with corrupt politicians whom they would be powerless to remove from office, adapt to streetwalkers who smile one day and betray them the next, and do it all in the relentless, perfectionist glare of a media spotlight. It would be challenging, to say the least.

Nevertheless, when American and Mexican citizens in specific locales clamor repeatedly for reinforcements to police and civilian law enforcement, the U.S. Army and/or Marine Corps should rightfully be considered a viable alternative. If mayors are regularly bribed, and police chiefs are routinely killed on either side of the border, then the American and Mexican governments have a moral obligation to respond to their people. When 86 percent of Mexicans say they need soldiers walking the streets to protect them from organized crime, then military forces are, by default, the last, best hope.

The negative perception of employing the U.S. military as a tool along the border has evolved because of the 1997 death of Esequiel Hernandez in Redford, which was a tragedy borne from poor training, bad intelligence, and regrettable decisions. Ten years later, a new generation of soldiers toughened and tenderized from counterinsurgencies are more likely to know that mission accomplishment may depend on preventing—not conducting—wonton destruction.

In a recent *Marine Corps Gazette* article, an officer described how exercising restraint during a tense 2004 patrol in Ramadi may have saved the lives of both innocent civilians and his own Marines. The men were walking in formation down an alley and encountered a corridor that appeared eerily empty. All of the shops were closed, and there were no women or children. A pair of rocks hit two Marines, thrown from an unknown direction by unseen assailants. "There was a palpable tension in the air," writes the officer, who was the senior Marine on the patrol.

Suddenly, a group of young Iraqi men formed a crowd. They were slowly walking down the other end of the alley, but they were not carrying weapons or threatening the Americans. Regardless, the Marines sensed something was about to happen. "My heart rate was racing and adrenaline was pumping through my veins," he writes. "My thumb rested on the safety of my rifle. I really thought an attack was imminent."

The expected attack never came. The Marines patrolled another thirty minutes, and no shots were fired. The crowd of young men dispersed. Women and children returned to the streets and the shops resumed their activity. The officer summarized his conclusion:

> Marines and soldiers are required to make tough decisions every day in combat on the use of force....Counterinsurgency operations are so complex, and the stakes are so high that we owe it to small unit leaders to educate them in the philosophy of the use of force, and how restraint can and should be exercised for moral and pragmatic reasons.

The author of the article, "Restraint in War," was Lt. Col. Lance McDaniel, who, as a captain, had been in charge of the ill-fated JTF mission in Redford, Texas. After his 2004 tour in Ramadi, McDaniel was one of several officers who contributed to the new Army and Marine Corps Counterinsurgency Manual. In January 2008, Lieutenant Colonel McDaniel—now commanding an artillery battalion— began his third tour in Iraq.

━━━━━━━━━➣-◉-⬅━━━━━

Security issues notwithstanding, since the poor will inevitably seek opportunity in *El Norte*, opponents of immigration enforcement often ask why America prolongs the fiction of a border in the first place. After all, the European Union maintains a nation-state consortium whose borders appear no more regulated than those of the forty-eight continental U.S. states. Many ask why America could not adapt a similar system with Mexico.

The borderless European Union is not as carefree as it appears. A treaty called the Schengen Agreement governs the crossings between EU nations. Twenty-four European nations have full participation in the 1990 accord; five others maintain varying degrees of compliance. In exchange for the removal of border controls, the Schengen regulations mandate the support of law enforcement and security organizations in other countries. This happens by permitting intelligence agencies to conduct investigations, granting hot pursuit to the police of neighboring nations, and sharing information on potential threats. If a criminal sprints from France into Germany—seeking refuge on the other side of the border while the local French police are giving chase—the cops will switch to the German radio frequencies, notify the German authorities of the situation, and chase the villain into Germany.

An ideal future scenario for the U.S.-Mexico border would include a similar accord. But given the disparity between the U.S. and Mexican legal codes, the prospect for such a treaty is dubious at best. The Schengen Agreement happened because the twenty-plus European countries could reform their own similar legal codes and structures into a common approach. Decades from now—assuming a twenty-first-century security system became the standard in both nations—a Schengen-like open border would be the most stable in North America.

Although ideal, the right for police and *policia* to pursue suspects into each other's country is still a long way off. The U.S. and Mexico do not even have the same laws about who can legally cross their borders, and an open border can only be developed within a framework that enables countries to support one another's laws. This may work right now for the U.S. and Canada, but the U.S. and Mexico have a way to go. The Mexican government's decision to grant their citizens free passage to the north—in open defiance to U.S. laws—hinders prospects for a stable future, as does the American refusal to renegotiate the status of the All-American Canal with Mexicali.

These illustrations only scratch the surface. Employee verification programs will inevitably affect both nations; the biometric scanners and fingerprint cards may reduce illegal immigration, but could also drive companies to move their factories and farms to Mexico. Drugs are tacitly legal south of the border and firearms are openly sanctioned to the north; the pair of smuggling industries feed off of each other. The debate continues over birthright citizenship. And although the current model of rewarding illegality with labor may provide short-term rewards, shoving millions into the shadows is ultimately destructive for both nations.

"I can't say over the miles that I had learned what I had wanted to know, because I hadn't known what I had wanted to know," wrote William Least Heat-Moon in *Blue Highways*, a story of his 1978 road trip through America. "But I did learn what I didn't know I wanted to know." As I walked back across the Stanton Street Bridge on that Friday night in March, I sensed that these Mexican soldiers who frisked me—along with their American counterparts—would eventually join together and play a much larger role in securing both sides of the border than inhabitants of either nation could currently appreciate.

In May 2008, Mexico's Chief of Police was assassinated and the annual Mexican death toll passed 1,300. As the growing anarchy haunted and terrorized residents, the anti-military graffiti plastered on Juárez culverts that lined the border had never seemed so ironic. And both Washington D.C. and Mexico City had never seemed so remote.

# NOTES

## Prologue

The exact length of the border comes from a November 2007 phone conversation with the U.S.-Mexico International Boundary and Water Commission's public affairs office. Border and immigration statistics in the prologue were published on *The New York Times* website as part of a series on global migration. The compilations cite United Nations reports.

Statistics from and statements about the U.S. Border Patrol, Department of Homeland Security, and Immigrations and Customs Enforcement come from their official websites as well as interviews with agents. Also useful throughout the book as reference for border law enforcement were William Langewiesche's *Cutting for Sign*, Ken Ellingwood's *Hard Line*, Clifford Perkins's *Border Patrol*, John Myers Myers's *The Border Wardens* and Lee Morgan's *The Reaper's Line*.

Articles from the Cato Institute and *The New York Times*, as well as *NAFTA Revisited*, provided the statistics about NAFTA, the *maquiladoras*, Mexican job loss to China, and narcotics use. The gross domestic product of northeastern Mexico was cited by José Antonio Fernández of the Free Trade Alliance San Antonio. The comparisons between northeastern Mexico–Texas and the rest of the border, as well as the absence of a Mexican-American culture clash in south Texas, jumped out during numerous 2007 interviews and observations.

## 1

Many descriptions of history along the border were initially observed on a tourist landmark and then researched on the Web. In Brownsville, the Texas State Historical Association's "Handbook of Texas Online" confirms various Civil War anecdotes. The Brownsville Affair story comes from John Weaver's 1970 book, *The Brownsville Raid*, whose publication drove the Nixon Administration to grant justice to Dorsie Willis.

Clifford Alan Perkins's 1978 memoir *Border Patrol* illuminates the organization's origins. Perkins was one of the three men charged by the U.S. Department of Labor with developing the original "strategic plan" for securing the border. His team selected the sector construct on the southwestern border, and it has changed little since its 1924 inception. Mae Ngai's excellent spring 2003 *Law and History Review* article, "The Strange Career of the Illegal Alien," illustrates the Wilsonian background of passports, immigration, and border controls.

I rode along with and interviewed Agent Walter King in May 2007. The post–Operation Rio Grande statistics were reported in the *Brownsville Herald*. The 2006 Gallup Poll was taken from April 7–9, 2006, and reported—strongly—by FOX News. The Gateway International Bridge statistics were published by the Texas Department of Transportation. My interview with José and encounter with the deported painter occurred in September 2007.

### 2

The population notes and projections come from the Texas State Data Center. The August 24, 2007 online exchange was publicly available on a City-data.com electronic bulletin board.

In addition to online material from the Texas State Historical Association, the primary sources were Paul Horgan's *Great River* and T. R. Fehrenbach's *Lone Star: A History of Texas and the Texans* and *Fire and Blood: A History of Mexico*. Published in 1954, Horgan's four-volume Pulitzer Prize–winning opus chronicles the story of the Rio Grande through the eyes of Native Americans, Spaniards, Mexicans, Texans, and Americans. For any interested scholar of Texas and Mexico, Fehrenbach's work is a most effective starting point.

In *Lone Star*, Fehrenbach details the influence of Scots-Irish culture after their Appalachian migration in the early years. In his 2004 sociological history *Born Fighting: How the Scots-Irish Shaped America*, James Webb—now a U.S. senator from Virginia—chronicles the Scots-Irish migratory influence on the continent. Although Webb does not discuss Texas statehood explicitly in *Born Fighting*, his characterizations of the settlers of the American south mirror Fehrenbach's comments on early Texans. The migrations were one and the same.

This is significant on the border because Texan culture appears to blend Scots-Irish and Mexican-Spanish tradition. The bombastic, fiery independence of Texans seems to be rooted in Hadrian's Wall and Bannockburn, but the quiet charm, good-ol'-boy courtliness, and social caste system originate from within the Catholic customs and rituals of Castilian Spain.

The footnote on the Mexican-American War as being one of five congressionally declared wars that sent troops to foreign soil has been circulated on military websites, but is primarily my own conclusion after query and research. A strong case, however, could be made for the many declared Indian Wars as Congress sending U.S. troops onto "foreign land."

My anecdotes about Isaac Guerra's personal magnetism came from firsthand observations in May and August 2007. I also interviewed Isaac, Don Medina, and Eric Ellman in May 2007.

### 3

Tom Lewis's *Divided Highways* provides the background on the Interstate Highway System, as does Dan McNichol's *The Roads that Built America*. Laredo's beginnings are chronicled in *Great River*, Leon Metz's *Border*, and by the Texas State Historical Association. As with McAllen, the population statistics were reported by the Texas State Data Center.

All freight-related interviews—Veronica Reyes, George Gonzalez, and the Coyote Creek trucker—took place in August 2007. Three visits to Laredo and a read through the October 2007 issue of *Overdrive* broadened my view of the trucking industry, as did Kim Reierson's photos in the November 2007 *National Geographic*.

I interviewed Chief Carlos Carrillo in May 2007. I also received a copy of his letter to the agents in the Laredo Sector after his August 2007 comments in the *Laredo Morning Times*. The cost estimates for the carrizo cane removal were reported in a four-part series on border security and illegal immigration by Michael Riley of the *Denver Post*.

Articles in the *San Antonio Express-News* informed my description of the drug plazas, as did the work of Sam Logan, a trilingual journalist (English, Spanish, Portuguese) based in Rio de Janeiro. I also used an October 2007 report on Mexican drug cartels by Strategic Forecasting Inc. (Stratfor.com).

Information on the Merida Initiative came from the *San Antonio Express-News*, *The Economist*, the U.S. State Department, a report to the Senate Foreign Relations Committee, and interviews with U.S. government sources.

## 4

Mayor Chad Foster, whom I interviewed twice in May and August 2007, provided me with a timeline of Eagle Pass history prepared by Al Kinsall of the Eagle Pass Public Library. I checked the timeline's facts against the Texas State Historical Association's "Handbook of Texas Online."

The nacho story is oral tradition in Eagle Pass, but it has been verified by several reporters. Adriana Orr's article in the *Oxford English Dictionary News* provides a thorough account.

I interviewed Agent Randy Clark in May 2007. I would later learn that Michael Riley of the *Denver Post* interviewed Clark two months before I did on the same issues of catch-and-release. Unsurprisingly, Agent Clark told me many of the same things that Mr. Riley also reported.

All information about Bo Pilgrim was available through links to the Pilgrim's Pride Chicken company website. The statement about immigration law enforcement consequences was made in a November 13, 2007 press release covering their Financial Report for the fourth quarter, 2007. Joel Garibay-Urbina's story was reported by the Associated Press in July 2007.

The coming of Corona to the border and the story of Ambassador Tony Garza and his bride were reported by *Southwest Texas Live*, the *San Antonio Express-News*, the *Washington Post*, and *Texas Monthly*.

## 5

The definitive source on the Pecos is *Judge Roy Bean Country* by longtime Langtry resident Jack Skiles. Also helpful were Douglas Lee Braudaway's *Railroads of West Texas*, Keith Bowden's *The Tecate Journals*, William Smythe's *History of San Diego*, Anne Seagreaves's *Women Who Charmed the West*, and Cormac McCarthy's *No Country for Old Men*.

I interviewed Robbie Dudley at the Judge Roy Bean Visitor's Center in May 2007 and Pete Billings a few months later. The Texas State Historical Association, *Houston Chronicle*, and *Texas Monthly* reported stories about the Big Bend area. The castration of Mayor Clay Henry stirred the interest of writers from the *San Antonio Express-News*, *Los Angeles Times*, and *The New York Times*.

The 2006 testimony of Sheriffs Sigifriedo Gonzalez, A. D'Wayne Jernigan, and Arvin West is accessible online through the U.S. House and Senate Web sites. The January 2006 IED discovery in Laredo was reported in a press release issued by the U.S. Immigration and Customs Enforcement.

In addition to *Great River,* numerous studies on the influence of the Río Conchos on the Rio Grande are available, including Mary Kelly's 2001 report for the Texas Center for Policy Studies. *The New York Times* reported on the Rio Grande Valley water shortage, as did *SourceMex Economic News* and other Texas newspapers.

Beyond the obvious political explanation, I was unable to understand why the Rio Grande and Río Conchos are not referred to as a single river. In hydrological terms, the stream that flows south from Colorado to Presidio—which I renamed the Northern Rio Grande in this narrative—clearly has a lesser effect on the body of water that empties into the Gulf of Mexico. The nomenclature should be corrected, if for no other reason than so Americans can understand the source of their national boundaries. We should not be confused about where the water that separates the U.S. and Mexico flows from, and the current name of the river is, frankly, neither accurate nor useful.

The material on Pablo Acosta and Mimi Webb-Miller comes from William Langewiesche's *Cutting for Sign,* Terrence Poppa's *Drug Lord,* and "A Rio Runs Through It," a five-part series by *San Antonio Express-News* travel writer Rod Davis.

## 6

The list of all U.S. ports of entry and their definitions, classes, and designations can be found in Title 8 of the U.S. Code of Federal Regulations.

The primary sources for the background on JTF-6 and the account of Esequiel Hernandez, Jr.'s death were Maj. Gen. John Conye's April 1998 investigation for the First Marine Expeditionary Force and Congressman Lamar Smith's November 1998 report to the House Judiciary Committee. In Major General Coyne's 132-page report, every principal character mentioned in this story added statements to the investigation. A total of sixty people were interviewed, along with 640 documents that totaled 13,000 pages of evaluated material.

Congressman Smith (R-TX), then Chairman of the House Judiciary Committee, added additional information. In part, the Smith report was an analysis of Coyne's investigation. Smith credits the Marine Corps with being the only organization that demanded any kind of accountability from its officers—the entire chain of command received letters of reprimand—and vilifies the Border Patrol for its failure to conduct any kind of detailed internal review on their own mistakes for the public. Smith points out that if agents had responded in fifteen minutes, as they had advertised, the shooting might not have happened.

Both investigations question whether or not Hernandez's rifle was aimed at Lance Corporal Blood when Banuelos fired. Since the bullet hit Hernandez on his right side, the angle doesn't match up with the statements. All other Marines say they were looking away when Hernandez was killed. Only Banuelos knows what he saw.

Supplementary sources included articles by Robert Draper in *Texas Monthly*; Monte Paulsen in the *San Antonio Current*; an August 13, 1997, transcript of a "PBS News Hour with Jim Lehrer" report; and stories in *The New York Times* and *Los Angeles Times.* Timothy Dunn's *The Militarization of the U.S.-Mexico Border: 1978–1992* provides statistics on missions from the early JTF-6 years.

Kieran Fitzgerald's *The Ballad of Esequiel Hernández,* a documentary that premiered at the 2007 TriBeCa Film Festival was also helpful. Fitzgerald's work features updated interviews with all the Marines involved except for Banuelos, as well as investigators, supervisors, and the Hernandez family. Subtly, but not offensively, political, Fitzgerald grants all sides a chance to tell the story in their own words. It's a compelling, insightful film. As of January 2008, it has not been publicly distributed. (For more, see: *www.heyokapictures.com.*)

The Marfa Sector of the U.S. Border Patrol recorded the radio transmissions made over the Border Patrol frequency leading up to the shooting. Those were then reported as direct quotes in Major General Coyne's investigation. I reflected them as they were recorded by the Border Patrol and published in subsequent appendices.

## 7

As mentioned in the narrative, U.S. District Attorney Johnny Sutton has made the official transcripts of the *United States vs. Ignacio "Nacho" Ramos and Jose Alonzo Compean* trial available on his official Web site. I used the court transcripts, Loya's letters, and numerous articles for my research.

There were only three eyewitnesses to the shooting: Osvaldo Aldrete-Davila and the two agents. To me, each individual's relationship with and sympathy for each of those parties will affect who they believe and why. A person's opinion will also be driven by what they think should or should not justify the use of deadly force on the U.S.-Mexico border.

My education on the Tigua people, along with the remaining anecdotal events in the chapter, came from firsthand experiences, interviews, and online references.

## 8

Much of my knowledge of the raid into Columbus came from a visit to the museum at Pancho Villa State Park. Supplementary sources include *Huachuca Illustrated* and Max Boot's *The Savage Wars of Peace*, an account of low-intensity conflicts involving Americans that contains a chapter on Pershing's unsuccessful expedition into Mexico.

Be warned: Lee Morgan's perspective of Arizona-Mexico law enforcement, *The Reaper's Line*, is caustic, arrogant, and profane. It is also the most authentic account of a U.S. federal agent undercover with drug cartels on the market. In January 2008, I asked Morgan if he had received any lawsuits for defamation of character from the current or former leaders of Douglas. "They know everything I said is true," he said. "They also know I've got more ammo that I held back."

I cross-referenced Morgan's account of the Borane brothers with other Arizona residents, including Border Patrol agents from the Tucson Sector. Although the Boranes have not been proven guilty in court, the jury of public opinion says otherwise. Other sources on Douglas include *Cutting for Sign*, *Hard Line*, and a *New York Times* article about Borane's indictment.

Statistics for the 2008 Pentagon budget—annual appropriations, plus supplemental costs for the wars in Afghanistan and Iraq—came from *Congress Daily*, October 1, 2007. The rankings of the world's nations in GDP for comparison were from the International Monetary Fund's "World Economic Outlook Database." I interviewed Dan and Connie Finck at the Copper Queen Hotel, and Agent Zulma Gomez at the Nogales station, in May 2007. My night in Nogales, Sonora, was recorded in September 2007.

## 9

The statistics on Mexican army incursions come from a 2005 annual report of the same name that was generated by the El Paso Intelligence Center.

The quotes on hybrid wars come from the articles referenced. Since 2005, a significant body of academic literature has primarily discussed the theory of hybrid wars to twenty-first-century conflicts in Iraq and Afghanistan, as well as the Global War on Terror in general. Mattis and Hoffman distinguish a hybrid war from the "Three Block War" of USMC Gen. Charles C. Krulak primarily through a disparate, sustained use of information operations. They might not agree with my classification of the chaos along the U.S.-Mexico border as a "hybrid war." Based on their article, I believe my use of the term they coined is accurate.

D. Rick van Schoik, the Managing Director of the Southwest Consortium for Environmental Research and Policy, provided me with a bound compilation of documents involving border ecology. Monograph Series 13, "Lining the All-American Canal," was helpful for exploring the Colorado River/Mexicali Valley history and issues. I also recommend *Aquafornia.com* as a useful Internet resource on California's water challenges.

My comments on California were informed by the longevity of the immigration debate in the Golden State, as well as my own observations and interviews. Victor Davis Hanson's *Mexifornia* was an insightful read from the right wing of the political spectrum, as was Peter Laufer's *Wetback Nation* from the left.

Sgt. Rafael Peralta's heroism, and immigration status, was the subject of the 2007 History Channel documentary *Act of Honor*. The show was broadcast in both English and Spanish.

# BIBLIOGRAPHY

## Articles/Documents

Althaus, Dudley. "Calderón Urges Continued Donations." *Houston Chronicle*, November 10, 2007.

Alvarez, Capt. Steve. "Mexican Forces Wind Up Humanitarian Mission." *American Forces Press Service*, September 26, 2005.

Arrillaga, Pauline. "What really happened in border shooting and agents' convictions?" *Seattle Times*, February 17, 2007.

Aued, Blake. "Unions Work to Lure Hispanics." *OnlineAthens*, September 2, 2007.

Author unavailable. "Four States Go Dry Out of Six Voting: Colorado, Oregon, Washington, and Arizona Decide to Close their Saloons." *The New York Times*, November 5, 1914.

Author unavailable. "Largest Employers in Southern Arizona." *Tucson Relocation Guide*, 2007.

Author unavailable. "Plan Mexico." *The Economist*, August 16, 2007.

Author unavailable. "Smuggler shot by Border Patrol agents denied bond." *Associated Press*, December 13, 2007.

Author unavailable. "The Tiguas: People of the Sun." Ysleta Del Sur Pueblo; Tigua Indian Cultural Center, 2007.

Author unavailable. "World Economic Outlook Database." *International Monetary Fund*, October 2007.

Ballí, Cecilia. "Continental Rift." *Texas Monthly*, October 2004.

Barker, Allison. "El Paso Index." *El Paso Magazine*, July 2007.

Bell, Alistair. "U.S. Envoy Riles Mexico." *Reuters*, August 18, 2005.

Brezosky, Lynn. "Funding is set on levee-fence for Hidalgo," *San Antonio Express-News*, May 6, 2008.

Caldwell, Alicia. "Mexico Army Likely Part of Border Incident." *Associated Press*, January 27, 2006.

Carpenter, Ted Galen. "Mexico is Becoming the Next Colombia." *Cato Institute: Foreign Policy Briefing No. 87*, November 15, 2005.

Carroll, Susan, and Billy House. "Border Patrol's 'Progress' Unclear." *The Arizona Republic*, September 23, 2005.

Coloff, Pamela. "Badges of Dishonor." *Texas Monthly*, September 2007.

Corchado, Alfredo. "Drug Gangs Extort Money from Nuevo Laredo Business Owners." *The Dallas Morning News*, October 17, 2007.

Coyne, Maj. Gen. John T. "Investigation to Inquire into the . . . (JTF-6) Shooting Incident That Occurred on 20 May 1997 Near the Border Between the U.S. and Mexico." U.S. Marine Corps, Camp Pendleton, California, April 7, 1998.

Cuomo, Capt. Scott A., and Capt. Brian J. Donlon. "Training a 'Hybrid' Warrior." *Marine Corps Gazette*, February 2008.

Davis, Rod. "A Rio Runs Through It." *San Antonio Express-News*, June 3–July 8, 2002.

Dibble, Sandra. "Calderón Stands Firm against Lining the All-American Canal." *San Diego Union-Tribune*, May 5, 2007.

Dillin, John. "How Eisenhower Solved Illegal Border Crossings from Mexico." *Christian Science Monitor*, July 6, 2006.

Dillon, Sam. "Small-Town Arizona Judge Amasses Fortune, and Indictment." *The New York Times*, January 30, 2000.

Draper, Robert. "Quitter's Paradise." *Texas Monthly*, September 1996.

———. "Soldiers of Misfortune." *Texas Monthly*, August 1997.

Espinoza, J. Noel. "Border Patrol Touts Improved Quality of Life Operation Rio Grande: Fewer Illegal Immigrants Apprehended." *The Brownsville Herald*, March 17, 2002.

Fernández-Carbajal, José Antonio. "Shaping our Region from a Business Perspective." *Free Trade Alliance San Antonio*, October 18, 2007.

Finley, James P. "Villa's Raid on Columbus, New Mexico." *Huachuca Illustrated*, Vol. 1, 1993.

Foreno, Juan. "As China Gallops, Mexico Sees Factory Jobs Slip Away." *The New York Times*, September 3, 2003.

Gambrell, Jon. "Illegal Immigrant Rents American Dream for $800." *Associated Press*, July 3, 2007.

Gonzalez, Sigifriedo, Jr. "Outgunned and Outmanned: Local Law Enforcement Confronts Violence along the U.S.-Mexico Border." *U. S. House Judiciary Committee*, written testimony, March 2, 2006.

Heyman, Josiah McC. "The Mexico-United States Border in Anthropology: A Critique and Reformulation." *Journal of Political Ecology*, Volume I, 1994.

Jernigan, A. D'Wayne. "Federal Strategies to End Border Violence." *U. S. Senate Judiciary Committee*, written testimony, March 1, 2006.

Katz, Jesse. "Marines Faulted in Own Report on Teen's Death." *Los Angeles Times*, September 20, 1998.

Knowles, Gordon James, Ph.D. "Organized Crime and Narco-Terrorism in Northern Mexico." *Military Review*, January–February 2008.

Lehrer, Jim. "Casualties of the Drug War." "PBS News Hour with Jim Lehrer," August 13, 1997.

Lobeck, Joyce. "Work Under Way on All-American Canal." *Yuma Sun*, July 1, 2007.

Logan, Samuel. "Mexico's Uppermost Threat Is Organized Crime." *International Relations and Security Network*, April 26, 2006.

———. "The Scourge of Ice in Michoacan." *International Relations and Security Network*, July 12, 2006.

Loya, Joe. "The Ramos-Compean Affair: What Really Happened." http://ramos-compean.blogspot.com/2006/12/ramos-compean-affair-what-really.html, December 5, 2006.

———. "Open Letter to Congressman Walter Jones (R-N.C.)." December 25, 2006.

Lugar, Sen. Richard G. "The Merida Initiative: Guns, Drugs, and Friends—U.S. Senate Foreign Relations Committee." *U. S. Government Printing Office*, December 21, 2007.

MacCormack, John. "Corona to be Toyota of Border." *San Antonio Express-News*, December 12, 2006.

———. "Top Bid for Lajitas Resort Short of Auction's Goal." *San Antonio Express-News*, November 2, 2007.

Marizco, Michael. "Border Patrol Agent's Murder Trial Sure to be Interesting." *The Border Report*, April 30, 2007.

Mattis, Gen. James N., and Lt. Col. Frank Hoffman. "Future Warfare: The Rise of Hybrid Wars." *U.S. Naval Institute Proceedings*, November 2005.

Mattson, Sean. "American Intervention Suddenly Looking Better." *San Antonio Express-News*, August 19, 2007.

McDaniel, Lt. Col. Lance A. "Restraint in War." *Marine Corps Gazette* (Web content), November 2006.

McKinley Jr., James C. "Mexico Hits Drug Gangs With Full Fury of War," January 22, 2008.

———. "Mexico Drug War Causes Wild West Bloodbath," April 16, 2008.

Montgomery, Dave. "U.S. forces Texas city to give up land for border fence." *McClatchy Newspapers*, January 16, 2008.

———. "Border fence faces obstacles." *McClatchy Newspapers*, April 27, 2008.

Moreno, Sylvia. "Along Part of the Border, A Zero-Tolerance Zone." *Washington Post*, June 18, 2006.

Moore, Evan "Trial Nears in Castration of Town's Beer-Swilling Goat Mayor." *Houston Chronicle*, August 17, 2002.

Navarro, Carlos. "Controversies Arise at Border Governor's Conference" *SourceMex Economic News*, August 30, 2007.

Neuman, Johanna. "Border agents' case gets holiday push." *Los Angeles Times*, November 24, 2007.

Ngai, Mae M. "The Strange Career of the Illegal Alien: Immigration Restriction and Deportation Policy in the United States, 1921–1965." *Law and History Review*, Vol. 21, Issue 1, Spring 2003.

Nuñez, Claudia. "People Smuggling Has the Scent of a Woman." *La Opinión*, November 9, 2007.

Official trial transcript. *United States vs. Ignacio Ramos and Jose Alonzo Compean*, U.S. Department of Justice.

Olsson, Karen. "Keep Out!" *Texas Monthly*, November 2007.

Orr, Adriana P. "Nachos, Anyone?" *OED News*, July 1999.

Osbourne, James. "Erotic Ball fans outrage in downtown McAllen." *The Monitor*. October 26, 2007.

Padgett, Tim. "It Starts in Mexico: Rethinking Immigration Reform." *America—The National Catholic Weekly*, October 15, 2007.

Paulsen, Monte. "Drug War Masquerade." *San Antonio Current*, September 10, 1998.

Powers, Ashley. "They've Got Their Goat . . . for Mayor." *Los Angeles Times*, December 9, 2005.

Preston, Julia. "7-Year Immigration Rate is Highest in U.S. History." *The New York Times*, November 29, 2007.

Reierson, Kim. "Photo Journal: On the Road Again." *National Geographic,* November 2007.

Reuters. "Bush Seeks Funds to Help Mexico Fight Drugs." *The New York Times,* October 22, 2007.

Riley, Michael. "Fortress America." *Denver Post,* March 4, 2007.

———. "Building a Border." *Denver Post,* March 5, 2007.

———. "Criminal Crossing." *Denver Post,* March 6, 2007.

———. "Moving Targets." *Denver Post,* March 7, 2007.

Roebuck, Jeremy. "Weslaco Scientist Offers Insects as Solution to Weed's Growth." *The Monitor,* July 14, 2007.

Rodriguez, César. "BP Eyes Terrorism, Area Chief Declares." *Laredo Morning Times,* August 16, 2007.

Root, Jay, and Tom Pennington. "The Dividing Line: A 2,000 Mile Journey Along Our Troubled Border." *Fort Worth Star-Telegram,* April 19–May 10, 2007.

Rowley, Heidi. "Border Sheriffs Give an Earful, Plea to Feds." *Tucson Citizen,* January 22, 2007.

San Diego County Water Authority. "Canal Lining Projects Fact Sheet," August 2007.

Sato, Kanji. "Formation of La Raza and the Anti-Chinese Movement in Mexico." *Transforming Anthropology,* October 2006, Vol. 14, Issue 2.

Schiller, Dane. "'El Chapo' is Mexico's Most Wanted Man." *San Antonio Express-News,* June 19, 2005.

Smith, Congressman Lamar. "Oversight Investigation of the Death of Esequiel Hernandez, Jr." *U. S. Government Printing Office,* November 1998.

Sneider, Daniel. "U.S. Isn't Only One Losing Jobs to Other Nations." *San Jose Mercury News,* August 16, 2003.

Sontag, Bill. "Giant Brewery Headed to Piedras Negras Region." *Southwest Texas Live,* January 28, 2007.

———. "Border Patrol Proposes POE Fence." *Southwest Texas Live,* June 14, 2007.

Stratfor. "Mexican Drug Cartels: The Evolution of Violence." *Strategic Forecasting, Inc.,* October 15, 2007.

Sullivan, Kevin. "Bilaterally in Love." *Washington Post,* February 7, 2005.

Susman, Tina. "Attack Really Got Town's Goat." *Newsday,* January 1, 2003.

Sutton, Johnny. "Myth vs. Reality: The Facts of Why the Government Prosecuted Agents Compean and Ramos." *U.S. Department of Justice,* January 17, 2007.

Taylor, F. J. "The People that Nobody Wants: West Coast Japanese." *Saturday Evening Post,* May 9, 1942.

Taylor, Guy. "Merida Initiative Would Provide Counter-Drug Aid to Mexico, but Congress Remains Skeptical." *World Politics Review,* December 13, 2007.

Teixeira, Ruy. "What the Public Really Wants on Globalization and Trade." *Center for American Progress,* January 18, 2007.

Thomas, Cathy Booth, and Tim Padgett. "Two Countries, One City." *Time,* June 11, 2001.

Thompson, Marc. "Oñate in Context." *CARTA Quarterly Journal,* January–March 2007.

U.S. Department of Homeland Security. "Mexican Government Incidents: 2005 Fiscal Year Report." *Border Patrol Field Intelligence Center,* September 30, 2005.

U.S. Immigration and Customs Enforcement press release. "ICE-Led Task Force Seizes Improvised Explosive Devices, Large Caches of Firearms, Silencers, in South Texas." *U. S. Federal News Service*, February 3, 2006.

U.S. State Department press release. "The Merida Initiative: United States—Mexico—Central America Security Cooperation." *U. S. Federal News Service*, October 22, 2007.

Verdugo, Eduardo. "Mexicans Missing After Flood, Landslide." Associated Press, November 6, 2007.

Verhovek, Sam Howe. "No Charges against Marine in Border Killing." *The New York Times*, August 15, 2007.

Weiss, Stanley A. "The United States Has to Move Against the Drug Trade in Mexico." *International Herald-Tribune*, July 1, 1995.

West, Arvin. "Armed and Dangerous: Confronting the Problem of Border Incursions." United States House of Representatives, written testimony, February 7, 2006.

White, Owen P. "Border Yearns to Lead its Own Life." *The New York Times Sunday Magazine*, March 21, 1926.

Wiegand, Daniel, and Leonel Sanchez. "The Harris Fire" (graphic). *San Diego Union-Tribune*, October 24, 2007.

Wilson, George C. "Just Your Money." *Congress Daily*, October 1, 2007.

Winograd, Ben. "Follow the Stat." *American Journalism Review*, February/March 2005.

Yardley, Jim. "Water Rights War Rages on Faltering Rio Grande." *The New York Times*, April 19, 2002.

———. "Because of 9/11, a Uniting River Now Divides." *The New York Times*, August 1, 2002.

———. "No One Shot the Sheriff, but Someone Cut the Mayor, a Goat. Got It?" *The New York Times*, August 5, 2002.

Zielinski, Graham. "Chili Cook-Off at Times Wild, Always Revered." *San Antonio Express- News*, November 3, 2007.

## Books

Annerino, John. *Dead in Their Tracks: Crossing America's Desert Borderlands.* New York: Four Walls Eight Windows, 1999.

Boot, Max. *The Savage Wars of Peace: Small Wars and the Rise of American Power.* New York: Basic Books, 2002.

Bowden, Keith. *The Tecate Journals: Seventy Days on the Rio Grande.* Seattle: Mountaineers Books, 2007.

Braudaway, Douglas Lee. *Railroads of Western Texas: San Antonio to El Paso.* Charleston: Arcadia, 2000.

Buchanan, Patrick J. *State of Emergency: The Third World Invasion and Conquest of America.* New York: St. Martin's, 2006.

Conover, Ted. *Coyotes: A Journey through the Secret World of America's Illegal Aliens.* New York: Vintage, 1987.

Dunn, Timothy J. *The Militarization of the U.S.-Mexico Border, 1978–1992.* Austin: Center for Mexican-American Studies, 1996.

Ellingwood, Ken. *Hard Line: Life and Death on the U.S.-Mexico Border.* New York: Random House, 2004.

Fehrenbach, T. R. *Fire & Blood: A History of Mexico.* New York: Da Capo Press, 1973, 1995.

———. *Lone Star: A History of Texas and the Texans.* New York: Tess Press, 1968, 2000.

Gill, Mary McVey, and Brenda Wegman. *Streetwise Spanish.* New York: McGraw-Hill, 2006.

Graves, John. *Goodbye to a River.* New York: Vintage, 2002.

Grossman, Lt. Col. David. *On Combat: The Psychology and Physiology of Deadly Conflict in War and in Peace.* Centralia, Ill.: PPCT Research Publications, 2004.

Hanson, Victor Davis. *Mexifornia: A State of Becoming.* New York: Encounter Books, 2004.

Horgan, Paul. *Great River: The Rio Grande in North American History.* New York: Rinehart, 1954. Reprinted in Austin: Texas Monthly Press, 1984.

Hufbauer, Gary Clyde, and Jeffrey J. Schott. *NAFTA Revisited: Achievements and Challenges.* Washington D.C.: Institute for International Economics, 2005.

Huntington, Samuel P. *Who Are We?: The Challenges to America's National Identity.* New York: Simon & Schuster, 2005.

Kaplan, Robert D. *An Empire Wilderness: Travels into America's Future.* New York: Random House, 1998.

Kelly, Mary E. *The Río Conchos: A Preliminary Overview.* Austin: Texas Center for Policy Studies, 2001.

Kerouac, Jack. *On the Road.* New York: Penguin, 1955.

Langewiesche, William. *Cutting for Sign.* New York: Pantheon, 1993.

Laufer, Peter. *Wetback Nation: The Case for Opening the Mexican-American Border.* Chicago: Ivan R. Dee, 2004.

Least Heat Moon, William. *Blue Highways.* New York: Random House, 1982.

Lewis, Tom. *Divided Highways: Building the Interstate Highways, Transforming American Life.* New York: Viking, 1997.

Logan, Samuel. *The Reality of a Mexican Mega Cartel.* Rio de Janeiro: Sam Logan, 2006.

McCarthy, Cormac. *No Country for Old Men.* New York: Random House, 2005.

McNichol, Dan. *The Roads that Built America.* New York: Sterling, 2006.

Metz, Leon C. *Border: The U.S.-Mexico Line.* El Paso: Mangan Books, 1989.

Mills, Nicolaus. *Arguing Immigration.* New York: Touchstone, 1994.

Morgan II, Lee. *The Reaper's Line: Life and Death on the Mexican Border.* Tucson: Rio Nuevo, 2006.

Morse, Ashley. *Calderon's Plan for Mexico and the Evolution of Mexican Organized Crime.* Rio de Janeiro: Sam Logan, 2006.

Myers, John Myers. *The Border Wardens.* New Jersey: Prentice-Hall, 1971.

Perkins, Clifford Alan. *Border Patrol: With the U.S. Immigration Service on the Mexican Boundary, 1910–54.* El Paso: Texas Western Press, 1978.

Poppa, Terrence E. *Drug Lord: The Life and Death of a Mexican Kingpin.* New York: Pharos Books, 1990.

Rak, Mary Kidder. *Border Patrol.* Boston: Houghton Mifflin, 1938.

Reich, Robert B. *The Work of Nations.* New York: Random House, 1991.

Riding, Alan. *Distant Neighbors: A Portrait of the Mexicans.* New York: Vintage, 1984.

Schlosser, Eric. *Reefer Madness: Sex, Drugs, and Cheap Labor in the American Black Market.* Boston: Houghton Mifflin, 2003.

Seagraves, Ann. *Women Who Charmed the West.* Post Falls, Idaho: Wesanne Publications, 1991.

Skiles, Jack. *Judge Roy Bean Country.* Lubbock: Texas Tech University Press, 1996.

Smythe, William E. *History of San Diego.* San Diego: San Diego Historical Society, 1907.

Southwest Consortium for Economic Research. *The U.S.-Mexican Border Environment: Monograph Series, no. 13 (All-American Canal).* San Diego: SDSU Press, 2004.

Stavans, Ilan. *Spanglish: The Making of a New American Language.* New York: Rayo, 2003.

Steinbeck, John. *Travels with Charley.* New York: Viking, 1962.

Stevenson, Robert Louis. *Travels with a Donkey in the Cévannes.* New York: Penguin, 1879.

———. *The Amateur Emigrant.* New York: Penguin, 1895.

Thompson, Gabriel. *There's No José Here: Following the Hidden Lives of Mexican Immigrants.* New York: Nation Books, 2007.

Weaver, John D. *The Brownsville Raid.* New York: W. W. Norton, 1970.

Webb, James. *Born Fighting: How the Scots-Irish Shaped America.* New York: Broadway Books, 2004.

Zaloga, Steven J., and James W Loop. *Soviet Bloc Elite Forces.* Oxford, UK: Osprey Publishing, 1985.

## Internet

Aquafornia.com. www.aquafornia.com

City-data.com. www.city-data.com

Collectron International Management, Inc. www.collectron.com

Border Reporter. www.borderreporter.com

European Union official Web site. Europa.eu

Eyes on the Border. www.eyesontheborder.com

Forbes.com. "The World's Billionaires." www.forbes.com

Gallup.com. Immigration Poll, April 7–9, 2006. www.gallup.com

Hossain, Farhana. "Snapshot: Global Migration." June 22, 2007. www.nytimes.com

International Boundary and Water Commission, official website. www.ibwc.state.gov

Joint Task Force North, official Web site. www.jtfn.northcom.mil

Justia.com, U.S. Code of Federal Regulations. law.justia.com/us/cfr/title08.html

Overdrive: The Magazine for Truckers. www.overdriveonline.com

Pilgrim's Pride Chicken, official Web site. www.pilgrimspride.com

Texas Department of Transportation, official Web site, www.dot.state.tx.us

Texas State Data Center and Office of the State Demographer, University of Texas at San Antonio. 2006 Texas Populaton Projections. txsdc.utsa.edu/tpepp/2006projections

Texas State Historical Association. "Handbook of Texas Online." www.tsha.utexas.edu

United States Customs and Border Protection, official Web site. www.cbp.gov

United States Department of Homeland Security, official Web site. www.dhs.gov

United States Immigration and Customs Enforcement, official Web site. www.ice.gov

Ysleta Del Sur Pueblo, official Web site. ydsp.stantonstreetgroup.com

## Interviews

Biegay, Ron; August 22, 2007; Laredo, TX
Billings, Pete; August 25, 2007; Langtry, TX
Bonner, T. J.; November 20, 2007; phone interview
Buer, Brother David; May 24, 2007; San Xavier Mission, AZ
Cafarelli, Gene; May 22, 2007; phone interview
Carrillo, Chief Carlos; May 14, 2007; Laredo, TX
Castañeda, Blas; August 23, 2007; Laredo, TX
Cerrillo, Agent Ram; May 14, 2007; Zapata, TX
Clark, Agent Randy; May 16, 2007; Eagle Pass, TX
Clothing store clerk, name withheld; August 30, 2007; El Paso, TX
Dennis, Sgt. Suzanne; May 18, 2007; Marfa, TX
de la Fuente Amaro, José Louis; September 11, 2007; Matamoros, Tamaulipas
Deported painter, name withheld; September 11, 2007; Matamoros, Tamaulipas
Dodson, Sheriff Ronny; September 10, 2007; Brewster County, TX
Dudley, Robbie; May 17, 2007; Langtry, TX
Duronslet, Agent Ulysses; May 22, 2007; Douglas, AZ
Easterling, Agent Lloyd; May 25, 2007; Yuma, AZ
Ellman, Eric; May 13, 2007; McAllen/Roma/Rio Grande, TX
Executive consultant, name withheld; August 18, 2007; San Antonio, TX
Federal agent, name withheld; August 30, 2007; Fort Bliss, TX
Federal agent, name withheld; September 5, 2007; Nogales, AZ
Fimbres, Agent Martin; May 22, 2007; Douglas, AZ
Finck, Dan & Connie; May 22, 2007; Bisbee, AZ
Foster, Mayor Chad; May 16/August 25, 2007; Eagle Pass, TX
Frers, Agent Lloyd; May 26, 2007; Calexico, CA
Gonzalez, George A.; August 22, 2007; Laredo, TX
Gonzalez, Staff Sgt. Julian; September 4, 2007; Tucson, AZ
Gomez, Agent Zulma; May 23, 2007; Nogales, AZ
Green, David; September 7, 2007; El Centro, CA
Guerra, Isaac; May 12, 2007; McAllen, TX
Gutierrez, Sammy; August 29, 2007; Tigua Indian Reservation
Halepaska, Douglas; December 10, 2007; email interview
Hectorio; August 31, 2007; Palomas, Chihuahua
Holguin, Iliana; May 19, 2007; El Paso, TX
Johnson, Agent Matt; May 28, 2007; San Diego, CA
King, Agent Walter; May 11, 2007; Brownsville, TX
Kolbe, Congressman (ret.) Jim; June 8, 2007; phone interview
Larkins, Elizabeth; May 20, 2007; Hachita, NM
LeBoeuf, Agent Michelle; May 19, 2007; El Paso, TX
Los Samaritanos volunteers, names withheld; May 25, 2007; Tohono O'Odham
    Nation
McDaniel, Lt. Col. Lance; December 20, 2007; email interview
Martinez, Luis; September 4, 2007; Nogales, Sonora
Medina, Don; May 12, 2007; McAllen, TX
Mexican migrants, names withheld; September 4, 2007; Nogales, Sonora
Montoya, Mike; August 30, 2007; Las Cruces, NM

Pérez, Javier; August 31, 2007; El Paso, TX
Portugal, Pedro; September 4, 2007; Nogales, Sonora
Reyes, Congressman Silvestre; May 19, 2007; El Paso, TX
Reyes, E. Veronica (no relation); August 22, 2007; Laredo, TX
Rodriguez, Martha; August 31, 2007; Columbus, NM
Salinas, Mayor Raul; May 15, 2007; Laredo, TX
Shimp, Maj. Chris; January 16, 2008; email interview
Shopkeeper, name withheld; May 15, 2007; Nuevo Laredo, Tamaulipas
Simcox, Chris; September 6, 2007; Phoenix, AZ
Smietana, Chief John; May 18, 2007; Marfa, TX
Spener, Sally (IBWC spokesperson); November 28, 2007; phone interview
Student, name withheld; September 7, 2007; San Diego, CA
Texas National Guard Soldiers, names withheld; May 18, 2007; near Neely's Crossing, TX
Tisdale, Brenda; August 29, 2007; El Paso, TX
Trucker, name withheld; August 21, 2007; Laredo, TX
Van Schoik, Rick; September 7, 2007; San Diego, CA
Valdez, Judge Danny; May 15, 2007; Laredo TX
Wasito, Janar; December 10, 2007; email interview
Williams, Sgt. Marlon; May 18, 2007; Marfa, TX
Zachariah, Bob; May 13, 2007; Laredo, TX

# ACKNOWLEDGMENTS

**M**y largest debt of gratitude goes to Robin Bhatty, a counterinsurgency warfare scholar, wildlife photographer, and globe-trotting bon vivant. Bhatty was my wingman on the initial May 2007 journey along the border and took two-thirds of the pictures that appear in the book. I also owe no small appreciation to Janice Kaplan editor of *Parade* magazine, who helped to commission that first trip and her news editor Daryl Chen, who waited over a year for me to deliver the final story.

E. J. McCarthy, my agent, promoted this project, and Chris Evans, my editor, sculpted the concept from the ethers into reality. Virginia Danieley has been tireless in her commitment and attention to detail towards this book and has done tremendous work as an editorial assistant, publicity advocate, and deadline negotiator. I'm grateful to the entire editorial, publishing, and sales staff at Stackpole Books for betting on a sophomore author tackling a controversial topic.

The interviewees—whose names are listed in the bibliography—shared their time, thoughts, and experiences. The Ameriks and Quinn families opened their homes to me in Las Cruces and Tucson for respite. Tim Feist and Tyson Belanger read the early drafts of several chapters, and their suggestions were invaluable. As longtime San Antonio residents, my parents Dan and Kathy Danelo shaped this book with helpful insight and priceless editorial eyes.

James Schaffer drove several hundred miles and almost helped me cross the border illegally. When that became unnecessary, he met me anyway and bought me dinner. I was grateful for both, as well as Schaffer's perceptive reading and editing of the full manuscript. Also of enormous value was an edit by an anonymous Border Patrol agent, whom I will note only by his off-duty call sign: Stevie Nicks. Two members of the Texas Philosophical Society, Raul Rodríguez and Jay Young, helped me maintain balance as I explored these complex issues.

Finally, thanks to my wife Mary, for sharing the journey of this book with me.

# INDEX

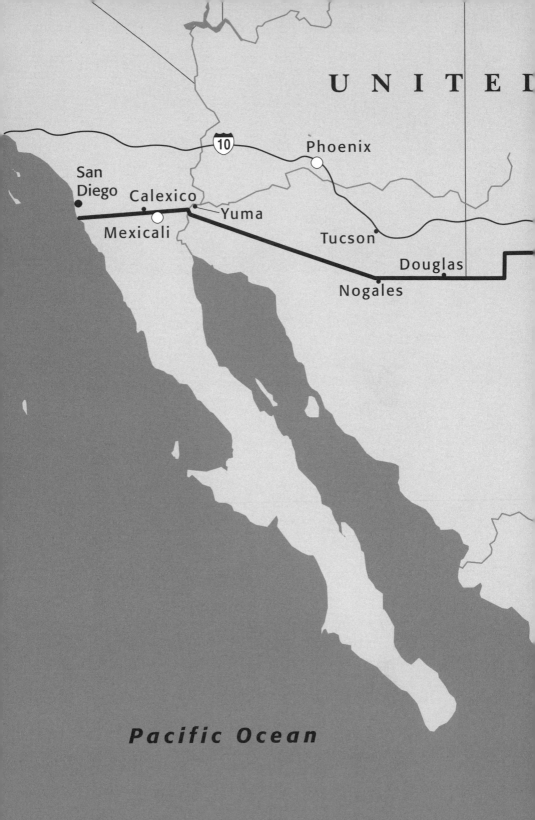

U N I T E D

10 Phoenix

San
Diego
Calexico
Mexicali
Yuma
Tucson
Douglas
Nogales

Pacific Ocean